W9-BHW-575

SHOOT ME

INDEPENDENT FILMMAKING FROM
CREATIVE CONCEPT TO ROUSING RELEASE

SHOOT ME

INDEPENDENT FILMMAKING

FROM CREATIVE CONCEPT

TO ROUSING RELEASE

ME

Rocco Simonelli and Roy Frumkes

ALLWORTH PRESS
NEW YORK

© 2002 Roy Frumkes and Rocco Simonelli

All rights reserved. Copyright under Berne Copyright Convention, Universal Copyright Convention, and Pan-American Copyright Convention. No part of this book may be reproduced, stored in a retrieval system, or transmitted in any form, or by any means, electronic, mechanical, photocopying, recording, or otherwise, without prior permission of the publisher.

07 06 05 04 03 02   5 4 3 2 1

Published by Allworth Press
An imprint of Allworth Communications
10 East 23rd Street, New York, NY 10010

Cover and interior page design by Annmarie Redmond

Page composition/typography by Integra Software Services Pvt. Ltd., Pondicherry, India

Library of Congress Cataloging-in-Publication Data:
Frumkes, Roy.
 Shoot me : independent filmmaking from creative concept to rousing
release / by Roy Frumkes and Rocco Simonelli.
 p. cm.
Includes index.
ISBN 1-58115-247-7
1. Motion pictures—Production and direction. 2. Motion picture
authorship. 3. Independent filmmakers. I. Simonelli, Rocco. II. Title.

PN1995.9.P7 F77 2002
791.43'023—dc21
                              2002013795

Printed in Canada

TABLE OF CONTENTS

ACKNOWLEDGMENTS

Many thanks to Bob Seigel, Brian Hershey, Ted Bonnitt, Michael Ellenbogen, Richard Dutcher, Liz Van Hoose, Olga Gardner Galvin, Nicole Potter, Birte Pampel, Tony Lover, Bill Chepil, and Denise LaBelle.

CHAPTER ONE

WHERE IT BEGINS

One week early in February of the year 2001, I was lying in bed at my mother's apartment, recovering from surgery to transplant cartilage in my knee. The procedure I'd undergone, known as osteochondral grafting, had entailed harvesting plugs of healthy cartilage and bone from a non-weight-bearing section of the joint and then inserting them into holes drilled in the damaged area. My case had required six plug grafts, meaning that between the harvesting and the transplanting, twelve holes had been drilled into my knee. And so both my judgment and concentration were considerably impaired by painkillers the night my long-time writing partner, Roy Frumkes, visited my bedside and informed me rather matter-of-factly that we would be shooting our script *The Sweet Life* that summer as an independent production.

At the time he told me this, it was a foregone conclusion within the industry that the Writers Guild (of which Roy and I are members) would go on strike when our union contract expired in July. In anticipation of this, the studios had shifted their focus away from leveloping projects to rushing as many films as they could into production before the strike stopped everything cold. Unless you were at the top of the screenwriting food chain, that short A-list of scribes the studios turn to again and again to doctor and rewrite other people's scripts, you were hard put as a movie writer to get work just then. Being East Coast–based only compounded the problem for Roy and me. Why not be proactive, Roy reasoned, and shoot our own picture while the industry hashed out the strike issues?

Lying there that cold February night in a medicated haze, I agreed it made sense. But where would we find the money to shoot the film? *The Sweet Life* was a character-driven script, with no complicated action scenes or special effects, a classic low-budget piece of material. Yet, produced at the most minimal level, it would still cost close to a million dollars. Even drugged, I didn't believe for a moment that we could raise that kind of money. Six figures, maybe, but never a mil.

"Digital," Roy uttered.

"What?"

"We'll shoot on digital video. I've been looking into it, and I think we could shoot the picture on digital for a fraction of what it would cost to do on film. That kind of money I think I can raise. But what about you? Will you be physically able to direct a film by July?"

It didn't seem likely. A month of virtual inactivity prior to the surgery had reduced my right leg to a spindly appendage. I was already overweight and out of shape. Now I would be on my back for seven more weeks before I could even begin physical therapy.

"Sure," I replied with an air of casual confidence. So what if in addition to my questionable physical condition I'd never directed a film before and had only the vaguest notion of what the job involved? The truth was I didn't believe it would really happen; that we would find the money and that I'd be faced with having to come through on my promise. So I figured I could afford to be cavalier.

This was my first mistake in judgment in connection with *The Sweet Life*.

It would not be my last.

CHAPTER TWO

JUST WHEN I THOUGHT I WAS OUT, I PULLED MYSELF BACK IN . . . !

Sixteen years ago, I get this call from an ex-student of mine at the School of Visual Arts in NYC. Rocco was the best screenwriting student I'd ever had. He was by no means great, but then again he'd only been a student. Twenty years old maybe. With a writing partner named Rico! Rocco and Rico. They'd better not have been writing anything but comedies with that alliterative moniker.

I was on the last few days of a grueling twelve-and-a-half-week shoot as screenwriter/producer of a low-budget feature called *Street Trash*. It was 1985, and Rocco had been out of my class for three years. The reason for his call: Rico had gone straight.

I'd better clarify that immediately; my partner is very sensitive about people misinterpreting our professional relationship as a sexual one. Rico had decided to abandon writing for marriage to the woman he'd been dating since high school, and for a safe job in a family-related business.

Rocco was in desperate need of a new writing partner. He asked me if I'd like to work on a screenplay with him. Rocco and Roy. Yipes.

I'd worked both with and without writing partners, and I liked it both ways (careful . . . !). However, not being the "driven" type (the quest for a creative chocolate dessert could lure me away from the typewriter without a moment's hesitation), I found myself more motivated with a partner on hand. Also, it was a relief to have someone close by who could supply the script with those elements I was less skilled at— such as dialogue. When I wrote alone, if I needed an esoteric voice—a mercenary, a psychic, et cetera—I would invite a person in that field out to lunch and tape them for a few hours, feeding them the lines their character would be responding to. I would then have these "character banks" at hand, and could easily modify them as the script underwent changes.

I'd had two writing partners simultaneously just prior to Rocco's call, and his call was serendipitous, to say the least, because both of them had died that year, leaving me in a vulnerable state not only of grief, but of compounded hypochondria.

Though I have no strong spiritual beliefs, I entertained the thought that one or both of my ex-cowriters had guided my future partner to me. I agreed to meet and kick the concept around. Roc lives in New Jersey, and the *Street Trash* production was shooting a scene at a liquor store the following day in his neck of the woods. Gary Cooper (not *the* Gary Cooper, but a good Gary Cooper nonetheless, who is currently editing *The Sweet Life*) was playing the liquor store owner, and the special-effects makeup crew was going to "melt" him all over the sidewalk in front of the store. (Curious about *Street Trash*, are you? Well, let me employ a little "narrative drive" here by not filling in too much about that film just yet. Over the course of this book you'll learn all, as you would in any well-constructed screenplay, where each scene supplies some vital new information, yet leaves a few questions unanswered, with the intent of drawing the viewer inexorably forward.)

Gary was miserable. Glop (a.k.a. methylcellulose with food coloring mixed in) was being spewed up through his clothing by hidden tubes, and out through his hair. It was dripping down his face, oozing from his pant legs; as I recall, he even had to keep some in his mouth and drool it out on cue. He was supposed to look transformed with pain; but he just looked mortified. Poor Gary was sorry he'd ever signed on for this thankless role. (He'd relive that experience at my hands fifteen years later, on *The Sweet Life*, and not in the editing room . . . but that, too, we shall catch up with in another chapter . . .)

It wasn't fun seeing Gary tortured, so I was happy when Rocco arrived and we adjourned to a nearby bar for a drink. The script idea we discussed was an Othello tale transposed to the modern boxing milieu, called *Killer Instinct*. We wrote it, but it was never produced. It was never even optioned. Neither are 75 percent of all the scripts written in this country, and of the 25 percent or so that *are* optioned, 75 percent are never made into a movie. Yet, Roc and I began a friendly, productive, and adventurous writing partnership that day, and after a decade we even made some money at it.

A writing partnership should be firmed and fixed in legalese. That way the partners will stand less of a chance of being at each other's throats a few months down the pike. Boilerplate agreements will include several cogent "what if's" and "who's." What if one of you dies? Who gets the rights and the revenue of the deceased, and will any heirs have "creative" or "business" say? Who does the negotiating on sales deals?

What if there are attendant costs? Who pays them? What if one of the parties goes on to do a book about the filming of the screenplay? Who gets what in that case?

Intriguing, yes? Let's up the ante. What if there are *three* parties involved? On occasion, Roc and I have written about the lives of real people, relying so heavily on interviews with said third parties that it became a three-way collaboration agreement. Then the above-listed questions become complicated by the subject's ownership of his or her own life, and a new question arises: What if he or she wants to do something else with it while we're working on it? Another question is, how long can we own it?

Following are excerpts from such an agreement, reprinted with the permission of Bill Chepil. Bill starred in *Street Trash*. Beyond that, he is a retired New York City police officer with an incredible story to tell. Apparently, the literary agents didn't think so, because three sample chapters of *Muscle*, a book which we hoped later to turn into a screenplay, didn't meet with overwhelming enthusiasm. The collaboration agreement, however, was a good one, and here it is, in part (with certain names deleted), for you to cannibalize for your own purposes:

COLLABORATION AGREEMENT

AGREEMENT dated as of _____ ,by and among ROY FRUMKES ("Frumkes"), (address), ROCCO SIMONELLI ("Simonelli"), (address), and BILL CHEPIL ("Chepil"), (address).

1. *Purpose of Collaboration.*

1.1 The parties hereto are collaborating in the writing of a book (the "Book") and screenplay (the "Screenplay") based upon autobiographical, anecdotal and other nonfiction materials (the "Materials") furnished by Chepil pertaining to Chepil's experiences as a New York City police officer.

1.2 Subject to Paragraph 1.3 of this Agreement, the parties intend to negotiate and enter into one or more agreements for the publication and exploitation of the Book and rights allied, ancillary and subsidiary thereto (each such agreement is called a "Publishing Agreement") and/or for the development, production and exploitation of the Screenplay and rights allied, ancillary and subsidiary thereto (each such agreement is referred to herein as a "Production Agreement").

1.3 Frumkes shall have the sole right to negotiate Publishing Agreements and Production Agreements. Frumkes shall keep Simonelli and Chepil fully informed of the progress of all such negotiations. No Publishing Agreement or Production

Agreement shall be valid unless and until approved and signed by all of the parties. [*This was a vital clause, which, if you think about it, saves mucho potential infighting down the road. I'm the business negotiator, but they get veto rights on any deals I've put into place. Fair enough.*]

2. *Rights to Exploit Materials.*

2.1 Chepil shall not use or exploit or authorize or permit the use or exploitation in any manner or medium of any materials used in the Book or Screenplay or in any work or production based upon or derived from the Book or Screenplay ("Production") without the prior written consent of Frumkes and Simonelli. Notwithstanding the foregoing, nothing herein shall be deemed to limit Chepil's right to use or authorize or permit the use other than in the Book or Screenplay of Chepil's physical description, date and place of birth, years of employment by the New York Police Department and such other similar autobiographical facts, the use of which will not be likely to diminish the unique appeal of, or interfere with the market for, the Book, Screenplay or Production. [*You can see the necessity for this. Word of the project gets out . . . other entrepreneurs decide to do something similar . . . Bill gets involved with them . . . a lot of our valuable time goes down the toilet. Not that Roc and I thought there was the remotest chance that Bill would do something like that, but it's your lawyer's job to hatch the worst-case scenario, and then prevent it from ever happening. The following clauses clarify the situation even further.*]

2.2 If a first draft of either the Book or the Screenplay is completed, and if Chepil wishes at any time thereafter to write, collaborate on, or cause to be written a book, screenplay, story, treatment, format, teleplay, radio play, or stage play based upon or derived from elements of Materials contained in the Book or Screenplay, including, without limitation, a sequel or remake ("New Work"), then Chepil shall so notify Frumkes and Simonelli and will negotiate exclusively and in good faith with Frumkes and Simonelli for a period of thirty (30) days for Frumkes and Simonelli to write or to collaborate with Chepil in writing such New Work. If the parties are unable to negotiate such an agreement within such thirty (30)-day period, Chepil shall have the right to write, collaborate on, or cause to be written such New Work, subject to the following:

2.2.1 If Chepil proposes in good faith to enter into an agreement with a third party for such third party to collaborate with Chepil on or to write a New Work, Chepil will give notice to Frumkes and Simonelli of the financial terms and conditions of such offer.

2.2.2 Frumkes and Simonelli shall have a period of thirty (30) days following receipt of such notice within which to notify Chepil of their election to accept such offer upon the same financial terms and conditions set forth in such notice. Upon Frumkes's and Simonelli's notification to Chepil of such election, the parties shall immediately be deemed to have entered into an agreement upon such financial terms. If either Frumkes or Simonelli does not wish to accept such offer, the other alone shall have the same right to accept such offer as set forth above.

2.2.3 If Frumkes and Simonelli both fail to accept such offer as aforesaid, Chepil may enter into the proposed agreement with such third party upon the same financial terms specified in said notice. In the event Chepil does not enter into the proposed agreement of which Frumkes and Simonelli have been given notice and/or if Chepil proposes thereafter to write, collaborate on or cause to be written a New Work, the same procedure set forth above shall be followed in each case.

3. *Name and Likeness.*

Chepil hereby consents to the use of the materials and of Chepil's name, likeness and biographical materials in the Book, Screenplay and Production, and in the advertising, promotion and publicizing of any of them.

4. *Copyright.*

The copyright in the Book and Screenplay shall be secured and held jointly by the parties.

5. *Sharing of Proceeds and Losses.*

5.1 Unless otherwise stated in this Agreement, all assets, claims, income, rights, profits, fees, receipts, and returns of whatever kind (collectively, "Benefits") derived by the parties hereto from the exploitation of the Book and Screenplay and, subject to Paragraph 5.2 hereof, any costs, expenses or losses, shall be divided by the parties as follows:

5.1.1 All royalties paid to the parties pursuant to a Publishing Agreement after the recoupment of any advances paid pursuant to such Agreement (except such royalties paid with respect to a disposition of the right to produce an audiovisual work based upon or derived from the Book, which shall be divided pursuant to Paragraph 5.1.2 hereof) shall be payable one-half (1/2) to Chepil, one-quarter (1/4) to Frumkes and one-quarter (1/4) to Simonelli.

5.1.2 All other Benefits derived by the parties from the exploitation of the Book and Screenplay, including, without limitation, any advances paid pursuant to a Publishing Agreement, shall be payable one-third (1/3) to Chepil, one-third (1/3) to Frumkes and one-third (1/3) to Simonelli.

6. *Credit.*

6.1 In all Publishing Agreements or otherwise in connection with the exploitation of the Book, the parties shall use their best efforts to obtain provisions providing that the parties shall receive appropriate credit as co-authors of the Book.

6.2 In all Production Agreements or otherwise in connection with Productions based upon materials written by the parties, the parties shall use their best efforts to obtain provisions providing that the parties shall receive credit in substantially the following form (or such other form as the parties may mutually agree): Written by Bill Chepil, Roy Frumkes and Rocco Simonelli.

6.3 All credits to be given to the parties shall be of equal size, prominence and style of type and in no event shall one name appear without the others.

7. *Term.*

The "Term" of this Agreement shall commence on the date set forth above and continue in perpetuity. In the event of the death of any of the parties hereto during the Term, the surviving party or parties shall have the right to act generally with regard to all artistic matters relating to the Book and Screenplay, as though he or they were the sole author or authors thereof, except that the provisions of Paragraph 6 hereof shall survive the death of a party hereto. The personal representative(s) of a deceased party shall receive his or her decedent's share of the Benefits, as provided in Paragraph 5.1. [*In the case of a subsequent collaboration with a former Liberian student of ours named Hawa Stovall, who returned to her country and became a kind of national hero during a bloody civil war, the Agreement had a time limit. We were unable to get the project off the ground within the time allotted, and Hawa allowed us to extend it for another several years for free. Keep in mind that time limits come creeping up on you faster than you would have imagined.*]

The portions reproduced here were written in accordance with New York State law. Different states may call for modifications in language and even in the content of the agreement. Be sure to have an entertainment lawyer in whichever state you reside look the agreement over, even if you use this as a template and create the agreement yourself.

So Roc and I became joined at the hip . . . aesthetically and businesswise. All my previous scripts suddenly became coauthored by him as part of the deal, whether he worked on them or not, and vice versa. It was an odd experience to get my mind around. I'd written *The Substitute*, for instance, before our partnership began. He read it and proclaimed: "This will not only make a great Hollywood film, it's a franchise! However," he added, "the ending's gotta go. The protagonist has to live in the end, go on to another school. And it's gotta be trimmed by thirty or forty pages; Hollywood won't do a samurai epic . . ."

"Oh, yeah . . .?" I responded sourly, "Why don't you just fix it yourself and don't show it to me." He did, and the script that went out to the coast had *my* ending, followed by a blank page save for one tiny word in the middle—"or"—followed by *his* ending. Later we heard that studio people were tearing my ending out of the script before passing it along to their superiors. The screenplay sold, became a franchise, and bought us a modicum of independence, so how miffed could I be that the project existed before we signed the agreement.

And it works the other way, as well. *The Sweet Life* is really Rocco's script, though it bears both our names. It's about his life, he did it in between our "paying" gigs, and I served as editorial advisor on it rather than actually contributing to the text. It all balances out. But the agreement makes it painless.

And so our career went. The success of *The Substitute* brought us in contact with all the needy people out there at the studios. But need us though they did, and provide work though they did, they just had to put in their two cents to justify their worth, or keep their jobs, and our work mutated and diminished before our eyes. The checks were good, but not as good for the soul as the interference was bad for it.

This was particularly painful for Roc. All this time he kept a mantra going. Like a window wiper set on ten-second intervals, every so often it would crop up: that he wished he could see just one of our scripts reach the screen uncorrupted by studio vermin. He thought one way to do this was to direct, and I explored raising money for him to direct one of our short installments for a proposed anthology feature called *New York Primeval*. But money just wasn't forthcoming for a short. It's too obvious that under no circumstances could money invested in that kind of project yield profits: where could it play other than on a cable station such as the Independent Film Channel, or the Sundance channel, which aren't big paying gigs. Certainly it could be entered into film festivals, but festival cash prizes aren't substantial for shorts. It could be bunched with other shorts on a DVD, but then your share of the profits would be small. So, you can't use profitability as a selling point to potential investors for something of this nature. To first-time filmmakers/ students I suggest offering a potential investor points not only in your short thesis/independent project, but in the first feature you produce, so that for the money they invest in the short, they go along for the ride and benefit down the road from your career. This scenario has worked for students. But it didn't fit two guys who'd already been in the industry for decades.

So Roc languished in his loathing, and, according to him, the reason I *didn't* was because at least I'd produced/directed a few films the way I'd written them, so I had *that* no matter what they did to my work now.

Then, as the new century rolled around, *The Blair Witch Project* seemed to validate the prediction of David Whitten, a brilliant distributor and former publicist who advised me that the coming millennium would see no-budget films made by young filmmakers on digital video, bypassing the studio system entirely and recouping their costs on Broadband. I became intrigued by a medium that had hitherto repulsed me.

The Sweet Life was our simplest screenplay, despite having thirty speaking parts and a number of locations. There were no big effects, no makeup meltdowns, nothing to give the insurance company the willies. It was essentially a character piece. We'd done a staged reading of it two years earlier and it had been optioned for eighteen months by a small company who planned to shoot it in 35mm. When their option ran out, they generously gave me their budget workup, and now, out of curiosity, I adapted it for digital video to see what the cost reduction might be. Same amount of shooting days. Lots of my little money-saving ideas inserted (which you'll read about later). But mainly it reflected the ways in which digital video impacted production and postproduction expenses. The budget plummeted from over a million to $250,000.

I'd produced seven feature films over the last thirty years, and one of the reasons I stopped was because while it's been relatively easy for me to raise money, it's always proved nearly impossible to get it back. The distributors and exhibitors, who lay between me and the greenbacks, were determined to keep them from reaching me in myriad nefarious ways, and they were armed with accountants galore, while I was just one vulnerable filmmaker with limited funds to fight back. And since the money I raised came mainly from people I knew, rather than from nameless entities like banks and investment funds, this back-end problem weighed heavily on me. Screenwriting, equally lucrative in my career, did not come with the financial burden that being a producer entailed.

But digital video introduced a new wrinkle into the scenario. A million dollars might be hard to recoup given the obstacles mentioned, but a quarter-million wouldn't be. And with new, evolving audience-access venues like Broadband, DVD, and digital theater projection, I might not have to deal with the distributors at all. The new century might just have rendered Hollywood an anachronism in the arc of independent production.

I wandered over one night to Rocco's mother's apartment, where my convalescing partner was being nursed back to health on chicken soup and maternal love, and told him he was going to get his chance.

CHAPTER THREE

WHERE IT REALLY BEGINS: THE SCRIPT

One of the most frequently asked questions I receive as a screenwriting teacher is, *Where do you get your ideas?* The truth is I'm not much of an idea man. I rarely come up with a story purely on my own that I feel is rich enough with potential to sustain a feature-length screenplay. But if you pitch me an idea I respond to, I'm pretty good at building on it, expanding it, and carrying it through to its conclusion. (This is why I've always worked with a writing partner, one whose strengths compensate for my weaknesses, and vice versa. Roy is terrific at blowing out story ideas; he fills notebooks with them. Thus our collaboration.) In other words, to use a football analogy, I'm not very adept at calling the play, but if you toss me the ball, I can usually run downfield with it and get it into the end zone. This is no small feat. The world is full of wannabe screenwriters who are great at conjuring story ideas, but when it comes to sitting down and actually writing a full-length script, of fulfilling the initial promise of the idea, they fall short, lose their way, run out of gas. Writing a screenplay is not unlike being involved in a serious romantic relationship, in that it takes time and effort and concentration, and *attention*, every day, to make it work. It is not a one-night stand.

That said, *The Sweet Life* is one of the few scripts I've been involved in the writing of that *did* begin with an idea of mine. Less an idea, really, and more of a desire. I wanted to save my soul.

A screenwriter for hire is always writing at the behest of others—studio executives, producers, directors and actors, as well as that elusive creature known as the "audience." You are always trying to please others, because if you don't, you will be dismissed, and another writer will be brought in. Which means that, by the third or fourth draft of an assignment, one begins to feel much more like a typist than a writer. You are being given orders in the guise of "suggestions," and you must carry them out no matter how moronic and clichéd you believe them to be. You do this because you want the screen credit, you *need* the screen credit. You need to eat and pay your rent. And, if you're like Roy and myself, you possess a sense of personal honor that will not allow you to quit on a job in midstream just because you're no longer enjoying it. So you slog on. And with each draft, with each diminishment of your original intent, another piece of your writer's soul is stripped away.

Then one day the film is completed and you see it for the first time, and there it is, your name up there on the screen. But the movie that follows bears little resemblance to anything you had in mind when you first started writing the script. It is, as you feared, as you warned them it would be, moronic and clichéd. At times, it doesn't even *make sense*. You grow dizzy as it goes on, and by the time the end credits are rolling, you can hardly breathe. You know you're not responsible for any of it, but that you'll be blamed for all of it, nonetheless. And it hits you—that's what they were really buying when they handed you the check. It's what you were selling when you accepted it. So, in the end, you're the guilty party after all. Because you're the whore. You're the whore because you took their money and agreed to their terms.

That's pretty much what I was feeling after watching the premiere of *The Substitute 2: School's Out* on HBO. Roy had created and I had rewritten the original *Substitute* as a spec script, which had been acquired by Live Entertainment and eventually produced as a feature film starring Tom Berenger. Though the film wasn't as gritty and perverse as we would have liked, neither was it an embarrassment to us, and it enjoyed modest success in theaters, opening number two at the box office its first weekend, behind the Richard Gere legal thriller *Primal Fear*. But where it really thrived was on cable and home video, and so we'd been approached to write a lower-budgeted sequel geared toward these latter markets. We took the money, and would again, for *The Substitute 3: Winner Takes All*. Each time, the experience of writing the scripts and then viewing the films which resulted would leave us disgusted and disillusioned.

Then why do it, you may ask? Why take the money if what goes into obtaining it leaves you so creatively and emotionally devastated? What could it buy you that could possibly be worth it?

What it buys you is this, and it is something more precious than material goods: it buys you *time*. Time to write rather than punch a clock at a job you hate that devours all your energy and your will. Time to write something *you* care about, something entirely personal, rather than take another creatively bankrupt studio gig. Time to buy your soul back.

Over the years, I've periodically written what I call file-cabinet scripts. These are screenplays I know have no commercial potential, no worth on the spec market, no real hope of being sold or optioned, let alone made. I write them simply because I want to, to remind myself of what it feels like to write something without a thought or concession to anyone but myself. I write them and put them in my file cabinet, and, for a while, the fires of Writers Hell burn just a little less hotly.

The Sweet Life began as a file-cabinet script. Its origins lay primarily in my relationship with my brother, coupled with my own at times rather ridiculous romantic life. My brother and I were born just fourteen months apart, grew up in the same town, went to the same school, even shared a room into our teens. Yet, we couldn't be more different—in our interests, our personal styles, and our philosophies about life and love. I've always told him that if I weren't his brother, he'd probably have nothing to do with me, or I with him. But, being brothers, we're forced to. That's always an interesting kind of situation to write about. But it's not enough, in and of itself, to sustain a full-length screenplay. What was needed was something for these two siblings to clash over, something to which we could see their disparate philosophies applied. A woman seemed the natural choice.

From that starting point, a story emerged, one that explores my belief that we are all the architects of our own misery, at least in regard to our troubled love lives. A New York story about characters searching for love and connection, in which *everyone* makes the wrong choice.

MICHAEL, a self-deprecatingly witty and insecure editor of an obscure cinema magazine, flashes back to the defining moment of his romantic life. As a ten-year-old boy just discovering the opposite sex, he develops a crush on the prettiest girl in class. Hoping to impress her, he leaves a large heart-shaped box of chocolates, along with a signed card, on her doorstep. But his well-laid plan goes depressingly awry when she arrives home with **FRANKIE**, Michael's fearless and more outgoing older brother. Hidden in some bushes across the street, Michael watches in horror as they laugh at his card, tear open the chocolates, and feed them to a neighborhood dog.

Forever haunted by that long-ago romantic humiliation, Michael never set his sights so high again, and a comic montage reveals to us the dating history which has resulted: an endless parade of troubled women, from the psychotically hostile to the painfully vulnerable. Meanwhile, his brother Frankie, a twice-divorced cad, partier, and gambler, is able to charm every woman he meets. He complains to Michael that his latest conquest, **LILA**, a tough and sexy foul-mouthed bartender with tattoos and a terrific body, is wearing him out sexually. "My heart bleeds," Michael responds dryly. "The last woman I dated told me she wasn't ready to have a physical relationship. And this was *after* we'd had sex." Frankie explains to Michael that his problem is he's too nice; that upon meeting him, most women (including Lila and the girls in Frankie's office) tend to think he's gay, and that Lila is the type of woman Michael could never handle. "You're right," Michael agrees. "I'd be afraid that if I entered her body, it might take hostage negotiations to get back out." Still, Michael trails along with his brother to the bar where Lila works, quickly fading into the background as Frankie becomes totally energized by the social setting. Cracking jokes, slapping the bar, and handing out cigars, he's a magnetic force to which everyone is eagerly drawn. It's a performance Michael could never hope to duplicate, and can only watch in bemused awe and silence.

When Lila finds out he isn't gay, she fixes Michael up with her room-mate **SHERRY**, assuring him that she's a "pussycat." The kitty, however, turns out to have a sharp set of claws, arriving at his apartment building clad in leather and straddled atop a Harley-Davidson. A harrowing (for Michael) cross-town motorcycle ride leads them to Sherry's favorite biker bar, where Michael could not be more out of place. He inadvertently insults some of the rough crowd, and has to talk his way out of trouble, a difficult task, given the beefy fingers of a hulking biker named **TICK-TICK** ("You know, like a bomb? Tick . . . tick . . .") are clutched around his throat at the time. Later, after getting a plastered Sherry back to the apartment she shares with Lila, Michael reluctantly goes to bed with her, then immediately regrets it when she handcuffs him to the bedposts and passes out on top of him.

A teary-eyed Lila arrives home and rescues him, then spills her troubles. She tells Michael that Frankie broke up with her because she was getting too serious. "I shoulda known I could never be good enough for him," she opines. "I mean, look at me . . . !" They spend the night walking and talking, and by dawn, moved by her unexpected sweetness and vulnerability, Michael's per-ception of Lila has completely changed. After she confides in him that she's always thought it'd be "kinda cool" to be a massage therapist, he urges her to follow that dream, and she's touched by the fact that Michael is the only man to ever give her any encouragement.

The next day, Michael seeks out his brother at lunch, and tells Frankie he thinks he's crazy for breaking up with Lila. Frankie takes a different view, saying she's great for "a steady piece on the side. But let's face it, she's trash." Michael tells him that maybe she could change, if only Frankie

Michael (James Lorinz) *foolishly needles a grim-faced Tick-Tick* (Axel Engmark).

would help her a little bit, but Frankie's cynicism is unshakable. "The leopard can't change its spots. It's natural law, Mikey. I didn't make it." They return to Frankie's place of business, and Michael grows even more frustrated with him when he refuses to tell the women he works with that Michael isn't a homosexual. "It's hard enough for me to find women I can date without the whole world thinking I'm gay!" Michael musters his nerve and makes the announcement himself, but it backfires horribly when some of the workers who actually are gay interpret his statement as either homophobia or denial, or both. Michael is still trying to explain himself as Frankie ushers him out.

At the magazine offices, Michael tells his friend and senior editor **JEFF** about Lila, and of how he thinks she could be a really special person if someone would just give her a little encouragement. "Well, you know what the Japanese say," Jeff offers. "Don't fix the blame, fix the problem." When Michael asks if he's suggesting that he should interfere in the girl's life, Jeff challenges him by saying, "Just be her friend, that's all I'm saying."

Responding to Jeff's challenge, Michael looks up the best massage-therapy school in the city and surprises Lila by taking her there and encouraging her to enroll. She hesitates, but after coming home that night to find a drunken Sherry sprawled out in front of their door, unable to get her key in the lock, Lila decides to go for it, fearful that if something doesn't change she's going to end up just like her roommate. But her first days at school don't go well. Feeling nervous and inadequate, and shocked by the graphic nature of an anatomy film, she throws up in her desk.

Embarrassed and downcast, she comes to Michael's apartment, looking for comfort. He does his best to cheer her up, and, while doing so, finds he's drawn to her. Much to his surprise, she returns his affections, and they make love. Afterward, Michael is in the bathroom when the phone rings, and he calls out to Lila to get it. When she realizes it's Frankie, she quickly hangs up and sinks into a guilty depression. Michael reassures her that everything will be okay. "We don't have to define this. We don't have to put a label on it. And nobody needs to know about it, not until we feel comfortable. Okay?" He rocks her gently in his arms. "You're so sweet," she coos. "I love it that you're so sweet . . ."

Frankie grows suspicious that Michael and Lila have begun seeing each other, and, like a jealous child, wants back the toy he tossed away. He doesn't tell Michael outright what he suspects, but suggests he could resume with Lila any time he wanted; that if she is with someone else, the guy is just "a way station," as he puts it—"A rest stop on the turnpike." But it's not his style to go begging for seconds; she'll have to come back to him. In other words, he'll give Michael his chance. But if he blows it, all bets are off.

And, of course, despite their affection for each other, the differences between Michael and Lila begin to cause friction in their relationship. He becomes frustrated at her inability to appreciate the serious films he loves, and she gets upset when he abandons her at her favorite dance club because he's unable to bear the noise and crowding. It all comes to a head when, for a homework assignment, Lila tries to give Michael a therapeutic massage. Unfortunately, her technique is so inept he lands in the emergency ward, looking like he's been mugged. Told that Michael's injuries are the result not of an attack but a massage, and one administered by a woman, no less, an ER doctor offers that she must be "one vicious, man-hating bull dyke." Believing she was a fool to think she could ever fulfill her dream, or sustain a relationship with a guy like Michael, Lila leaves the hospital in tears.

Using a cane to get around on his massage-injured leg, Michael goes to the bar where Lila works and is devastated to learn she's gone home with Frankie. He goes to his brother's apartment building, but Frankie won't let him up to see her; rather, he comes down to the street, where he and Michael have a heated verbal confrontation over which one of them really has Lila's best interests at heart. It concludes with Frankie revealing that he and Lila plan to get married—and they're counting on Michael to be the best man.

WHERE IT REALLY BEGINS: THE SCRIPT

Later, drinking alone in a West Side tavern, a disconsolate Michael tries to emulate his brother's fun-and-crazy barroom behavior, but the results aren't quite the same: two homophobic West Side twenty-somethings, offended by his unnervingly insistent offers to buy them drinks and taking him for gay, follow him into the men's room and beat him up. Bruised and dejected, he hobbles to a subway platform. Just before boarding the train, he offers a bag lady a dollar. She takes his hand in both of hers and calls him "a sweet boy." It's only after his train pulls out of the station that Michael realizes she's stolen his wristwatch.

At Frankie and Lila's wedding reception, a despondently tipsy Michael is urged, first by the guests and then his brother, to make a toast. He rises, lifts his glass . . . and hesitates. "Just say what's in your heart, Mikey!" one of his uncles calls out. And so, that's what he does. "I think everyone here knows that these two should not be getting married today . . ." After the initial shocked response, many of the guests, including Frankie's and Michael's tearful mother, begin to voice their agreement.

Frankie protests, but Michael is adamant. "You're the one who told me, Frankie, the leopard can't change his spots. And everyone here knows you'll never change yours. You've never been faithful to a woman in your life, and you're not gonna be faithful to this one." It all degenerates into a near brawl as Michael calmly walks out, pausing at the door to make a vaguely papal gesture over his squabbling relatives.

Lila catches up with him in the hall and tries to explain. Michael tells her he understands perfectly; the better man won. She tells him he's wrong. "I thought I wasn't good enough for Frankie. But you're the one I really wasn't good enough for. I mean, God, you're so much smarter than me. You must know it." Michael smiles weakly and takes her hand. "I'm not smart," he responds. "I'm stupid. Very, very stupid." He squeezes her hand, lets it go and walks away.

Outside, he encounters Lila's solemn stepsister **DEBORAH**, who's missed everything that's just happened inside. He asks what's wrong, and she tells him of how Lila was always the prettier one when they were growing up, and more popular. Her sister's marriage to Frankie "just sorta drives it home for me that I'll never find anyone as nice as she has." She's clearly sad, vulnerable, and screwed-up . . . what else can Michael do but ask her to go for a walk? As they stroll off into the night, SUPERIMPOSED OVER is a reprised image of Michael as a boy, running joyously hopeful with the doomed Valentine heart clutched in his arms, as we . . .
FADE OUT

Having read this, you might be wondering what, precisely, makes this a file-cabinet script—a piece of material that needed to be made independently or not at all? It doesn't appear to be an esoteric, inaccessible, art-house movie. It's a romantic comedy, a familiar genre. It's a conventionally structured three-act story, and New York City is a popular and attractive setting. It seems to have humor and conflict. So, what's the problem?

Well, for one thing (and it's a *big* one thing), it doesn't have a *hook*, at least not in the Hollywood sense—a big, glaring, obvious gimmick that can be used to sell the picture. A *concept*. Something like having the girl fall in love with a guy in a coma, or a visitor from another planet. The second thing (and it's an even bigger thing than the first thing) is that there's no happy ending. Lila doesn't run off with Michael at the conclusion. No one learns anything. Nothing positive is affirmed. Love doesn't overcome all obstacles.

The Sweet Life is a script that needed to be an independent movie because it plays off all the clichés of the romantic-comedy genre and turns them on their ear. It was written specifically to do this, to dupe a reader (and later, hopefully, a viewer) into thinking he or she knows exactly where a scene or the story itself is going, and then twist it in an unexpected direction. Why is this such a potentially powerful approach? Because, thanks to home video and the proliferation of cable channels, modern audiences see a lot of movies. *A lot of movies.* They're very savvy about the formula elements inherent in the various genres. What this has created is an audience that is rarely called upon (by Hollywood, anyway) to participate in a film, to pay attention, to *think*. To truly wonder about what's going to happen next. Is there any real tension when you're watching *Pretty Woman* or *What Women Want*, or any of a myriad of Hollywood romantic comedies? Does anybody really think there's a chance in hell that Julia Roberts and Richard Gere aren't going to end up together in the end, despite how utterly implausible it is to believe that a Sunset Boulevard streetwalker could win the heart of a stunningly handsome *billionaire*? I mean, we're not talking a thousand-dollar call girl here. I've seen the hookers on Sunset Boulevard, and I wouldn't go near most of them unless I were wearing one of those *Silkwood* radiation suits. It's utterly ridiculous, but it happens all the time—in the movies. So we're not surprised, we're not concerned. We know it's coming, inevitable as a sunrise.

Don't get me wrong, I'm not condemning this. Not entirely. Hey, I'm listed as coauthor of *The Substitute*, a movie about a hardened mercenary soldier posing as a high school teacher. Not exactly a reflection of reality. What it is is wish fulfillment—like the situation in *Pretty Woman*, something that can only happen in the movies. And audiences do enjoy wish fulfillment. But *The Substitute* was a screenplay written for the spec market and meant to be a commercial movie, one that needed to appeal to a large audience. More specifically, as a script it needed to *appear to a reader* as if it *could* appeal to a large audience. This is the only reason studios shell out money to purchase material and shell out even more money to make films. To put asses in the seats. To make money. That is it. So, I'm as guilty as anyone of tailoring what I write to the perceived requirements of the marketplace. If you wish to sell a script, to make movies, to make a living, you do this. Because a screenplay, in and of itself, as a piece of writing, is nothing. It is not a novel, or a short story, or a poem, which are what they are whether they are published or not. They are completed things. But a screenplay, to quote Paul Schrader, is nothing more than "an invitation to others to make a movie."

Does that mean people make independent films for some reason other than to make money? Not a chance, shmendrick. To make an independent film, one needs to raise money. And the people who give you this money are going to want some assurance that there is at least a possibility of your film making it back for them, or—and talk about wish fulfillment—perhaps even turning a profit. This may not be *your* chief goal, but it will be theirs. What you've got to do is create a situation in which your differing interests don't cancel each other out.

How do you do this? By moving the game, by changing the playing field. Will your film, when completed and brought out into the marketplace, generate the kind of revenue even a bad Hollywood film can generate? Probably not. In fact, most definitely not. What a classic independent film does is adopt an approach in which it doesn't have to. Simply put, you spend less to make it. Much less. Gobs and gobs less. The entire production budget of *The Sweet Life* would not get even a low-budget Hollywood studio film through a single morning's shoot. To give you a clearer idea of what I mean, Live Entertainment produced *The Substitute* for $11 million, a figure considered staggeringly low by Hollywood studio filmmaking standards, where a $20–30-million budget is considered thrifty. Another $5 or $6 million was spent in promoting and releasing the picture. It was a profitable venture for the company because it generated $15 million at the domestic box office and over $20 million on video. Other money came in from overseas, pay-per-view, and cable, and it needed every dollar to get over the hump and into the green. (*Entertainment Weekly* called the picture "a low-rent victory for Live Entertainment.")

The Sweet Life doesn't need to make anywhere near that kind of money to break even, and this is its primary appeal to investors. Is it a risky piece of material? Compared to the romantic comedies Hollywood makes, yes. It defies the clichés, breaks the rules, and refuses to give the audience what Hollywood tends to think it wants. It's not written for mass appeal. It is funny, though, and it is marketable, and it doesn't require a mass audience to break even. Thus, our interests (primarily, to make a film in which our script is shot *as written*) and the investors' interests (to make money) don't cancel each other out. With a little bit of luck, everyone will get to go home happy.

And maybe I get a piece of my soul back.

CHAPTER FOUR

STALKING THE MONEY

With Rocco alerted about our summer plans, the next few months were up to me. Raising the money for independent films is the most painful part of the process for most people. Where do you find it? (Relatives and friends are invariably the first in your infrared sights, sadly.) How do you ask for it? (How painful is that?!) I can perform both of these tasks, which doesn't mean it's effortless for me. In fact, I only do it because I must. And if I must, then my goal, my liberation, my weapon, is to do it with panache.

FIRST COMES *DEVELOPMENT*

This is kind of your dry run for soliciting the big bucks. For some reason, most books on film production, most classes on producing, most words of mouth, neglect to mention this crucial stage. It precedes pre-production and you can't accept a cent from anyone without having gone through it. So, let's define it by posing this simple question: What expenses must you incur *before* you can ask a potential investor to part with his or her hard-earned shekels? I wish this were on the bottom of a page so that you would really have to think about it, rather than just glance down at the next paragraph.

LEGAL FEES

Well, first off there's got to be a legal/financial entity already in existence when you approach the money folks. They have to see, in writing, what kind of business entity they're dealing with—Corporation, Limited Partnership, LLC (Limited Liability Company), Joint Venture, et cetera—and also the agreement they will be signing when they fork over the wampum. That's not something you can provide by scrutinizing and replicating preexisting contracts you've managed to lay your hands on (though anything of that sort will be helpful). And this legal work further must include any agreements between you and your partners in the project. You can see that we're already talking thousands here, for an entertainment lawyer. And no, the family practitioner won't do; your uncle who specializes in divorce law won't do; nor will a friend's father whose legal forte is real estate . . . Nobody will do except an entertainment lawyer, since entertainment law is as different from divorce law as, let's say, "silent films" are from the "talkies." They're both on celluloid, light shining through them is casting shadows on a screen, but beyond that, there are a great many conspicuous differences.

I know from where I speak. On one of my first films, I used a friend of the family, an old and generous friend who offered to work free in exchange for a small percentage. I ended up losing substantial amounts of money on the deal because little clauses that are "givens" for an entertainment lawyer, which he wasn't, never even entered my friend's mind. Such as *they* provide transportation, lodging, and per diem if they request (read "demand") a meeting at their offices in Los Angeles, and since there was no clause like that, I had to foot the bills whenever I was summoned from my aerie in New York. It would have been sleepwalking time for an entertainment lawyer to anticipate such a costly problem. So, under no circumstances attempt this severe a shortcut around the rubles you need to spend on legal matters. If you are destitute, there is an organization called Volunteer Lawyers for the Arts (212-319-2787; Web address *www.vlany.org*), which will recommend attorneys who will work for less than "full rate," or "on spec" if you are not eligible for a volunteer attorney. Whether you are eligible for VLA's services depends on your level of income, of which you will need to show them proof. But they're not available in all cities, and in any case, eventually you'll have to move on.

Back to percentages. Sometimes a lawyer will work for less, plus a percentage. Almost every area in the filmmaking process can be bargained down in such a way. But you tend to get nothing for nothing, so beware the lawyer who defers *all* costs. Down the road, when things get rough over music rights, or distribution contracts, your golden deal will suddenly reveal its tarnished side when said lawyer is no longer readily available, or claims that all this back-end work wasn't in the deal and attempts to renegotiate. If people are paid *something*, they tend to stick to their end of the deal. Half off their asking price is do-able without sacrificing performance.

Another tip here. If you refuse to heed my advice about the family attorney, if you're so strapped for cabbage that he constitutes an opportunity that simply can't be ignored, then find an entertainment lawyer who, for a nominal sum, will *review* what you are doing. That might work in a pinch. But oh, how I hate to see things veer off in the wrong direction from the start. It's all a montage, this process, and when it deviates from the correct scenario even slightly, it gathers negative weight with each step forward.

VARIOUS ENTITIES TO CHOOSE FROM

So, in development you've got legal expenses. Even if your lawyer comes gratis, which I advise against, there are the fees involved in the incorporation or other business entity formation process itself, which you must go through to protect yourself and your film, not to mention your slim chances of finding someone who will put money into a venture that doesn't have a legal corporate structure. And different business entities have different costs. For a lawyer to create an LLC might cost upward of ten grand (inclusive of lawyer fees, federal and state filing fees, et cetera), whereas a Joint Venture might entail an expenditure of less than ten grand. You figure out which entity you should apply for ahead of time, by polling potential investors and seeing at what level they can invest.

With *Street Trash*, that in-your-face black comedy about melting winos, with no socially redeeming values and a certainty of either an X rating or an unrated release, I didn't stand a chance of raising half a million dollars from thirty-five people or less. What a little investigating showed me was that I stood a reasonable chance of getting the money from middle-income people, for whom a fun risk was going to Atlantic City twice a year for a weekend and dropping a few thousand. So, my goal became to sell two hundred shares at $2500 each. Some investors bought multiple shares; some bought one. We used a Joint Venture for this film.

The Sweet Life, at a quarter-million dollars, with a soft R rating and a broad audience, and at least one notable name in the credits . . . *that I* could scavenge from fewer than thirty-five people, so we had ourselves an LLC to create.

And *Burt's Bikers*, an upbeat, comedic docudrama about a big bike race for mentally handicapped children in the Greenwich School System . . . for that I had aligned my nominally for-profit company with a parent-based non-profit organization—The Greenwich Association for Retarded Citizens (GARC)—and it acted as our fiscal sponsor and executive producer, accepting donations (that were tax-deductible) on behalf of the project from major corporations in the area. I had no credentials in the field of special education, but they did. *Burt's Bikers* was the kind of socially significant film that would attract tax-exempt contributions. IBM, Pepsico, and several others saw the virtue of having their names associated with this kind of subject matter. *Street Trash's* bubbling derelicts would not have produced the same positive feeling in their wallets. We partnered with GARC and raised all our money in a matter of months, and since these were donations and not investments or loans, none of it ever had to be returned, which led to a relaxed creative situation, one of the best I've ever experienced. *Burt's Bikers* eventually played on NBC, which gave the investors the kind of exposure that justified their financial gifts, whereas *Street Trash* has never played network TV or any kind of TV in prime time, and I doubt it ever will. Maybe in a half-hour version . . .

So, there you have three different types of legal structures for three different types of movies. Think out your target market ahead of time, and what kind of investors might like to be involved with that kind of project, and proceed accordingly. I will advise you of this, however: the reason 95 percent of the films made in this country are made with Limited Partnerships is that, by definition, the investors are "limited" to their investments both in terms of their vulnerability to any legal problems the film may encounter, and in terms of the legal damage they can impose on the filmmakers if problems arise. Film budgets are written in water, and the final budget may not resemble the budget the investors originally saw in the Memorandum or Business Plan. This could come back to haunt you with a Joint Venture where, for example, if even five investors become dissatisfied with how they perceive you to be doing your job, and if there are only four of you in the corporation venturing with them, they outnumber you and can take over your production. I found myself writing many more letters to the investors in *Street Trash*, and inviting them to the set, to screenings, calling them with pep talks, because I didn't want them turning against us for any reason. With a Limited Partnership, you don't have to worry nearly as much about the damage a rampaging investor can inflict. You can spend your time in more effective ways than nursemaiding them through the year or two it will take to get your film into the marketplace.

OTHER DEVELOPMENT EXPENSES

What other expenses might there be in development? If you didn't write the screenplay yourself, or if your partner didn't write it, you may have to pay someone part of their fee up front for it. If it comes from a book, or a short story, there will be option rights, and that definitely will involve money, for even if the author gives you a free option, there's the legal fee for drawing up an option agreement.

How about the Private Placement Memorandum—the formal summary of a proposed commercial, literary, or other venture, containing all the information on the type of corporate entity as well as the definition of gross and net, and the way in which investors will recoup their investment and share in profits? Potential investors need to *see* something of this sort, which comes laced with heavy, boilerplated legalese.

Then there is a separate, optional document, a Business Plan, which is generally used as an informational marketing tool. This should contain a synopsis of the script, a budget top sheet, a time frame for production and release, narrative bios of the talent involved, positive comparisons with other films like the one you're producing, a detailed statement of the risks involved, and coverage of any special aspects of the production (e.g., in our case, shooting digital video; with *Street Trash* it was having free access to a Steadicam). It does not contain the legal entity, and the terms under which an investment would be recouped; all of that is in the Memorandum. It is a more seductive document. In fact, the contents of the Business Plan should be couched in beauty, meaning it should be designed by an art director, and include such graphics as a logo for the film. Potential investors need to see both the Business Plan and the Memorandum, but the Business Plan should be placed before the Memorandum: It's all about appearance in this industry. (How often did your mother remind you about tucking your shirt in?) A gorgeous presentation does half the work for you. I bring an art director on board long before the director. In fact, the art director comes on board right after I do. You'll need stationery, business cards, mailing stickers, all with that same logo, to allow people to perceive you as professional. (That is, I'm assuming, if you're doing a film for more than ten or twenty thou. If your budget is miniscule, things may never reach the stage of preparing a Memorandum, or even a corporation, and your investors will find out if you're professional or not when you're done.) Go to the art department at a local college and get a student to do a logo for free, copy it onto your stationery, and keep your fingers crossed.

So, now we've got legal fees, a legal/financial entity, possible literary rights to deal with, and an art director to have a hand in the preparation of the Business Plan. But that's not all: we can't forget duplication costs, mailing costs, phone bills, lunches with potential investors, transportation, stationery supplies. It goes on and on.

And it could go even further, depending on what kind of film you're making. With *The Sweet Life*, a bittersweet romantic comedy, there was no inherent problem in familiarizing potential investors with the genre.

But with *Street Trash*, there most definitely were going to be difficulties in that regard, so on that film, as part of development, we shot a three-minute promotional trailer to show to investors in order to help them visualize what we were doing. It was shot on film and then transferred to video. Today, it could, theoretically, all be done digitally. But no matter how it's done, there will be expenses involved—a day's shoot or more, with lunches for cast and crew, possible minimal compensation for cast and crew, transportation, equipment rental, supplies purchases, making multiple copies of the video.

Let's put it another way: On *Street Trash*, we raised $35,000 for development, all of it to be spent before a single penny was raised from investors for the film itself. With *The Sweet Life*, the development figure was only $8,000. *Street Trash* ended up costing around $900,000. *The Sweet Life* looks like it'll come in at around $250,000. Is there a relationship between the budget of the film and how much one has to raise for development? Only in that it makes sense, if the budget is low, not to spend too much on development. Just keep in mind, certain costs—such as incorporation—don't go down just because the budget for the film is less. Alas, the cost of making copies at your local copy store remains constant, too.

DEVELOPMENT MONEY FOR TALENT

Are we done? Not by a long shot. What about the possibility of having to pay talent for a letter of commitment, so that you can use their name recognition in your Memorandum as a selling point? Back in the eighties, I worked for a year as creative director of a Dutch development company based in America, called R A Entertainment. We were well funded, and our purpose was to develop two screenplays for preproduction. The two we chose for development were *The Substitute*, which I wrote, and *The Johnson-Blues*, which Rocco wrote. Then we prepared Memorandums, budgets, et cetera. For *The Johnson-Blues*, a perverse black comedy-thriller about a single mother and her daughter fending off an attack on their brownstone in Lower Manhattan by inbred Ramapo Mountain hillbillies, we felt a "name" in the Memorandum might help to overcome the weirdness of the plot. Of our development budget, ten thousand dollars was allotted to secure such a commitment. I approached Glenda Jackson, with whom I'd worked once before, on *Burt's Bikers*, and out of sheer luck, she was at a point in her career where a change of pace seemed strategic. Also, it didn't hurt that her sixteen-year-old son, after reading the screenplay, urged her to get involved in our high-class horror flick. She agreed to give us a letter of commitment, and didn't ask for money. We had snagged the participation of a great actress who needed us as much as we needed her. Moreover, she suggested her friend Oliver Reed as the head of the mutated mountain clan, a brutish actor with whom she'd done battle previously in *Women in Love*. A great idea. One casting coup had led to another. We never had to use our development allotment, but we might have had to.

(R A Entertainment was dissolved after one year, and as part of my settlement, I was given full rights to *The Substitute*, while the company took *The Johnson-Blues* back to Holland with them. I informed Glenda that I was no longer involved with the project, and she laughingly replied that she'd be willing to jump over a few canals. Eventually it was produced as *The Johnsons* by Dutch filmmaker Rudolf van den Berg, and though they would have benefited from having the participation of a two-time Academy Award winner for Best Actress—since they were hoping for a crossover film, one with international cache—they ended up not using her. *The Johnsons* was the number-one film in Holland when it debuted, doing better box office than *The Prince of Tides*. It has achieved a noncommercial but highly visible cult status in the States. And where did Glenda end up? As a member of the British Parliament.)

Now if, after all this, you've accepted the fact that money must be spent before you can raise money for the film—and, in addition to what I've mentioned, there are also the little matters of copyright protection and WGA (Writers Guild of America) registration for the screenplay, title protection with the MPAA (Motion Pictures Association of America) if you feel so inclined (which I don't, as a rule), and myriad other mini-expenses a diligent producer will attend to—if you've accepted the fact of development as a reality in your film's life, *how then does one go about raising these funds?*

THE DEVELOPMENT PITCH

Put yourself in an investor's position. It doesn't matter if your potential investors are friends, family members, or people one step further removed (though with development, it should ideally be no more than four or five investors, and they should be people you know): They are going to carefully consider what they are being asked to do. And what you are asking of them is to invest money several months prior to, and outside the reality of, your project. Their five or ten thousand doesn't guarantee that you will get the film off the ground, merely that you will be brought up to the point of asking for money to produce it. In other words, they're taking a longer risk than the actual investors in the film, and a bigger risk as well: they stand to lose all their money if the film's budget never materializes, something the investors in the film truthfully don't face. Oh yes, they can lose their money, too, but the chances are they'll have a film to show for it, an investment that, down the road, could still yield earnings. How do you justify to a potential development investor the transfer of cash from his or her pocket to yours, with the distinct possibility of nothing to show for it?

Surprisingly, I've always found it easier to raise development money than the actual budget of the film. So, there must be something compelling about this kind of investment. And indeed there is. Let me go through the development fund-raising pitch from the beginning, and you'll see how it gathers momentum and finally becomes an investment opportunity that is hard to resist.

PRODUCER: So, Nicole, how'd you like to invest five thousand into the development of our new project?

POTENTIAL DEVELOPMENT INVESTOR: Well, I need to hear more about it . . . but why are you calling me Nicole?

P: Oh, that's just for the purposes of this chapter on development. You could be anyone.

PDI: Okay. Well then, about the money. I'm not doing great this year, but maybe I could afford a few thousand . . . but, uh, you explained what development is, but why would I want to invest in your new film so early? Why don't I just jump in when you're closer to getting it off the ground?

P: Well, that's a good point. You could. But I need this capital to get to the next plateau, and there are incentives for being a development investor. For instance, if we use the tired but classic metaphor that the entire earning power of the film, 100 percent of the film, is a pie, with 50 percent generally going to the investors and the other 50 percent going to the producer, and we say—just for the purposes of this example—that the budget is a half-million dollars, if you do the math, then each investor percent is worth ten thousand dollars. What the producer does with the other 50 percent of the pie is up to him, but it's his job to hang onto as much of that percentage as he can. Some of it may go to a lawyer, some may go to the director, or the screenwriter, or a name actor, or a name cinematographer, or for an otherwise unaffordable location . . . whatever. When he's given away whatever he's had to, what's left of that 50 percent is the producer's.

The development investors' percentage *also* comes from the producer's 50 percent, not from the 50 percent that represents the investors' half-million. So . . . we've said that for the investors in the film's budget, $10,000 would buy one percent of the film. Right?

PDI: Yep.

P: However, as a development investor, and not an investor in the budget of the film, your investment would be made equal to twice the percentage that an investor in the film's budget would get for the same amount of money . . . which is only fair, since you're taking a longer shot.

PDI: So, for five thousand, I'd get 1 percent of the producer's share, whereas the other investors would have to pay ten thousand for one percent of the investors' 50 percent.

P: Yes, and what's more, that money—your $5000—would show up as an expense item in the film's final budget . . . as "Development Expenses" . . . so that when the budget is raised—the half-million—you would get your money back immediately, off the top, in preproduction, and still retain the one percent you were given from the producer's piece of the pie. You would no longer be at risk financially, and you would stand to share proportionately more than the other investors in the film's profits.

PDI: Gotcha. Interesting. Now, when money starts coming in, do I get money from my 1 percent at the same time that the other investors do?

P: Well, no, because you've already made all your money back. So it's only fair that they be allowed to make all *their* money back first. Then everyone shares equally—you, me, and the investors. And there may be a few deferred amounts, for a name actor for example, that come even before the investors, but right now, there aren't any.

PDI: Okay. So if it takes you six months to raise the budget, using what I invested separately with you to enable you to get that far, if it takes you six months, at that point I get paid back off the top, and the other investors have to wait until the film comes out.

P: More or less. There could be a distribution deal that gives a large enough advance to get them clear, but yes, that's the general idea. You get twice as much as they do in terms of profit participation, and, if we raise the capital to shoot the film, you get your money back immediately, and they have to wait out the production, post-production, the film festivals, and marketing conventions and distributor screenings, the period of time it takes from having made a distribution deal to the time the film plays . . .

PDI: How much longer would that be?

P: Could be as long as a year. Could be longer if we self-distribute, which is becoming more and more of a reality these days, with digital video and all the cable outlets. If you look at it that way, you may actually be waiting a shorter period of time to get your money back than they will, even though you've invested several months earlier than they have.

PDI: Yeah, but . . . I see why it's a good deal, for me . . . to invest in development. But it's a long wait, and I might be able to better use that money in the meantime.

P: Well, it's not *that* long a wait, since you'll be getting it back off the top from the budget.

PDI: I understand. But you might never raise the money to make the film, and you'd have spent all the money I gave you trying.

P: True . . .

Okay. Now that's a relatively common perch to have jostled a potential development investor on to. She's up on the fence. She's teetering. I can feel her slipping off into my arms with that check. There's grease on that fence. But she needs one more little tweak, one more piece of good, legitimate bait dangled in front of her to do the job.

And the great thing is, you've had that final chess move in your pocket all this time. But you've saved it, waiting to see if your potential investor needed the whammy. And if she didn't, if she forked over the cabbage without it, then you give it to her anyway, because she's got to know, and she's gonna be very happy to hear it . . . but this way you're actually letting her set herself up for the denouement. All roads lead to this final piece of information, and it's the one that makes the development money yours:

P: . . . and that's a good point. Which leads us to the area of tax write-offs.

PDI: Can film investments be written off?

P: Actually, no. And of all people, it was Reagan who saw to that. Before his administration, there were fairly seductive tax incentives, but he knew, being a film person, that if a film earns 10 percent of its money back in the first year, it can still keep earning for the next twenty years. So, you can't write off the other 90 percent. There is a small tax write-off, but it's not enough for me to use it as a major incentive in raising money.

PDI: *[staring, waiting . . .]*

P: However, a *development* investment can be written off entirely.

PDI: Really?

P: Yes, because of the nature of the investment. Think about it: If, after a while, I've raised the budget, you get your 100 percent back immediately. If, on the other hand, a reasonable amount of time passes, say two years, and I haven't been able to raise enough money to produce the film, I will inform you and, at your request, send you a letter declaring that your money is a complete loss, and then you can write off 100 percent of your investment.

PDI: That's really great. Does it have to be in two years?

P: No. In two years I'll inform you that the film isn't going to happen—god forbid—and you can tell me to wait with the letter for a later year, when you've earned a lot and need a good deduction to balance it. One investor had me wait six years before requesting the letter. And it still worked.

PDI: So, give me this again . . .

P: So, either you make it all back in several months and stand to profit without risk, or, down the road, you get to use 100 percent of your development investment as a tax write-off. It's actually a no-lose situation. Obviously you'd like the film to make money for you, but at least, either way, you do okay. And that's only the case with *development* money.
      [Pause.]

PDI: Okay. I'll do it.

P: You'd have to be out of your fucking mind not to!

Sorry; scratch that last outburst. That was just me thinking.

There are other ways to sweeten the deal. You could offer the potential development investors double their money back out of the budget, or you could structure it as a bonus in a first position after the investors have recouped their monies.

A development agreement is brief and to the point. It protects you, but it reads like a loan rather than an investment in a corporate entity, and, in fact, that's really much closer to the truth, a kind of a loan between the investor and yourself. Here's one version of a development agreement for you to peruse, bearing in mind that a lawyer should be consulted if you plan to adapt it to your own purposes, because in some states it might violate security laws.

NAME & ADDRESS OF PERSON
SEEKING DEVELOPMENT MONEY

DATE

NAME AND ADDRESS OF INVESTOR

"NAME OF FILM PROJECT"

Dear _____ :

This letter will constitute an agreement between us concerning certain monies to be advanced by you to me [*or us, accordingly*] for use in connection with expenses incurred and to be incurred for my proposed motion picture ("the Motion Picture") presently titled "_____."

1. Upon the execution of this Agreement, you agree to pay me the amount of Five Thousand Dollars ($5,000) (the "Advance"), to be used by me, in my sole discretion, for preproduction and production expenses incurred in connection with the Motion Picture.

2. In consideration of the Advance paid to me hereunder, you and I agree as follows:

A. Out of my Producer's Share of the net profits, if any (as hereinafter defined), from the exploitation of the Motion Picture, you shall be entitled to receive a sum equal to __% of my Producer's Share of net profits.

As used herein, "my Producer's Share" shall mean the aggregate monies received by the Production Entity from the Motion Picture after the deduction of theatre owner's percentage or fee, distribution fees, the cost of prints, advertising, and distribution expenses, the equity interest (if any) due to suppliers and financiers of, investors in and guarantors of the "Main Finance" of the production, the production budget and negative costs and all other participations in gross and net receipts.

B. I shall have no obligation to repay any of your Advance to you except as follows:

(i) If, and only if, a final production budget is set for the Motion Picture, you shall receive out of the initial expenditure of funds from such production budget a sum equal to twice the amount of the Advance.

(ii) If we abandon the production of the Motion Picture (as provided in paragraph 3 herein), I shall return any unused portion of the Advance to you pro rata with any other persons who have made similar advances, if any.

3. It is understood that I shall have the right, in my sole discretion, if I shall deem it appropriate, to abandon the production of the Motion Picture at any time, whether before or after the commencement of principal photography, without any obligation to you hereunder, except for the pro rata return of any unused portion of the Advance.

4. This Agreement is made in the State of New York, and shall be governed and enforced in accordance with the laws of the State of New York.

5. Nothing herein contained shall be deemed to make you a partner or joint venturer with me in connection with the production of the Motion Picture.

If the foregoing fully sets forth our understanding, please sign below where indicated, and thereupon this will constitute a binding and enforceable agreement between us.

Very truly yours,

[Producer's signature]

[Producer's name]

ACCEPTED AND AGREED TO   DATE

[Signature of development investor]   _____

[Name of development investor]

I know what one or two of you are thinking. A crafty individual could just keep making development deals and live off them for an entire lifetime. Tell investors the budget is $5 million and raise $50,000–$100,000, only to send out the letter in two years while living high on the hog in the meantime.

Exactly how many times do you think you'd be able to pull that off? How many close potential investors do you have? Remember, you can't reach out too far for development money. So you might be able to do it once, or even twice if they're soft touches, but not for a lifetime. And besides, is that how you plan to write your life in stone? By scamming development money and never making films? Good luck.

And just so you know, after all this in-depth explication about the nature of raising development money, I put up the $8,000 for *The Sweet Life* myself rather than go searching for it, and concentrated my time on the creation of the Business Plan and Memorandum, which would serve to secure me the funds necessary to put the film in the can, or the digital video on the tape . . . whatever.

CHAPTER FIVE

CASTING

After the writing and preparation of the script, casting is the most important part of the filmmaking process. Cast well and you'll have a shot at making something decent. Cast not so well and it won't matter how good the script or the photography is, your picture probably won't play. And I don't mean just casting actors who turn out to be no good; you can cast tremendously talented actors—hell, famous actors, *stars*—but if they're wrong for the parts they're playing, it won't matter how talented they are. You're multiplying by zero. But Hollywood studios, more often than not, don't cast based on the criteria of who's right for the part. They cast based on who can get the project a green light at that particular moment in time. How the movie will turn out is beside the point.

If you've seen *The Substitute*, you know that as the battle-scarred, world-weary, middle-aged mercenary Shale, Tom Berenger was a great choice. And when asked at the time of the film's release, Live Entertainment studio executives, to a man, all said he was their first choice, their only choice.

Of course, they were lying.

Here's how it really went. And remember, this is a typical Hollywood casting story, the only exceptional element being that it has a reasonably happy ending.

Let's look at the character of Shale again, read the description above: battle-scarred, world-weary, middle-aged. Want to know who Live Entertainment approached first?

Denis Leary.

You read that right: Denis Leary. This was 1995, and Leary was the flavor of the moment, hot off his one-man stage and HBO show *No Cure for Cancer*, and his well-received performances in *Demolition Man* and *The Ref*. A talented guy, no doubt, but what could he have been at the time? In his thirties? And he looked twenty-five. But as I said, he was hot at the moment. So, who cared if he was completely wrong for the part? He might have been effective in the teaching scenes, but the rest of it? I think it would have been a disaster. In any case, they offered him a million bucks. No one had offered him that much before.

And he turned it down. Which meant he was not only talented, but smart, too. A lot of others in his position would have jumped at the payday and not worried about being wrong for the part.

Fine, you might say. A casting disaster averted. Given a second chance, they chose more wisely, right?

Wrong.

The next actor they went after was Kevin Bacon. Another brilliantly talented guy, but as a battle-scarred, world-weary, *middle-aged* mercenary? Please. But again, he was hot off a lot of movies that had done good box office. All *I* could see was the image I had of him in *Footloose*. What was he going to do to the bad guys in *The Substitute*—dance them to death? He was an even more ridiculous choice than Leary. But he was a name, he meant a green light. So, they offered him a million and a half.

And (gulp!) he said *yes*.

Huzzahs from Live Entertainment. Deals began to be worked out, and papers drawn up. It would take a couple of days at least.

And in that couple of days, he changed his mind.

I don't know exactly what happened, but I can guess. Why had he accepted the role in the first place, one that was so wrong for him? Precisely for that reason. I can imagine him reading the script and thinking, wow, this is a ballsy part, a kick-ass action part, I never get offered parts like this, I've got to do it. Then a few days passed and he had time to think: *Why* don't I ever get offered a part like this?

Because I'm all wrong for it, that's why.

Thanks, but no thanks. Another smart guy.

Choice number three, and this was one of our suggestions: David Caruso.

Remember, this was 1995, and Caruso, like Leary, was a flavor of the moment. But unlike Leary, we felt Caruso brought more weight and gravity with him from his role on the hit series *NYPD Blue*. He looked older and somewhat world-weary. His face suggested a *past*, one that hadn't always been rosy. And no matter what anybody may say about him now, he was and still remains a terrific actor. If Live Entertainment had to have a flavor of the moment, David Caruso was one we could live with. He read the script, and liked it. So, they offered him $2 million. More than he'd gotten for *Kiss of Death* or for *Jade*.

And he passed. Why?

We knew him a little, had worked with him on a short film called *Swirlee*, which, over the years, has become something of a cult item. So we called him. He told us, yes, he did like the script, a lot, the script wasn't the problem. Nor was the money they were offering. But *Kiss of Death* and *Jade* had been perceived as failures. More importantly, they had been perceived as *David Caruso* failures. He felt he only had one more big screen shot, and he did not believe that Live Entertainment, which, at this point, had never fully financed a picture and was known only as a video distribution company, possessed the clout to get the movie in enough theaters. So he passed. (His concerns were legitimate at the time, but would prove to be wrong. *The Substitute* opened in April of 1996 on 1,800 screens across the country.)

And so finally, FINALLY, they came to Berenger. The guy most right for the part. A great actor, the correct age, with some box-office clout, who, for the audience, brought with him the echoes of all his past military roles in *The Dogs of War*, *Platoon*, and *Sniper*. This was a guy you could believe as a battle-scarred, world-weary, middle-aged mercenary. And, for $2.5 million, they got him.

Thus, the reasonably happy ending I mentioned earlier. However, if Leary or Bacon or Caruso had made their decisions based on greed (usually the most common motivating factor in Hollywood) rather than good sense about their own limitations or concerns about Live Entertainment's, it could easily have been otherwise.

When we first began the process of casting *The Sweet Life*, Roy and I were of slightly different minds as to how it would go. We'd raised the money ourselves to make the film, so we didn't need stars to get a green light; we were our own green light. All we needed to concern ourselves with was casting the best and most appropriate actors for the roles that we could find. Of course, our tiny budget meant we would have to use mostly nonunion actors. In spite of my inherent propensity to worry about everything, this didn't concern me very much. I was excited at the prospect of "discovering" people, and felt a little like Santa Claus in that I was of the belief that we had a variety of really good roles to offer. Roy, however, wasn't so sure of our being able to find all the actors we needed from among the deep pool of nonunion talent making the rounds of casting offices all over Manhattan, and conveyed his uncertainty to me about it on a number of occasions. Now, if you're wondering which of us turned out to be right, the answer is: We both were.

But I'm getting ahead of myself.

In May of 2001, the following ad appeared in *Backstage Magazine*:

> INDIE FEATURE:
> *Casting for a low-budget non-SAG digital feature, shooting July/Aug. Transportation, meals, slight pay provided. No nudity. Romantic triangle involving two brothers, mid-30s, and a feisty female bartender, 28–38. Also seeking several other smaller roles, biker chicks and guys, various participants at gaudy wedding (the jaded parents, etc.).*
>
> *Seeking—MICHAEL: 30s, sensitive, attractive, but insecure and self-deprecating; LILA: late 20s–early 30s, tough, sexy, attractive-but-hard-looking bartender; YOUNG MICHAEL: 10, sensitive; YOUNG FRANKIE: 11, outgoing; SHERRY: 20s–30s, loud, kinky biker chick; MIRANDA: late 20s–early 30s, appears and acts perfectly sane, but isn't; ER DOCTOR: 40s, dry and professional; DEBORAH: stepsister of the bride, early 30s, attractive, sweet and subdued.*
>
> *Send pix & resume to Sweet Life Productions, LLC, Box 925, Planetarium Station, NYC 10024-0546. NON-SAG PERFORMERS.*

What were the two key pieces of information we'd included in this ad of which actors would take particular notice?

Number One: *Transportation, meals, slight pay provided.*

We'd read the ads for other digital and/or low-budget features shooting around New York that were soliciting nonunion actors, and none of them were offering any of these. As many of the actors we ended up casting would tell me later, most low-budget productions expect you to find a way to get to the set on your own and to then shut up and just be grateful for the opportunity. But Roy believes (and I agree with him) that when you pay people, even if it's a small amount, and decently feed them, you create more of an atmosphere of mutual respect and professionalism. In short, people show up, and work harder, when you pay them.

Number Two: *No nudity.*

So much of what actors find themselves auditioning for, so much of what they're asked to do in front of a camera, is gratuitous crap. Actors want to work, desperately; but even more than this they want to do work they feel is worthwhile, or, at the very least, not demeaning. Talk to any aspiring actress and ask her how many times she's gone to an audition and found herself being asked to bare her breasts, or worse. We wanted actors who wanted to be a part of what we were doing not just because it meant an acting job but because our project might turn out to be something they could be proud of having participated in and helped to make better. We wanted good actors, talented actors, *enthusiastic* actors, but if we were to have any hope of luring them, we first needed to get them to respond to our ad. *No nudity*, I think, along with the prospect of actually being paid and fed, sent a message, created a hope in some of the more talented but struggling individuals we were reaching out to that maybe, just maybe, this *Sweet Life* project could be something worth getting involved with.

So how'd we do with the ad?

Here's how: Within a matter of weeks, my apartment was littered with *over fifteen hundred* head shots and resumes. Now, on a studio film, or a larger-budgeted independent feature, a casting director would have pored through this mountain of photographs and narrowed down the selections before presenting them to me. But we had no money to pay for a casting director, and so I had to do it.

It was a daunting and sometimes depressing task. Every time I glanced at a photo and then rejected it, I felt guilty. But there was also the excitement, the anticipation that perhaps inside this next envelope I'd discover a face that spoke to me, that made me think, yes, yes, this could be my Lila, or my Deborah. But each time I spotted one of those faces, new anxieties would immediately set in: Sure, she looks perfect, but can she act?

Well, that's what auditions are for. I'd go through the photos, separate my selections into their appropriate piles—here are the Lilas, here are the Mirandas, et cetera—then I would run them by Roy and he would narrow them down further. Then we scheduled a few days in a room at the School of Visual Arts and began making phone calls to the actors we'd selected.

How do you run an audition? I didn't know. So, I approached Nicole Potter, a friend of ours who had experience on both sides of the table—as an actress who'd been on countless auditions, as well as a director of numerous stage productions—and asked her, how does it normally go? How much time is allotted for each actor? How are they generally treated?

Like cattle usually, came the reply. Maybe five minutes a slot, reading with someone who often doesn't even look you in the eye.

It didn't seem necessary to us, or even productive, to be so rushed and cold. We decided on ten-minute slots, and, rather than hand the actors script pages when they arrived, if we were considering them for one of the four main roles, we arranged to have them pick up the pages (or "sides," as they are called) in advance, so they'd have a few days to familiarize themselves with the material. In some cases, we faxed or e-mailed the pages. Some would call me back and ask questions about the characters, and I always tried to oblige their queries with as much detail as I could. With actors we were considering for the smaller supporting roles, we went with a process we'd learned about from a filmmaker Roy had interviewed named Sal Ciavarello. He'd directed a digital feature called *Hardcore Poisoned Eyes*, and told Roy that when he was auditioning actors, he'd dispensed with having them read scenes from the script and had instructed them instead to come in with a prepared monologue. What he was interested in gleaning from the first go-round was whether they were talented or not, and whether he liked their look and voice in person. This seemed like a useful process for us, since we had any number of parts that called for only a few lines, or just one. How much could you tell from a person coming in and reading one line? We adopted this process, and it worked out well for us.

Something Roy liked to do if we were intrigued by a particular performer was to ask for an adjustment of some kind, to see if the actor could respond to direction and alter his or her performance on the fly. This was of paramount importance to me. I possessed neither the skills nor the background to manipulate or intimidate a performance out of anyone. I'm not an actor. I've never taken an acting course. I was clearly not going to be the kind of director who could teach anyone how to act. I knew the script and I knew the characters. Most importantly, I knew what I wanted. Beyond that, they were going to be on their own. We needed to see if they could handle that.

Many of them couldn't. It's a strange thing to watch when, after you've made a suggestion to, say, play it bigger, or smaller, or happier, or angrier, the actor comes back with . . . *the very same reading he or she just gave.* Over and over again. There's nothing for you to do then but thank them and move on.

But the good ones, they respond to the challenge. Thrive on it, actually. They enjoy the exploration. They surprise you by finding things in the text you didn't know were there. And those are the ones you have to hang on to.

Now, remember when I said I wasn't worried about finding enough talented nonunion actors to fill all the roles we needed to fill, while Roy was concerned we might not? And that, in the end, we both turned out to be right?

A contradictory statement, I know, but accurate. You see, we didn't have any trouble finding talented actors—from among the women. But the men, well, that was a different story. And I have no definitive answer as to why this should have been the case.

Here's one theory: Of the 1,500 head shots we received, over 1,000 of them were women. A two-to-one ratio. (True, we had more women's parts available than men's, which might have contributed *somewhat* to the disparity of the response, but I can't believe that was the entire reason.) There just seem to be more female actors than males. Maybe the women feel the increased competition, and so they work harder, train more, and come in more thoroughly prepared. All I know is this: the women to whom we provided sides in advance generally did not need to read from them when they came in to audition. They'd learned the lines and mapped out a performance. The men, on the other hand, more often than not had *not* learned the lines and *did* need to read from the pages. There was a discernible gender gap when it came to preparation.

Here's another theory: Women are more connected to their emotions than men, and less reserved about exposing them. While men have to overcome their natures to act well, a woman's nature serves the process of acting.

I don't know if either one of these theories holds any water in fact, so don't get steamed at me for being gender-biased or any other politically incorrect label these statements might prompt you to pin on me. I'm just conveying what we experienced in casting *The Sweet Life*. What can I tell you? The women were better. That's just the way it was. Thankfully, there were more female characters in the script than male. If it had been the other way around, I'm not sure what we would have done. As it was, most of the male characters we were forced to cast with SAG actors—union actors. It stretched the limits of our budget, but we had no choice.

Still, for the most part, I enjoyed the process, and think Roy and I did a good job choosing our cast. I loved hearing all these varied and marvelously talented people performing dialogue I'd written, and doing so helped me in rewriting lines that proved difficult, and in cutting others I now realized were unnecessary or too on the nose.

So with the movie cast, only one thing remained: to shoot the damn thing. All this preproduction work—the rewriting and the storyboarding, the hiring of the crew and the casting of the actors—you can liken to the long slow climb up a steep hill a roller coaster makes just after you've been strapped in. Now we'd reached the top, and the real ride was about to begin.

Or so I thought. To use another *Godfather III* reference, at this point, just days away from principal photography, our true enemies had yet to reveal themselves. But they were about to . . .

CHAPTER SIX

THE NAME AND MR. NO-NAME

Adapt. Improvise. Prevail.

This is what marines are trained to do in the face of adversity. How do you react when the terrain differs from what you see on the map? When the enemy (or worse, your supposed ally) behaves in a way that is unexpected? When the battle plan you've laid out suddenly and simply no longer applies? You can cry and curse your luck, fold your tents, and retreat. Or you can adapt, improvise, and, hopefully, prevail. If you're planning on making a film independently, without the safety net of a studio's money and power, you'd better adopt this mind-set, or you'll never make it past the first day of production. In our case, we would never have made it *to* the first day of production.

When you're producing a low-budget feature and trying to convince potential investors that there is a tangible possibility of their (at least) getting their money back, it helps immensely if you've got a "name" in the cast. What is a name? In this context, it's an actor or performer of some kind that people have heard of—someone they've seen on television or in other movies. The level of the "name" will vary accordingly with the budget. If you're Joel Silver and trying to get a big studio to green light your $80 million action picture, you need a name like Nicolas Cage or Mel Gibson. When *The Substitute* was being prepared with a budget of $11 million, Tom Berenger's was the name that got it green-lit. (This was 1995, and Berenger, coming off the modestly surprising box-office success *Sniper*, was still on the "A" list of leading men, though at the very bottom of it, as it was explained to us.) If you're Avi Lerner and you're making an exploitation crime thriller for $2 or $3 million, well, the name of Eric Roberts will do just fine.

Why are names important? Because they represent brand recognition, and help to ensure cable and video sales. ("Have you got a name for the box?"—meaning the video box—is a question you'll be asked frequently.) To help ease our investors' anxieties, and increase our ability to market an intimate, character-driven romantic comedy, Roy felt we needed a name. Given our miniscule budget, I feared this was going to be a tough bill to fill.

We had four major roles, four "leads"—Michael, his brother Frankie, their mutual love interest Lila, and Lila's roommate Sherry. When Roy broke down the schedule to see how many days it would take to film each role, it came out like this:

Michael—twenty-five days

Lila—seventeen days

Frankie—eleven days

Sherry—four days (this would increase to five later on, when we decided to include Sherry in the wedding reception sequence that climaxes the film.)

Clearly, if we were going to get a name, it would have to be in the role of Sherry. It was a flashy part, one that a name could jump into and be done with in less than a week, and one for which we could offer a decent daily payment amount. I asked Roy if he had someone in mind.

He did. Someone he'd often spotted shopping at Zabar's, a rock-and-roll icon from the eighties whom we'll call "The Name." We were both big fans of her music, Roy especially, and we shared the opinion that in the few movies she'd appeared in, she'd never been properly utilized as an actress. We had a role she could be a hoot in, on top of which we would be shooting in New York, which meant our project might appeal to her in that she wouldn't have to leave home and family to do it. Even so, I didn't think we had much of a chance of getting her, but told Roy if he felt strongly about it that it couldn't hurt to try.

Now, do you remember those mistakes in judgment I spoke of making, back in chapter 1? Well, this one was a *biggie*.

Flash-forward a few weeks. Roy had gotten the script to The Name via her agent and had actually received a long phone message from her in response, saying she loved the script and would like to do it. Nice, huh?

Ah, but there's more. Roy handed me the receiver and let me hear it for myself. The voice, instantly recognizable, began speaking not of herself, but of . . . *her husband* (let's call him "Mr. No-Name"). "You know, my husband is a really good actor, and I think he'd be great in the part of Michael. He's just like this guy, he could be really funny . . . ." I was instantly on the defensive. I hadn't even spoken to this woman yet, and she was already pressuring me into casting choices. And her husband, no less? What kind of nepotistic diva bullshit was this? Roy talked me down, reminding me, as he repeatedly has over the years, that in all human situations, the cooler head prevails.

Okay. I'm cool, I thought. Let me find out about this guy.

I looked him up on the Internet Movie Database, and found he possessed a solid list of acting credits. Some big Hollywood movies, some respected independent and art-house films. We were sent his reel and took a look at it. Saw that he was good. Very good, in fact. His look was okay, and he could play the character's age range. I started to become more enamored of casting him than The Name herself. The character of Michael is in almost every scene in the picture, he's the anchor of the story, the heart of it, and if we didn't place a good actor in that role, the participation of The Name or any name wouldn't matter at all, because we wouldn't have a movie. Finally, he came in and read for us. He seemed like a nice enough guy, and knowledgeable about low-budget filmmaking. We explained very clearly and openly what our budget was and what we could afford to pay both him and The Name. If that wouldn't do, we should just walk away from each other now, without any hard feelings. He said he understood, that the role was one he very much wanted to do, and that he and his wife had long been hoping to find a film project in which they could work together. Our script, the roles, and the fact we'd be shooting in New York added up to a perfect situation for them. The money was acceptable, in his case almost beside the point, but we would have to work out the specifics with their respective agents.

Another flash-forward, to Friday, July 21, 2001. We were set to begin shooting on Monday, the 24th, and the last week had been spent rehearsing the actors we'd cast in the major roles. In addition to The Name and Mr. No-Name as Sherry and Michael, to play Frankie we'd chosen Robert Mobley from the Actors Studio, who had played the part well in a staged reading of the script we'd done a few years earlier. As Lila, we'd cast Barbara Sicuranza, whose dark and provocative look was not what I'd originally had in mind for the character. But something in her head-shot spoke to me, and when she came in to read for us, both Roy and I knew we'd found our Lila.

While I'd spent the last weeks storyboarding the script, scouting locations with Roy and our line producer Brian Gunther, as well as auditioning and rehearsing the actors, the negotiations with The Name's agent had dragged on without any final resolution—though as far as I'd been made aware there were no glaring red flags to speak of, no indication that we were in any way terribly far apart. The way I saw it, we were working with a budget well under $200,000. We'd be shooting on digital video with a crew of no more than twenty. We were not flying the

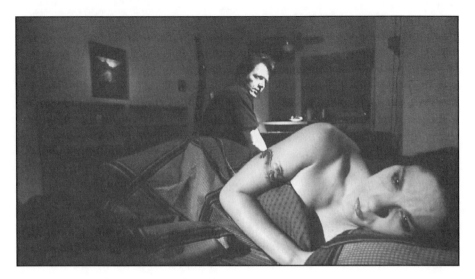

Frankie (Robert Mobley) *and Lila* (Barbara Sicuranza) *reunited, and it feels so good . . . or does it?*

banner of a major studio with millions of dollars in the coffers to throw around. We were just two guys making a glorified home movie. Either you loved the script and wanted to do it for that reason, or you didn't. It had seemed this was understood.

On this particular Friday morning, I had rehearsed The Name and Mr. No-Name in the living room of their vast apartment. I'd told them how grateful I was for their participation, that I was "humbled" that they had both been willing to throw in with an inexperienced first-time director such as myself.

Only I guess I wasn't humbled enough. Because by mid-afternoon, the calls from The Name's agent started coming in, after we hadn't heard a peep from her in over a week. Suddenly there were all kinds of new demands, back-end deals that would have put our investors in even riskier positions than they were already in, and to which, in good con-science, we simply could not agree. She apparently wanted cash bonuses every time one of us sneezed. As the afternoon and the phone calls wore on, Roy and I became increasingly disgusted. We came back with a counteroffer, but by this point, we were, in truth, hoping she'd back out.

Then, contemptibly, No-Name's agent got into the act, and also started making new demands. Looking to ride on his more-famous spouse's coattails, No-Name now wanted the same deal as The Name. All this just two days before we were supposed to start shooting.

Then came the final threat: If we didn't agree to The Name's terms and forced her to leave the project, No-Name would leave with her. This was particularly offensive to us, since Roy and I had gone out of our way to make it clear to No-Name that we wanted him in the role of Michael whether his wife played Sherry or not; that we'd cast him based on his own merits, apart from The Name's participation. Now he and The Name were holding us up. For money. They had waited till the eleventh hour to double-team us, believing we couldn't possibly say no to any of their demands so close to the start date. It was underhanded, and it was obvious, and it made no sense to me. We'd conveyed to them from the very beginning that good roles, rather than money, were what we had to offer. But they were creatures of the industry, and in the end, I suppose, they couldn't deny their natures. In their own minds, I'm sure, they were beyond accountability.

I called No-Name on the phone. Neither Roy nor I wanted to hear later on that we had misinterpreted the situation. I told him what had been related to me, and asked him flat out if the information was accurate: Was he going to walk if we didn't come to terms with his wife?

"Rocco, I've done a number of independent films, and these kinds of back-end deals are pretty much standard. The Name is a big international star, and we feel the only reason this project is happening is because of her, so . . ."

I didn't bother to tell him we hadn't raised a dime based on his wife's involvement, because we hadn't been using her name in any of our promotional material. We didn't have her signed on the dotted line, and Roy felt it wouldn't be ethical to use her name for such purposes until we did. Even if I had told him, I doubt No-Name would have believed me. One has to be capable of ethical behavior to fathom it in others.

"That's not what I asked you," I said, cutting him off. "Are you going to walk if she doesn't do the picture?"

He sighed heavily. "Rocco, I've gotta live with this woman, you know?"

And there it was. "I have my answer then," I responded. "I was looking forward to working with you, but I guess it's not going to happen. Have a nice life."

I hung up the phone, shaking. I then called Roy and recounted to him my exchange with No-Name. They were out, both of them. Two days till principal photography, and we'd lost half our cast. What in the name of all that is cinematically holy were we going to do?

Adapt. Improvise. And, godfuckingdamnit, prevail.

I rushed over to Roy's apartment to discuss our options. There weren't many. One was that we acquiesce to The Name's and No-Name's demands. I'm certain they were expecting us to do just that before the weekend was out. But neither Roy nor I could live with that option. The other, obviously, was to recast. We had a full week before any of the scenes involving the character of Sherry were to be shot, so we still had time to approach another name if we so desired. If we didn't, or if we did and failed, well, it was a city full of actresses, and we had seen a number of good ones who could step into the role and give us a performance. We attempted to comfort ourselves with the knowledge that *The Blair Witch Project* had done reasonably well in the marketplace without any names among its cast, as had *The Brothers McMullen*, and *Pi*, and any number of other independently produced films going back to *Night of the Living Dead*. Rather than be extorted into submission, we would just have to go forward without a name and let the chips fall where they may.

For the role of Michael, I couldn't think of anything else to do other than call on a friend. If we were going to begin shooting without any time for rehearsal or prep work, I needed someone who could not only play the part but with whom I already had a relationship—with whom I shared some common frame of reference. Someone I could communicate with right from the get-go. I turned to Roy and said, "We've gotta find Jimmy Lorinz."

I'd gone to film school with Jimmy, had known him for close to twenty years. Roy had given him his first big break as an actor in a movie Roy wrote and produced in 1985, a midnight classic called *Street Trash*. After that, Jimmy went on to appear in the films *Last Exit to Brooklyn* and *King of New York*. He starred in Frank (*Basket Case*) Henenlotter's *Frankenhooker*, then landed a regular gig on the Valerie Harper series *City*. When that ended, he and Roy and I collaborated on a project called *Swirlee* that spawned a fifteen-minute short film, which didn't succeed in convincing anyone to produce it as a feature, but did generate enough cult status to merit a chapter in Chris Gore's book *The Fifty Greatest Movies Never Made*. I then was involved in the writing of a picture starring Jimmy that *did* get made, but the experience proved so unpleasant for me, he and I ended up not speaking for something like two years. He moved out to Los Angeles, got married and had a child, and continued to appear in films and television shows. Eventually, we reconnected, and when Roy first suggested producing *The Sweet Life* ourselves, we'd considered Jimmy for the role of Frankie.

But he was still living in L.A., and, though he'd read the script and loved it, for a number of reasons, it just wasn't practical, for us or for him.

However, in the weeks just prior to our start date, Jimmy's circumstances had shifted dramatically. He and his wife had separated and decided to come back east, but rather than make the journey by airplane with his wife and daughter, Jimmy had chosen to drive cross-country. At the very moment The Name and No-Name were pulling their last-minute shenanigans on us, he was somewhere out there in the heart of the republic, motoring toward New York.

But where, exactly? And could he be reached? I tried phoning his wife's parents, but got only an answering machine. I had no number for Jimmy's parents, and wasn't even sure they still lived in the city. I called information and asked for any listing of a Lorinz in the five boroughs. There was only one. I dialed it. A woman picked up.

It was Jimmy's mother.

"Mrs. Lorinz, please tell me your son has a cell phone with him, and that you've got the number." He did, and she did. I thanked her profusely, hung up, and dialed the number she'd given me.

He was somewhere in Nebraska. I told him what had happened, and asked him if he'd like the starring role in our movie. He said yeah, sure, of course. How soon could he get back to New York? Monday or Tuesday, came the reply. Fine. (Roy had already told me we could push the start date from Monday to Tuesday, or even Wednesday if we had to.) I told him to call us as soon as he stopped for the night, and we'd fax the pages for the first week of shooting to the front desk of his hotel. This way he'd at least have a few days to learn the lines and be ready to jump in when he got here. I wasn't sure what we'd get from Jimmy in the role of Michael, but it was a part loaded with funny lines, and we knew that, if nothing else, he'd deliver a good comic performance.

I then called my leading lady, Barbara Sicuranza. I told her what had happened, and what we were doing to overcome it. I assured her that we were going to be making a movie, that she was going to play Lila, and that no one was going to stop us. Barbara is married to Chris Stein, of the band Blondie, and so she suggested offering the part of Sherry to Deborah Harry. We thought this was a great idea. Chris got on the phone and added that if Deborah passed, he could also put in a call to Joan Jett. (Before the weekend was out, Harry would pass, and we'd move on to Jett. In the end, it would turn out to be the luckiest thing that could have happened to us.) I thanked them both and hung up, feeling that now at least we had options.

It had been a nerve-wracking, gut-wrenching day, but we'd made it through and kept the project alive. Sure, all our well-laid plans and preparations had gone out the window, but we were still breathing, still moving forward. And at this particular moment in the project's history, that's all that mattered.

CHAPTER SEVEN

THE PRODUCER AS SEDUCER

Here comes a useful chapter about fund-raising for independent productions. But first, I'm going to digress for two minutes (that is if my partner is correct in his "minute-a-page" belief), because I see that Rocco has acquainted you with our little problem involving two of the actors originally scheduled to appear in *The Sweet Life*. Allow me to approach it from another angle . . . as a glass half full. Roc certainly feels that we ended up better off securing the services of Joan Jett. But I take pleasure in telling it as a cautionary tale for all of you, and if you benefit from it, and never fall into the trap they set for us, I'll feel that the soul-curdling horror we endured was worthwhile.

My not seeing it coming is one thing. I do a film every five or ten years. I could have been out of the tactical loop. However, I have advisors, and they should not have been taken in by such aberrant strategies. Why was my agent, who's been in the business forty years, unable to see it coming? What about my manager, who is younger, but in the thick of things and well connected? And then there was our lawyer, with whom I was on the phone practically every day; he, too, did not see the ambush that had been set, until he finally put the question to No-Name's agent, who told him that No-Name and his wife were a package.

And that is what it was: an ambush, cunningly planned and executed. The only thing the other camp didn't anticipate was our recalcitrance. In their minds, they certainly must have had us check-mated. There we were, low in budget, out of time, fully crewed-up with some of our staff already on salary, and we'd been in rehearsal with No-Name for a week, while The Name was already spending our art department's money on her wardrobe. They just hadn't considered our combined sense of ethical outrage. Devastated though we were, Roc and I were willing to shut the film down and reappraise our options, no matter what the damage such a decision would cause, just out of pure stubborn resistance to their duplicity. What I don't want is for this to happen to *you*. And what I've learned from the experience, particularly from all my worldly advisors' inability to perceive the threat, is that this must be a fairly new problem, one endemic to the turn-of-the-century wave of indie filmmaking.

The Name and No-Name's eleventh-hour ambush would, in a very real sense, have gained them control of the production. If we had acquiesced, not only would they have been getting several times more money, and three times as many points, but our capitulation would have set a precedent for them to make whatever further demands they wanted—otherwise they could hold up production and potentially shut us down. Even though SAG insists, as a precaution for their members' interests, that 40 percent of all SAG salaries be put into an escrow account, The Name/No-Name's agents had demanded that the remaining 60 percent be added to the protection fund. SAG, you will be interested to know (names off-the-record), agreed with us that such an actor/agent maneuver was underhanded. And perhaps something could have been done by their union to force them to retract their demands. But they hit us on a Friday, and we were forced to act with little time to think, and into the after hours of that day. With all the shrapnel raining down on me, I never thought to call SAG and protest. So, SAG didn't hear about it until after the fact.

In truth, my producer's paranoia began prodding me to call their hand about two weeks prior to shooting. In retrospect, I obviously should have. And this is what I urge you to do as well. Do not allow a situation to arise in which you will be held hostage. Get your "name"—be it SAG or non-SAG—and negotiate in good faith, but when the arbitrary two-weeks-until-production mark arrives, give the agents an ultimatum: Either it gets finished and signed now, by the end of this day, or we move on. And if they cajole you into continuing the negotiation (a mistake on your part), start seriously looking for a backup immediately. Then terminate the negotiations permanently within a few days of your first deadline.

I can name fifty films that went straight to video or TV with big-to-recognizable names in them. Names like Marlon Brando, Woody Allen, Jean-Claude Van Damme, Steven Seagal, Charlie Sheen, Whoopie Goldberg, et cetera. And I can name others that got a theatrical play with no names at all: *The Blair Witch Project*, *In the Company of Men*, *Girlfight*, *Pi*, et cetera. It has more to do with the nature and quality of the film than it does with star power at a small, indie level. It's great to have a name for a number of reasons—to help raise the money, to get your cast and crew excited and keep an energy going, to secure video sales in Europe and elsewhere, to keep the video on the shelves longer in all territories because of name recognition—but it isn't essential, and it's certainly not worth jeopardizing your production. As Rocco mentioned, we didn't even include our potential stars' names in the Memorandum we sent out to investors, because they hadn't signed on the dotted line. When we finally got our actors signed, they went in . . .

MAKE YOUR BUSINESS PLAN IRRESISTIBLE

. . . which brings me back to the Business Plan. It is this colorful document, positioned at the head of the Memorandum, which will go most of the way toward getting you the money necessary to produce your film. For some, particularly those with a proven track record, an elaborate investor presentation might not be necessary. But for first-timers, or for those who don't make films that often, like myself, it's a major consideration. I've been doing it for over twenty years.

On *Burt's Bikers*, a docudrama about mentally handicapped children in the Greenwich School System, our Business Plan presentation got us The Beatles' song "I Will" for free, because people at Apple Records saw it and responded to it; and it also got us Harry Chapin's commitment to write an original song (alas, he died before he could do that for us), and it got us Ennio Morricone's pledge to write an entire score for free (alas, we were afraid of the time and communication problems involved, and *we* backed out). Finally, we were equally fortunate to obtain the services of the gifted Frederic Hand, who had just done the score for *Kramer vs. Kramer*. Would they have gotten involved without a presentation full of color pictures and beautiful calligraphy by Al Kilgore (creator of the *Bullwinkle* comic strip)? I'm pretty sure the answer would have been *no*.

As I mentioned before, after researching what kind of people might want to invest in such a film as *Street Trash*—the bizarre black comedy about decomposing derelicts—we made the decision to approach middle-income bracketers, people who might risk a few grand at a time for fun, but not much more. With these people, I saw the colorful, seductive Business Plan work its charms over and over again. And this approach has been successful with *The Sweet Life*, too. Every investor has taken the time to compliment the Business Plan as practically a work of art. It's been as much a player in securing the money for these films as I was.

A Business Plan has to contain a certain amount of information: statement of risk (which appears in the Memorandum, too), the screen treatment, information about the filmmakers, a budget top sheet, a timetable indicating how long it will take to get from investment to release, an overview of the marketplace, a comparison with other films in its genre that have performed well, and information about anything unique to the production that enhances its salability. (The Memorandum repeats some of this in a dryer form, but mainly covers the legal and financial structure, an explanation of what the investor's money gets him/her, and the legal relationship of the corporation's partners.)

The "Risk" and "Timetable" pages are always painful to include in a memorandum. One imagines potential investors dropping out as soon as they read them. But, generally, investors understand that you will be held legally culpable if they haven't been adequately warned. Nonetheless, I've resorted to embroidering these with artful distractions in order to lessen the blow. Behold the "Timetable" page from the *Street Trash* Business Plan.

The film's story treatment, anywhere from three to five pages, is sufficient for the Business Plan. Investors without filmmaking knowledge will not be conversant with screenplay form, and to give them the screenplay to read will be a waste of time; or, worse, it will confuse them; or, worse yet, they will feel motivated to offer criticism of what they've read, which is the last thing you want. Don't even offer it to them. (I'm not including the treatment in the Business Plan you are about to see; I ordinarily do, but Roc already included it in chapter 3.)

The "Filmmakers" section would include professional bios (narrative format preferable to a cold list of credits) of the producer, director, screenwriter, actors, or anyone on board who has a track record . . . cinematographer, special-makeup designer, composer, et cetera. In the case of *Street Trash*, the director owned his own Steadicam rig, which gave the film a much more expensive look. I not only put a full page in the Business Plan about the Steadicam, but a picture of the director at work with the Steadicam harness on. This was an image that conveyed a mysterious sense of movie magic, or so it translated to the potential investor, who is partially considering his or her investment in your project because filmmaking has a romantic aura attached to it.

Also, with *Street Trash* we had a first-time director, so I approached a cinematographer with two hundred films to his credit and included his résumé, which enabled me to tell potential investors that no matter what the director did or didn't do, the film would probably look great, which is half the battle. So, the Business Plan is also a document in which potential negatives are balanced in the reader's eye, while I'm there, hovering over said reader, restating the positives. Rocco is a

STREET TRASH - TIME TABLE

Our tentative schedule for production
has already begun. Producer, Director,
Make-up Supervisor, and Art Director
have been working in PreProduction for
six months, preparing the Screenplay
and Preliminary budget.

As of completion of financing, the
remaining schedule will be:

Financing completed: Commence three
months of Special Make-up creation.

Nine Weeks of Production, scheduled
for a July 1st start.

Six months of Editing, to begin during
principal photography.

Six weeks for mix, final timing of
negative on Hazeltine Color Analyzer,
and striking of prints.

Film should be ready for release
approximately one year after
completion of financing.

first-time director as well, but as you will see, I stress his screenwriting accomplishments in the Business Plan, and no one has expressed any anxiety about his directorial gifts.

One last suggestion about first-time directors. If you prepare a list of other directors and their first films, it should diminish the risk factor in potential investors' minds. Orson Welles and *Citizen Kane*. Wes Craven and *The Last House on the Left*. The Coen Brothers and *Blood Simple*. The list is endless, since everyone started somewhere, and so many of them did exemplary work from the starting gate.

A budget top sheet is the one-or-two-page summary of all the categories of the budget. Again, this is all the potential investor is entitled to. Your actual budget is anywhere from fifteen to thirty pages long, and represents many weeks of work. You do not want to give it away. In my experience, 50 percent of potential investors who've been sent my way by other people are actually trying to learn about the business in the hopes of getting something off the ground themselves. They will wheedle everything they can from you, then drop out, using your info as their blueprint. The way to shortcut this dispiriting procedure is to give out only this compressed kind of information for free. If they continue to express interest in possibly investing, but request to see more, it's your opportunity to tell them that you're excited to show them more, but first you have to see their bank book, to make sure that the money they say they want to invest really exists. In other words, as you give more and more info away, they have to give something to you, as well, in terms of a commitment. Force the issue, but in a friendly way. If they stick with it, they may become investors after all.

A timetable is useful in allaying a potential investor's fears when nothing seems to be happening as the months following their investment drag by. This page should emphatically state that they will not be seeing any yield on their investment for at least a year, and possibly for two to three years. Think about it. Preproduction, production, postproduction. Then testing the film in festivals, arranging screenings for distributors. Then, after it's sold, the distributor has to first plan publicity, then book play-dates, or get it into video stores, or onto cable. We're talking a year at the very least, longer when you include overseas revenues. The potential investor must know this up front.

The marketplace is the world, and in each territory there's the potential of theatrical, TV, home video, armed forces, airlines, and media yet to be devised. Before each of the major marketing conventions— Cannes, MIFED (in Milan), the AFM in Santa Monica, the IFP in New

York City—your entertainment lawyer should be able to advise you as to what minimum bids you can expect from each of these markets based on recent market results for his other clients. This way you can keep on top of your foreign-sales agent, and write encouragingly to your investors, as well. *Variety* also reports after each of these conventions as to how films are selling for the various markets, and often divides the results into budgetary zones (e.g., films made for $500,000–1,000,000 went for a certain range, films made for $1,000,000–3,000,000 went for a different range, et cetera.)

A nice way to make a potential investor feel safer about his potential investment is to reduce pages from *Variety*'s Top 50 chart, which is published every week, and highlight films that are similar in genre or budget to yours. If they're even *on* the chart, that's a good sign. With *Street Trash,* I used *Repo Man* and *Blood Simple* in the Business Plan as successful models of what we were going after—low-budget black comedies that performed well. With *The Sweet Life,* as you'll notice, I actually left that category out. Why? Because the digital indie genre is in its infancy and I didn't trust the rather random performances at my disposal. Would you, if you were a potential investor, believe that *The Blair Witch Project* was typical of the new indie marketplace? I wouldn't. But by the time you've read this and are organizing your own Memorandum and Business Plan, the comparisons will be far more available and believable.

The financial/legal entity is generally boilerplate, and there's no way to gussy that up. So it comes last, in the Memorandum, along with the relationship of the partners. By this time, the potential investor isn't reading quite as thoroughly. All the fun-to-read stuff was up front.

What follows is the "fun-to-read stuff" from the *Sweet Life* Business Plan. You'll see just how much I relied on my art director, Denise LaBelle, to bring my vision of this document to reality. With modern computer graphics, there is simply no excuse for a Business Plan that fails to dazzle the potential investor. I supplied Denise with categories, text, and pictures, and she supplied the concept, fashioning it all into a cohesive whole. She also created the effective title page. What you won't see is the color palette, a shame, because those soft yellows and greens looked *so* lovely.

The description of the corporate entity is saved for the Memorandum. As previously discussed, there are several types of corporate entities you can structure, depending on how you think your financing will be obtained. Most film productions in this country have used the more advantageous, tax-wise, Limited Partnership, S-Corp, or LLC, in which

SweetLife Productions, LLC

Presents

THE SWEET LIFE

THE PRODUCER AS SEDUCER

The contents

of this informational packet
are confidential and are disclosed pursuant to
a confidential relationship and may not be
reproduced or otherwise used except for
the purpose intended herein.

THE SWEET LIFE

**Key
Creative
Forces**

Roy
FRUMKES

Producer/
Co-screenwriter

is co-author of **THE SUBSTITUTE,** produced by Live Entertainment, which not only rose to the number two position on Variety's Box Office chart, but subsequently earned twenty-two million in domestic video sales and spawned a lucrative franchise.

Enchanted by his grandfather's stories of the golden days of vaudeville (Bernard Burke was the leading Keith Circuit Booking Agent of the 20's and numbered, among his client list, Houdini - the greatest vaudeville act of all time), Roy followed his childhood dreams of filmmaking, and has been producing, writing and/or directing motion pictures for thirty years.

His first, as Assistant Director and Associate Producer, was **THE PROJECTIONIST** starring, in his film debut, a then-unknown Rodney Dangerfield. It developed a cult following and was chosen by The Museum of Modern Art as one of the three best films of 1971.

Roy directed the TV special **AN EVENING AT DANGERFIELD'S,** and later wrote and directed **BURT'S BIKERS,** a docudrama about Down's Syndrome children narrated by Academy Award winner Glenda Jackson. It was telecast on NBC and won the coveted D.W. Griffith Award.

In 1987, Roy wrote and produced the feature **STREET TRASH,** which was released through Vestron's Lightning Pictures division. An aggressive black comedy destined for cult status, **STREET TRASH** enjoyed wide theatrical exposure here and abroad, winning several foreign festival awards, and subsequently broke into Billboard's Top 40 chart for home video rentals. It is still shown globally in film festivals, most recently at Fantasia Montreal and Fantasia Toronto, both in 1998.

In 1989 Roy's long-awaited feature-length documentary **DOCUMENT OF THE DEAD** was released direct-to-video by Off-HollywoodVideo. In production for 12 years, **DOCUMENT OF THE DEAD** is a comprehensive study of independent filmmaking in the U.S., focusing on the career of director George Romero. It won the Gold Award at the Houston International Film Festival, and was named one of the ten best horror videos of 1989 by *The Phantom Critic* of the *New York Daily News.* A special edition of **DOCUMENT OF THE DEAD** was released on DVD by Synapse Films in 1998, featuring commentary by Roy and others involved in its production.

With writing partner Rocco Simonelli, Roy has written several screenplays over the past few years. **DUST** has been twice optioned by Gary

Roy FRUMKES

2

Shusett, and **THE SUBSTITUTE,** directed by Robert Mandel and starring Tom Berenger, created a franchise - hence their **SUBSTITUTE 2** was premiered on HBO in the Spring of '98 to high ratings, this time starring Treat Williams, and **SUBSTITUTE 3,** again with Treat Williams, was an HBO premiere in 1999. **SUBSTITUTE 4** premiered on HBO in 2000, with Williams reprising his role in the popular series yet a third time.

A supernatural thriller for which Roy created the original story idea and Rocco penned the script - **THE JOHNSONS** - filmed in Amsterdam by director Rudolph Van Den Berg, developed a loyal genre following and had its US video release in the Spring of 1999. The DVD features a spirited commentary track by Roy, Rocco and Rudolph.

From 1985 to 1994 Roy produced and directed the annual **D.W. Griffith Awards Ceremony,** working with the likes of Paul Newman, Bette Davis, William Hurt, Steven Spielberg, Kirk and Michael Douglas, Sidney Poitier, Jodie Foster and Sean Connery.

In addition, from 1994 to 1995 Roy was Managing Editor of *The Perfect Vision,* America's leading home theater magazine, and brought its circulation from 15,000 to 25,000. He has since assumed ownership of *Films in Review Magazine,* America's oldest and most prestigious film publication, and has brought it into cyberspace as www.filmsinreview.com, where it currently garners thousands of hits a day.

For two decades, Roy has taught courses in film production and screenwriting at the School of Visual Arts in New York City, and has lectured at many other respected institutions including Harvard University and Cornell Medical Center. He sits on the Board of Directors of the prestigious National Board of Review of Motion Pictures, has served as Vice President

in the Charge of the BBC's Film Archives in America, has managed movie theaters for the United Artists circuit, and has hosted his own film-oriented talkshow on WVOX radio.

Upcoming projects include a movie-of-the-week for TNT, tentatively entitled **Troubled Water,** for which Roy and Rocco have written the screenplay, with Emmy-award winning actor Andre Braugher in the lead, and **Triptych,** a psychological thriller to be helmed in Amsterdam in 2001 by legendary film director Alejandro Jodorowsky (**El Topo, The Holy Mountain, Santa Sangre**), again with a script by Roy and Rocco.

**Rocco
SIMONELLI**

*Director/
Co-screenwriter*

3

is the co-author (with writing partner Roy Frumkes) of
THE SUBSTITUTE, an action-adventure directed by Robert
Mandel (FX) and starring Tom Berenger, Ernie Hudson and
Diane Venora. Produced by Live Entertainment and distributed theatrically by Orion, the film opened number two
on the domestic box office charts, then went on to
become one of the most successful video releases of 1996.
THE SUBSTITUTE 2: SCHOOL'S OUT, a sequel shot on
location in New York City and starring Treat Williams, was
also penned by Rocco and Roy, and was a highly rated
HBO premiere in the spring of '98. The following fall they
were enlisted by Artisan Entertainment to write a third
installment of the popular franchise, with Williams returning
as the title character. **THE SUBSTITUTE 3: WINNER
TAKES ALL,** co-starring Claudia Christian (Babylon Five, The Hidden),
proved just as popular with HBO's over twenty million subscribers when
it premiered on the cable network in August of '99. The series continues
with **THE SUBSTITUTE 4: FAILURE IS NOT AN OPTION,** which hit
the video charts in the spring of 2001.

Most recently, for Turner Network Television and Davis Entertainment, Rocco & Roy have
written **TROUBLED WATER,** the inspiring true story of American swimmer Nelson
Diebel, who overcame both personal and physical problems to win a gold medal at the
'92 Barcelona Olympics. Emmy winning actor Andre Braugher (Glory, City of Angels,
TV's Homicide and Gideon's Crossing) is attached to star as Chris Martin, the intimidating
coach who helped turn the youth's life around. They've also completed a major rewrite
of a thriller script titled **TRIPTYCH** for Cadenza Films and producer Pierre Spengler
(Superman I, II & III) with legendary South American filmmaker Alejandro Jodorowsky (El
Topo, Holy Mountain, Santa Sangre) attached to direct.

They are also the authors of **SLAY THE BULLY!,** a sharp-witted satire of American huck-
sterism set in the milieu of a suburban junior high school, which has been purchased by
Promark Entertainment. For producer Robert Harris' Davnor Productions (The Grifters),
they wrote the psychological thriller **IN THE DARK,** an adaptation of the novel Soul
Snatcher by Camerin Grae. Other scripts by the duo include **DUST,** a thrice-optioned
action script, and **THE COMPOUND,** a contemporary action thriller with a sci-fi twist.

In addition, Mr. Simonelli's original screenplay (from a story by partner Roy Frumkes)
served as the basis for the mystical thriller **THE JOHNSONS.** Directed by noted
Dutch helmer Rudolf Van Den Berg (Cold Light of Day), it proved a theatrical hit in
Europe, and has become a cult favorite among American horror enthusiasts. Mr.
Simonelli also wrote the script for **ME AND THE MOB,** a gangster comedy
filmed in New York and featuring Sandra Bullock in a memorably raunchy cameo.
Released in 1994, the film garnered positive reviews from Variety and The New York

Rocco SIMONELLI

Director/
Co-screenwriter

4

Daily News. His screenplay for **SWIRLEE**, an independent short starring David Caruso, was the subject of a major article in Film

Threat Magazine, and was also featured in Chris Gore's book The Fifty Greatest Movies Never Made. Magazines in which Mr. Simonelli's writing has appeared include *The Perfect Vision*, *Films in Review* and *Expressions of Dread*. He is the recipient of three awards for screenwriting from the Houston International Film Festival for his scripts **A TICKET TO PARADISE** (a romantic comedy), **REBEL, REBEL** (an escape adventure), and the aforementioned **DUST**. He studied both art and film at the School of Visual Arts in New York, where he now teaches screenwriting. Other schools at which Simonelli has taught or lectured include Marymount College and SUNY.

THE PRODUCER AS SEDUCER

JAMES LORINZ AND
BARBARA SICURANZA

The droll craftsmanship of **James Lorinz** was a perfect matchup for the role of Michael, the witty, self-deprecating protagonist of *The Sweet Life*.

The versatile actor has appeared in many films over the last fifteen years including *Last Exit to Brooklyn, The King of New York, Robocop 3, Me and the Mob, Mr. Wonderful, Frankenhooker* and, for producer Frumkes, *Street Trash,* the black comedy cult classic of 1987 which featured Lorinz's attention-grabbing debut performance.

On TV, Lorinz has been equally prolific, co-starring in the tv series *City* with Valerie Harper, and also appearing in *The Practice, Brooklyn South, The Fighting Fitzgeralds, Becker, Judging Amy,* and *NYPD Blue.*

In the role of Lila, the feisty yet forlorn barmaid whom Michael is motivated to help and love, relative newcomer **Barbara Sicuranza** makes a vivid impression. Her only previous film appearance is in the soon-to-be-released indie feature *Margarita Happy Hour,* which is making the Film Festival circuit and winning rave reviews.

Also starring in *The Sweet Life,* as Michael's self-confident cad of a brother is **Robert Mobley** of the Actor's Studio in New York, who completed a role in Macbeth in Central Park just days before stepping into his cinematic shoes.

OUR HELL'S ANGEL FROM HEAVEN

Joan Jett, who plays the role of Sherry the Biker Roommate in *The Sweet Life*, was born in Philadelphia, Pennsylvania, and moved with her family first to Baltimore, and later, when she was twelve, to Los Angeles.

In L.A., passionate about Rock and Roll, she met song writer Kari Krome, and together they came up with the idea of a five-girl, teenage band playing the kind of aggressive rock that until then had been reserved only for guys. Dubbed *"The Runaways"*, and featuring Jett on guitar and vocals, the group achieved a formidable reputation, and released their first album via Mercury Records in 1976.

By '77 they had soon-to-be-huge bands Cheap Trick and Tom Petty and The Heartbreakers opening for them. A tour of Japan was an enormous success. Members came and went, though Joan remained consistent. In the Spring of '79, *"The Runaways"* dissolved.

Jett toured solo, released a single in Holland, and produced the *"Germs"* highly acclaimed first album, "GI". After this, and a six week hospital bout with heart valve infection, came a fateful meeting with producer/songwriter Kenny Laguna. With Kenny as her manager, they formed Blackheart Records. In December, 1981, the album *"I Love Rock-n-Roll"* was released. The title song single climbed the charts to #1 in America, the first song by a female-fronted band to do so, and it remained there for seven weeks. The album sold over ten million copies worldwide.

In 1985 Jett acted in Paul Schrader's *Light of Day* opposite Michael J. Fox. In 1989, the song *"I Hate Myself For Loving You"* was nominated for a Grammy, and *"Up Your Alley,"* her album from which the song came, went platinum.

In '92 she portrayed the villainous Felicia Martinez in the television series *"Highlander"*. In '95 she appeared on the television programs *"Unsolved Mysteries"* and *"America's Most Wanted"* to further the investigation into the brutal '93 sex murder of Mia Zapata, one of Seattle's most talented and popular performers. In '96 she appeard in the documentary *"Not Bad For a Girl"*, about hard-rocking women. Starting in '98, amid constant touring work and live appearances, she began hosting *"Independent Eve"*, a showcase of indie films for Maryland Public Televison. '99 saw the release of Joan Jett and The Blackhearts' Compilation CD *"Fetish"*.

In 2000, after guest starring on the popular TV series *"Walker, Texas Ranger"*, Joan ascended the Broadway Stage as Columbia in the successful revival of "*The Rocky Horror Show*." She left in May of '2001, and by July was essaying her colorful tour de force in *The Sweet Life*. We were thrilled to have her: her generous spirit and professionalism added greatly both to the experience of making the movie, as well as in making it come alive in post production.

THE
SWEET LIFE

**Budget
Summary**

The optimum budget - the one for which producers strive - is the magic figure that will result in a maximum return on the invested dollar without compromising the quality of the film. The Producer attempts to divine this balance of expenditure against the projected income the film will generate.

In the past, a standard industry rule of thumb maintained that a picture must gross approximately three times its negative cost to break even. This multiple of three took into account the Exhibitor's (theater owner) cut, the Distributor's cut, and the distributor's costs in promoting the film and striking prints. It didn't take into account Exhibitor and Distributor bookeeping 'sleight of hand', an appalling prospect to which all filmmakers are subject.

The Sweet Life will cost $250,000 both to complete and to take as far as distribution. Another $100,000 may be raised depending on various contingencies once we reach that point. A total of $350,000.

However, times have changed dramatically in the last two years. In some instances there may be no Distributor and no Exhibitor involved in the dissemination of the film to the paying public. The Internet and Broadband Cable TV have seen to that. And, as explained in the "Why Video?" section of this memorandum, there is no longer necessarily even a Negative!

So...what once was a figure of three times the monies spent as a goal for recoupment has to be substantially reduced to reflect the changing marketplace. No true figures are available at this time: the industry as it is presently evolving is just too current to have generated detailed studies. However, individual cases suggest that with a budget as low as ours, it would not be outside the realm of possibility to recoup all expenses - and bring the investors to the level of profit participation - from earnings of between $400,000 and $700,000.

Until recoupment is reached, all monies received by The Sweet Life Productions LLC will go to the investors. After this breakeven point is reached, profits will be shared equally by investors and producers.

Following is the 'Budget Top Sheet', which summarizes the various categories of the Development, Pre-production, Production, Post-production, and Securing Distribution phases of the film. It will continue to evolve and shift during production, but will always stay within that magic number.

| DEVELOPMENT | Memorandum, opening bank account, QuickBooks, stationary, legal fees, test shoot for video *format, website registration, etc.* .... .10,000. |

PRODUCTION	
Producer's Unit	.10,900
Director of Photograhy's Unit	.17,000
Sound Recordist's Unt	.5,300.
Art Director Unit	.8,100.
Dialogue Coach - Nicole Potter - rehearsals + several days	.1,000.
Cast - Leads, Bits, Xtras	.12,000.
Rehearsal food & trans	.500.
Equipment Rental & Purchase	.12,000.
DigiBeta shooting stock 60 hr. X 20	.1,200.
Locations (include construction, materials)	.7,000.
Costumes, props, make-up	.5,000.
Transportation	.11,000.
Food:	.10,500.
Stills	.2,000.
Insurance	.6,000.
Accounting	.1,500.

Post Production	Editor's Unit	10,000.
	PAL Deck	4,000.
	Transfer to VHS for edit 8 hr. X $300.	2,400.
	Slave of master - 100 per hr. + stock	2,200.
	3 Firewires for storage	1,500.
	On-line edit including dissolves - $600 per hr. X 8	4,800.
	Sound stock	600.
	Foley / ADR	4,000.
	Mix - $300 per hr. X 40 + Mix stock	12,000
	Titles	500.
	Music - include pub rights to one song	15,000.
	Editing Supplies, etc.	3,000.
	Contingency - 10 % approximately	18,000.
	TOTAL:	**199,800.**

Securing Distribution & Beyond	Phone	3,000.
	Accounting (distribution arrangements)	4,000.
	Copies (VHS, Beta SP, Digi Beta, PAL, etc)	5,000.
	Postage, office supplies, etc.	3,000.
	Poster Art	500.
	Distribution Publicity Kit	7,500
	E&O Insurance	7,000.
	Copyright registration, MPAA	500.
	Dialogue continuity for foreign sales	500.
	Festivals, marketing conventions, etc	10,000.
	Website (2 yrs)	700.
	2 years accounting, etc.	5,000.
	Contingency - 8% approximately	4,500.

TOTAL: **250,000.**

THE
SWEET LIFE

Markets &
Timetable

THE SWEET LIFE
Markets

The Sweet Life has many markets from which to earn revenue.

These include:
- *Domestic theatrical*
- *Foreign theatrical*
- *Non–theatrical (colleges, airlines, armed forces)*
- *Domestic television*
- *Foreign television*
- *Pay television/Cable*
- *Home Video (VHS, DVD)*
- *"Making of" documentary*

Any one of these markets could recoup the entire investment, considering our low budget.

THE SWEET LIFE
Time Table

The Development stage of the Production is already over. We are now in Pre-production. This will continue through a week of rehearsals in mid-July.

Production will begin on July 23rd, twenty-six days of shooting over a five week period, ending late in August, to be followed by a week of Sound pickups.

Then the meticulous Post-production process, begun during the shoot, continues until late in the year. By 2002 we will have our finished film, ready to begin to showing in strategic Film Festivals, at Marketing Conventions, and to various Distributors.

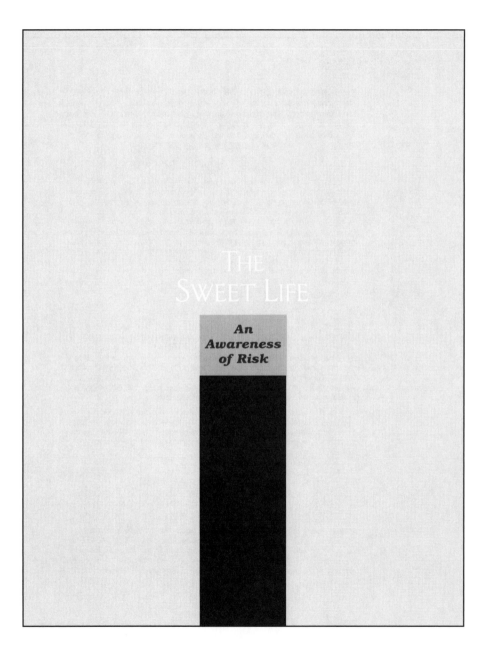

THE SWEET LIFE

An Awareness of Risk

An AWARENESS of RISK

1

Bear in mind that an investment in the Company involves a high degree of risk and is suitable only for Investors who can afford to bear those risks and have no need for liquidity from such investment. Each prospective investor should consider carefully the risk factors attendant upon such investment, including, without limitation, those discussed below, and should consult his own legal, tax, and financial advisors with respect thereto.
ROY FRUMKES & ROCCO SIMONELLI

Investment in an independent motion picture is highly speculative.

To provide a return to the Investors in this offering, the Managers must either a) sell the Motion Picture outright, b) license the distribution rights to a major or minor studio or distribution company, or c) consider self-distribution, a recent, realistic option afforded by the nascent field of low-budget digital video feature production. To reach this stage, the Managers must successfully complete the pre-production, principal photography, post production and marketing processes. Each of these steps is characterized by certain unique risks, many of which are beyond the control of the Managers. The inability to complete any of these steps could result in a complete loss of the investment. Consequently, an investment in the Motion Picture is highly speculative and should only be undertaken by those who are able to lose their entire investment.

There are no existing sale or distribution arrangements and the Management does not anticipate entering into any such agreements prior to completing the Motion Picture.

The Management has made no arrangements for the sale or distribution of the Motion Picture and does not expect to do so until after completing production. Ordinarily, any cash distributions to the Company would be derived from such sale or distribution agreements. There can be no assurances that the Managers will be able to enter into any distribution or sale agreements or that the proceeds from these agreements, if any, will be sufficient to recoup or provide any return on investment. Consequently, even if completed, the Managers may be unable to sell or license the distribution rights for an amount sufficient to provide a return for the Investors.

While the current and evolving state of digital video distribution, the internet, and Broadband, as delivery mediums   for a Motion Picture such as ours allows for routes of revenue beyond and outside those normally considered for feature length films even two years ago, such concerns as expressed in these paragraphs must be understood and weighed.

All or a portion of the cash flow from certain sale or distribution agreements may be based upon the box office receipts generated by the Motion Picture. In such instances, the financial success of the Motion Picture may be substantially dependent upon the marketing efforts of the Distributor.

In certain sale or distribution agreements, all or a portion of the cash flow received by the Company, and ultimately the Investors, is based upon a percentage of the box office receipts. Under these arrangements, the Distributor incurs all marketing and advertising costs associated with distributing the Motion Picture. Such agreements generally require the recoupment of all marketing expenses before cash distributions to the Production Company. The Company may enter into this type of agreement, rather than an outright

THE PRODUCER AS SEDUCER

sale, which may contain certain payments based on box office receipts. Under such agreement, the Managers will have either limited or no control over additional expenses that need to be recouped by the Distributor before the Investors receive any cash distributions. The performance of such marketing and advertising expenses could reduce the cash distributions to the Investors. If the marketing costs incurred by the Distributor exceed total box office receipts and proceeds from television, cable and video sales or rentals, the Distributor could cross-collateralize these losses into areas of profit, and consequently the Investors could potentially lose their entire investment.

If this scenario were to present itself - if this sort of distribution deal were entered into - then the Managers would endeavor to hold out certain territories as insurance against just such a contingency. Still, it is prudent for potential Investors to consider this chess move in the game of Securing Distribution.

The Company could enter into loan agreements or incur advances or deferred production costs that would have priority over cash distributions to the Investors.

The managers may, if the funds raised through this offering are insufficient to finish production, borrow, obtain advances, or defer certain production costs on behalf of the Company. Repayment of these loans, advances, or deferrals will have priority over cash distributions to the investors on the proceeds from any sale or distribution agreements. Consequently, even if the Motion Picture is completed, sold or otherwise distributed, such loans, advances, or deferrals, could delay or eliminate any cash distributions made to the Investors.

The Units do not possess votings rights. Consequently, the investors must rely on the Managers for the management and day-to-day operations of the Company. The Managers, jointly or individually, may be involved with other business ventures that may compete with the business of the Company.

The Investors will not have a right to participate in the management of the business of the Company, or in the decisions of the Managers. Accordingly, no prospective Investor should purchase Units unless he or she is willing to entrust all aspects of management of the Company to the Managers. The Managers have the ability to be involved in other business ventures (eg. the development of additional motion pictures) that may create a conflict of interest with the Company.

The Company is unlikely to make any cash distributions within its initial year.

Any cash distributed to the Investors will be derived from the sale or licensing of the distribution rights to, or from, the proceeds of self-distribution from the Motion Picture. The ability to enter into a sale or licensing agreement is generally dependent upon completing and marketing the Motion Picture. Marketing efforts may include participation in regularly scheduled events such as film festivals and film buyers' markets. Although the Managers anticipate that the production of the Motion Picture will be completed early in 2002, a comprehensive marketing process may be necessary in order to sell or license the distribution rights to, or lend credence to, the self-distribution of the Motion Picture. Consequently, the Managers do not anticipate making any cash distribution during the 12 months following the start of Production.

It's cheaper!
But there's more to it; much more:

1

In the century preceding the new millennium, the major Distributors (MGM, Disney, Universal, Warner Bros, etc.) and the minor Distributors (Miramax, New Line, Lion's Gate, etc.) exerted a stranglehold over the income they received when a filmmaker's work was released by them. Although Distributors claim to take as little as 35% of the gross after reasonable distribution expenses, those 'reasonable expenses' could include such items as $500. dollars a week for xeroxing. In other words, their bookkeeping could see a film's producer waiting for years before extracting a portion of the money he or she is owed for the film's distribution. Similarly, the Exhibitors (the theaters), who may take 50% of each dollar of the filmgoers' money, notoriously take a year or more to send the remaining 50% to the Distributor, who then does their magic with it before what's left filters down to the Producer. And the Exhibitors, as well, can lay claim to "reasonable expenses", some of which may indeed be reasonable (split advertising costs), while some may be just more bookkeeping magic.

The new century has given rise to high quality video modes of filming and projection, and suddenly the Exhibitors and Distributors are no longer indispensible. With the further venue of the Internet, where, as the speed of delivery increases with Broadband, entire films can be delivered to subscribers with relative ease, Hollywood begins to look like an anachronism in the making.

The field was opened up in 1999 with **The Blair Witch Project,** the first part-video feature film to earn as much money at the boxoffice as most of the major Hollywood releases (over $150,000,000. to date, not including home video, DVD, tv, etc.) Many major filmmakers and cinematographers have since experimented with this new, evolving form : including Lars Van Triers' **Dancer in the Dark,** Spike Lee's **Bamboozled,** Barbet Schroeder's new feature **Our Lady of the Assassins,** and the upcoming Alan Cummings/Jennifer Jason Leigh film **The Anniversary Party.** Many more digital video films have been announced as going into production this year.

To meet the demand of digital video, new theaters are being built, and existing theatres are being equipped, to project digital video to audiences. Technicolor has announced 500 of these theaters across the US in the next year. The pre-existing chains (Clearview, Sony, etc), are adding digital projection to some of their multiplexes. Already almost a hundred of these theaters exist in the US. By next Summer, when **The Sweet Life** is ready for release, the figure may be well over a thousand. This is a sound business shift on the part of the theaters - several hundred million dollars will be saved each year by not transporting film cans from theater to theater by truck, let alone by not having to manufacture thousands of prints of a film on cumbersome 35mm reels. The delivery system will probably be replaced by having the film/video beamed down to the theater projection booth via satellite. Soon a digital video feature may have access to a major theatrical release without having to incur the substantial cost of being blown up to 35mm film.

Why DIGITAL Video?

2

Recent News Item

Executives of four of Hollywood's major studios have held discussions about forming a nonprofit company that would help financially troubled theater chains replace traditional film projectors with digital ones, the 'Wall Street Journal' reported today (Thursday, May 17th, 2001), citing people familiar with the matter. According to the newspaper, Disney, Sony, Warner Bros. and Paramount have been involved in the discussions, with Universal and 20th Century Fox indicating that they may also participate. "We think the studios need to play a role in accelerating the deployment of digital cinema on favorable terms to theater operators," Phil Barlow, executive vice–president of Walt Disney Motion Picture Group told the 'WSJ'. However, the newspaper reported that the chains are worried about giving studios too much control over how films are exhibited. "Whatever structure is developed has to leave the existing players in the same position as they are today, vis–a–vis the relationships on film booking, control of the projector within the theaters and so on," United Artists Theater Co.'s CEO Kurt Hall told the 'WSJ'.

Clearly the above news article reveals the panic setting into the formerly complacent Hollywood machinery. While the Dream Factory and the Movie Theaters thrash out their problems, the independent filmmakers are finding more and more avenues by which to reach the public.

Recent News Item

Writing from Cannes in Britain's 'Guardian' newspaper, critic Roger Ebert suggests that digital projection could be a boon – indeed, perhaps the savior – of independent filmmaking. "If films were supplied [to theaters] on cheap high–definition discs, the same title could play simultaneously in 50 cities, with a national publicity campaign," Ebert writes. "Even as an opponent of digital projection of big–screen, mainstream movies, I can see how this would help the independent filmmakers sneak around the multiplex gridlock."

At this stage in digital video's evolution, many formats are vying for supremacy: NTSC, PAL, and HDTV to name three major ones, and many hardware systems are available to house them. With the good council of our talented Production and Technical crew, we are exploring these choices presently. Whatever format and hardware is chosen, we are determined to stay within the budget limit of $200,000 for getting the film through post-production, since certain vital deals depend on that ceiling.

But it is, finally, important to remember the sentiment of the opening salvo in this section of the memorandum: that shooting **The Sweet Life** on film would have made the project far less viable for the investors. Budgeted for 35mm, the film was closer to a million dollars than to our current $250,000-$350,000 figure.

the entity doesn't pay income tax, but the entity's limited partners, share-holders, and members respectively do. This tax treatment is different from the more traditional C-Corp, in which there is double income-taxation: once on the C-Corp itself, and then on its shareholders. For *The Sweet Life* we used the fairly recent LLC, which follows the rules of a Limited Partnership in many respects, but has distinct advantages. Under an LLC, the producer has the same limited liability as a corporate officer, whereas under a Limited Partnership, the individual general partner has unlimited liability. Therefore, with an LLC, the producer doesn't have to form two entities; a single-purpose corporation as a general partner (to avoid unlim-ited personal liability) and the Limited Partnership itself. With the LLC, the producer only has to form that one entity.

In some offerings, money that's been raised has to be placed in escrow, and if a minimum amount of money is not raised before a cer-tain date, the producer is required to refund all of the money to the investors. With our film, I eliminated this inhibitor completely. The exact wording was:

> There is no projected minimum amount (The "Minimum Capitalization") needed for the "breaking of escrow" [as such term is customarily defined in the motion picture industry], and the Company shall have the right to imme-diate access and use of funds which have been raised and secured in connec-tion with the Picture.

Nonetheless, I had set my own minimum in mind, and I started on *The Sweet Life* when it seemed clear we could raise the money neces-sary to complete production, approximately $150,000, including a con-tingency. If I'd been able to raise the entire budget, I obviously would have, but at the very least, I raised enough to finish shooting and get us into post.

After production, you can revise the Business Plan, eliminating all language about the production stage, and adding a jubilant page up front, proclaiming that filming has been completed. When pitching the revised Business Plan to raise completion funds, you can rightly tell potential investors that they are getting the same deal as the orig-inal investors, but with less risk now that the film is in the can.

To whom did I go with this elegant package? Again, considering the paltry cost of getting this film all the way to release, I studied my little black book and compiled a list of all the people I knew who I thought might be interested, or might know one or two other people

IT'S A WRAP!

The Sweet Life completed twenty-five days of principal photography on August 25th, on schedule and on budget. The cast and crew celebrated at Neva, a Russian Dance Club in Greenwich Village where one of the film's scenes had been shot.

Now the meticulous process of editing unfolds, four months of shaping the footage into its final running time. Then the score will be created by composer Kenny Laguna. Joan Jett's music will also be heard on the soundtrack.

The Spring of 2002 will be spent entering the film into select film festivals to get a buzz going, then testing the market place for the best possible distribution deals. Publicity will be generated, promotional work will be done by the Director, Producer and Cast.

By Summer of next year, *The Sweet Life* will be ready for release.

to turn me on to. Also, I find that in raising money for a film, having it helmed by a first-time director is an asset, not a handicap. Said director hasn't burned anyone yet by getting him to invest and then not returning his money. And, no doubt, everyone the new director knows—from friends and family members to business contacts and acquaintances—is aware that he has pursued a rarified and glamorous career outside the mundane nine-to-five world, and is interested in seeing him succeed. This is virgin territory, and unless the film earns its money back, most of these people won't be around next time. But on a first go-round, I expect the debut director's contacts to pan out. And they do. Roc's contacts, so far, have come through with about 20 percent of the necessary funds to make the feature. With *Street Trash*, the director's family and business contacts pulled in over 70 percent of the budget.

There are also professional party-throwers, who will organize a fund-raising event at their apartment, hand-picking a dozen or less people who might fit into the right economic category to possibly invest, and either take a percentage of the night's receipts, or charge a nominal sum. This has never failed for me, though it has also never produced huge amounts of investment capital. Maybe two or three shares. Nonetheless, it's a good opportunity for you to hone your spiel, and it's usually an enjoyable evening.

FAST-FORWARD TO LATE IN POSTPRODUCTION

Now, although chronologically I'm only at the beginning of production in this book, I'm going to jump ahead several months (chapters) to let you in on how fundraising is going in the month of June 2002. And it's actually not going so well. In the past, this approach has worked just fine—raising enough to get through filming, then going after more. Potential investors who were on the fence generally get shaken off and take the plunge when they can look at not only the revised Business Plan and Memorandum, but also a little demo reel of scenes from the film, as we did with *The Sweet Life*. Seeing footage is a very tangible persuader.

So why am I encountering difficulties in procuring the finishing funds? Well, there was 9/11, which occurred two weeks after we'd wrapped. That tragic event, added to a year-long flagging economy, resulted in people's installing padlocks on their wallets. In the wake of all this, the prevailing investment sentiment is against motion pictures. It was not anticipated, and it's proving to be an uphill battle. But this is a fluke convergence of worrisome events that may never happen again.

The economy ebbs and flows, but mostly it flows. Look at it the positive way: our problem is your good fortune. We're encountering it, and addressing it, and you are the beneficiary, because anything I learn, you learn.

Now I'm not saying the well has dried up completely; there *is* money trickling in, just not enough to support the correct speed with which our little adventure should draw to a close. What does a flexible producer do in a case such as this? He starts calling in favors and freebies. If you look at our top sheet, you'll see sums for music, for mixing, for ADR (dubbing or looping actors' voices). I don't believe in persuading people to do good work for free. Matter of fact, I fear that people don't *do* their best work for free. Nonetheless, there are ways and there are ways, particularly if you are situated near a film school, for instance, which has a sound studio that you can use for your ADR work rather than renting professional studio space for $1,800 a day. Or if there is a music school in your city, full of talented students with demo CDs who need a break. You get the point. Where there's a will, and a film that's in the can, there's a way.

But let's get back to the production. Roc's just about ready to start Day One. Always a creepy moment for a first-time director . . .

CHAPTER EIGHT

RS
SHOOTING THE MOVIE

In a *Star Trek* episode titled "Where No Man Has Gone Before," the *Enterprise* encounters a mysterious energy field at the edge of the galaxy, and Kirk is faced with a dilemma: Should he turn back, or go forward into the ominously pulsing, vaporous mass? Kirk decides to continue the probe, reasoning that "other vessels will be heading out here some day and will need to know what they'll be facing."

Directing a film the first time you do it is equivalent to taking a journey like that, and it's a good bet that if you're reading this book it's because you're hoping and planning to do the same some day and want to know what *you'll* be facing.

The truth is no one can fully prepare you for what directing a film is like. As with making love or having a baby or going to war, it can't be taught or entirely comprehended without firsthand experience. Ultimately, you can only learn by doing. But that doesn't mean you shouldn't gather as much information beforehand as you possibly can. Or, once you've gone through the experience as I have, share with others what you've learned.

In the chapters of mine that follow, I've made use of excerpts from a diary I kept during the shoot. I usually wrote things down as soon as I got home from the set, or, at the latest, the following day. I offer these accounts in much the same spirit as the dying Dr. Soberin in *Kiss Me Deadly*, urging would-be filmmakers to heed what I'm telling you "as if I were Cerberus barking with all my heads at the gates of hell."

The italicized paragraphs that open the chapters, as well as italicized comments in parentheses that appear within the text of the journal excerpts, have been added at the time of the preparation of this book.

FIRST WEEK—OR, LEARNING HOW TO SWIM BY DIVING IN THE DEEP END

There's an old saying: Men plan; God laughs. There is no pursuit in which this proves to be more true than in filmmaking. In a house located out in the Howard Beach section of Queens, we had built three different apartment sets: Michael's living room and bedroom, Lila's room, and Sherry's room. In light of my total inexperience as a director, Roy had scheduled all the scenes that take place in these sets for the first four days of shooting, the thinking being that we would be hunkered down at one location, shooting only interiors, making these the easiest scenes to shoot, thus giving me some time to get my feet wet and build up my confidence.

That was Roy's plan to avoid problems and overcome my shortcomings. Mine was to be as prepared as I could be, to have rehearsed our actors thoroughly enough so that when we came to filming, there would be little more for me to do than block the movements and call "action"—that the actors would be familiar with each other and somewhat in tune to each other's rhythms, and that major questions about the script and the characters would have already been asked and answered. But, in reading the previous chapters, you've seen how God laughed at my plan when we lost The Name and No-Name just prior to the start of production. And when my plan fell apart, it undermined Roy's as well, since now what should have been the easiest part of the shoot became one of the toughest, for me and the actors.

TUESDAY 7/24. First day of shooting. Tried to rehearse Jimmy and Barbara at the school.[1] Bob[2] loses my car keys (fuck!), then forgets to take the contracts Roy wanted him to bring. Jimmy's hair is bleached blond (fuck!) and must be dyed darker before we can start filming. Denise[3] is supposed to meet us in the lobby at noon. 12:15 comes, and she still isn't there. I go upstairs and find her with a student on the fifth floor. What the fuck! I drag her down and after going to Jimmy's car to check his clothes, we head over to a hair salon called Dramatics. Jimmy gets the dye job, Denise returns to SVA, and we head off in Jimmy's car to Howard Beach. The air conditioning isn't working too well, and it is literally the hottest day of the year. (*This is not an exaggeration; the temperature was just under 100 degrees Fahrenheit. As if I weren't sweating enough already . . .*) By the time we get to the house, I'm already drained and aggravated, and we haven't even shot a second of footage yet. Our makeup guy, Terry Matlin, comes to me and says Denise has called and said something about sending someone out to a thrift store or something to get Jimmy a pair of black pants. I nix that. We begin after lunch as I'd planned. But I've also learned that I can only shoot until 8:00 P.M., rather than 10:00 P.M., which is what had been indicated to me earlier.

---

[1] The School of Visual Arts.
[2] Bob McMurdo, a friend who was helping us out.
[3] Denise LaBelle, head of our art department.

Day One of the Sweet Life *shoot:* Barbara Sicuranza *and* James Lorinz *upon hearing one of their first-time director's suggestions.*

The set looks great, but the coffee table is the size of a mausoleum slab. And it's much closer and much hotter down there than I'd anticipated. Barbara's gotten very quiet. I can't tell if she's just trying to stay in character all the time (Lila's supposed to be depressed and upset in the scene we're filming) or if she's personally distressed. We get the first part of the scene in, then set up to shoot the lengthy exchange on Michael's couch, which ends on the two of them locked in their first romantic embrace. My notion is to get this all in one long take, gradually pushing in to a tight two-shot for the kiss. I thought this approach, by letting the two of them get into a rhythm without breaking it up, would make the actors happy. But it gradually becomes clear to me that this isn't going to be the case. Barbara's told me she's going to get emotional, but it's not happening for her the way I think she'd like it to, and I can see her getting more and more frustrated after each take. (*For this, we have The Name & No-Name to thank. We'd felt comfortable scheduling such a crucial and emotional scene at the very beginning of the shoot because we knew we were going to rehearse the actors for a week prior to the commencement of filming. But in light of the last-minute recasting, we couldn't have picked a more difficult scene to kick things off with.*) I'm dying inside, because I don't have any idea how to help her. Another kind of director might try abusing her like Kubrick did Shelly Duvall on *The Shining* to get her appropriately tearful and distraught, but I simply don't have it in me. Even if

Michael's date (Roseanne Petsako) *having trouble adjusting to the gravity on earth.*

it worked, and later on I told her, "You realize I was only trying to create the effect I needed," and she replied that she understood, it would haunt me that some little part of her would never forgive me. On a purely practical level, it might not work and end up having the opposite effect, driving her even deeper into herself and shutting her down completely. All I feel I can do is to be as supportive and nurturing and calming as I can be. I continually reassure her and tell her how wonderful I think she is, and that she's just going to keep getting better and better.

I drive Barbara home after we wrap, and I can tell she's upset with herself. I tell her today was just a fucked-up day, starting late, only meeting Jimmy this morning, the heat, et cetera. Tomorrow we'll have a normal day, we'll start early, we won't be so rushed, she and Jimmy will feel much more connected after getting through this first day. Maybe she believes it. Me, I just want to drive the car head on into a cement wall.

WEDNESDAY 7/25. I get to the set by ten. It is, once again, very hot outside. I find the basement not too bad though. Warm, but not as oppressive as the previous day. (It will get like that again later, but at least until we break for lunch at four it's much more bearable.) We start shooting before noon, and we cook through everything we need to get before the lunch break. We get scene #011 (Michael on the phone), we film the entire Miranda scene (Roseanne Petsako is simply wonderful, quietly cheerful and willing, she knows her lines, never screws up, and she and Jimmy seem to play well off each other), then go for close-ups on the scene Barbara and Jimmy had so much trouble with the previous day, for which we never got a good master. I don't know what's happened, but Barbara is completely transformed from what she was like yesterday. She tells me she's fine, she's feeling good, she's ready to go. My sense is that Jimmy has really helped us out with her, talked to her, bonded with her in some way. He nails his close-ups without a problem, then we turn the camera and put it on Barbara. Jimmy touches her hand, looks her in the eyes, and whispers a few words to her, I quietly utter "action," and her eyes are welling with tears, her expression full of emotion. We get three takes with her that are all marvelous, and my heart soars. She looks and sounds as wonderful on camera now as I thought she would when we cast her. It means I'll have to completely change my concept of the scene (keeping them both in one long shot that gradually gets tighter into the kiss that concludes it) and cut back and forth between them on the close-ups, but at least I've *got* a scene now.

After lunch, we start on Michael's bedroom scenes. It's even tighter in there, but I've brought a small fan and keep directing it toward the actors in between takes. Barbara is simply beautiful, while Jimmy is having difficulty with the lines. Keeps wanting to change them, or not say them. At one point he says, "This isn't me," and I, of course, respond

A troubled Lila (Barbara Sicuranza) perched on the edge of Michael's bed. Both the wall behind her and the tattoo on her arm are fake.

that he's right, it isn't him—it's Michael. I get a little frustrated with him, he appears to get pissed and closed off, but then he nails the lines on a couple of takes and we can move on. Between setups, I search the house and finally find him upstairs in the bathroom. I ask him if he's pissed at me, but he says no, he's just upset about what's going on in his personal life, and I believe him. The next setup, a two-shot of Jimmy and Barbara sitting side by side on the bed, keeps getting interrupted by jets taking off from JFK and noises from upstairs. I get very frustrated, but I think we have one or two takes we can use, and move on. We get a really lovely shot of Barbara sitting on the edge of the bed, her entire back exposed, head bowed. I boarded it this way, and my DP, James Carman, has captured just the feeling I was hoping to get. I'm once again thrilled.

We go for the last setup, get the fg/bg (foreground/background) two-shot with little trouble, but then the close-up on Jimmy reentering the room takes seven or eight takes because of focus problems. (We threw in an ad-lib here, having found a pig mask hanging over the door in the makeup room. Had the idea it would add a little something to the scene if Michael reentered the bedroom holding the mask over his face. Then, when Lila tells him it was Frankie on the phone, he lowers the mask and asks worriedly if he knew it was her. And that's how we shot it.) We wrap at 9:40, having not only gotten everything we needed, but more than I could have hoped in terms of images and performances. A total shift from yesterday. I also learn via a telephone call from Roy that we are *this* close to getting Joan Jett for Sherry. I'll find out for sure tomorrow.

THURSDAY 7/26. There were weather and traffic problems everywhere this morning, and so *everyone* was late getting to the set, me included. I try to talk with Barbara, but she's distant with me for no reason I can ascertain. I believe she'll be wonderful when things are cut together (*as indeed she is: provocative, sexy, vulnerable—everything I could have hoped for and more*), but the variety of her moods these first three days, the way she withdraws behind a kind of invisible wall, has me a bit on edge. She's an emotional person, and therefore an emotional actress (it's why we cast her), and I've got to figure she's saving her emotions for the work, hiding them away so they won't be wasted.

Jimmy is a borderline basket case today, emotionally. Clearly, he's having a hard time with what's going on in his personal life. He's increasingly recalcitrant as the day wears on, more and more openly unpleasant between takes, and though I laugh as if I know he's just joking, I'm sure he isn't. We're using a dolly move to shoot the master of the argument-before-the-massage scene, and after watching an early take on the monitor, I suggest a change in the blocking. We'd rehearsed it with Lila opening and putting her massage table together all through the scene, and actually setting it upright. But looking at it as we film a take, I see it's clumsy, and leaves too much of a distance for the actors to bridge at the end when the tension has been alleviated. So I tell Barbara to stop putting the table together at an earlier point and to leave it on its side, so that Jimmy can just kneel down in front of her and play out the conciliatory conclusion of the scene over the wall, so to speak. Carman moves the shot gradually in to a tighter two-shot for that, and it works terrifically. For a moment, I actually feel like a director: I saw something, suggested an adjustment, then watched it actually make the scene better. We shoot Jimmy's close-up, and save Barbara's for the end of the day—not something I want to do, but, time-wise, we have no choice. In my head, I'm thinking, I don't care if her close-up comes out very well or not, anyway, because the master is so damn good—both technically as a shot as well as in the performances—I'm already certain that's what I'm going to use in the film. But one is supposed to get coverage, just in case, so I'm getting it.

We do the massage scene next. This is our big comic scene, the only real physical comedy in the script, and I've been looking forward to shooting it. Part of that came from my belief the actors would be

"Now a firm stroke along the spinal column . . ." Lila (Barbara Sicuranza) gives Michael (James Lorinz) a disastrous massage.

looking forward to it too, that they'd have fun doing it. Boy, was I wrong. The whole thing becomes an ordeal, a real battle to get what I think the scene should be. Jimmy doesn't want to say some of the lines, and worse, doesn't want to play the scene as big as I believe it needs to be played, *has* to be played. Barbara is very withdrawn. The room is oppressively hot, and neither Jimmy nor Barbara seem to be able to remember all the lines, so that with each take, one or the other or both miss one or two lines, or more. However, I'm covering the action from different angles and close-ups, so even though I never get a single take where both of them get all their lines correctly, with all the takes combined I do get all the lines. Our editor, Gary Cooper, will just have to cobble the scene together from a lot of different takes, rather than me picking favorites. (*In the actors' defense, we never had the opportunity to really rehearse the scene, and work out the physical stuff in more detail. That's my failure, but there just wasn't time with Jimmy coming on in the eleventh hour. I let them both down on this, I guess, but it was such a battle just getting up and running with The Name and No-Name screwing us over as they did at the last minute.*) To make matters worse, on one of the takes where Lila is supposed to be sliding her hand along Michael's spine, but then slips on the oil and clocks him on the back of the head, Barbara really *does* clock Jimmy on the back of the head and knocks him loopy. He gets very unpleasant from this point on, but the poor guy is in pain, and dizzy, and just trying to get through the scene. Barbara feels guilty at having injured him, then injures herself while punching him in the thigh. Her hand turns red and swells a bit. They both go off between setups to get iced and pop Tylenols. I'm sick in my gut at my incompetence, at not having prepared them properly, at completely misjudging what filming the scene would be like, thinking it would be fun. Now I've caused them both physical damage, and will have to bring them back for more.

And I do. We labor through the remainder of the shots, and, despite everything, I think we've gotten enough to cut together a decent scene. I'd love to just say wrap it, but we've still got to get Lila's close-up from the scene we never finished shooting earlier in the day. Barbara is worried about matching the action of putting the table together and saying the lines the way she did in the master. We decide to push the shot in close so that the action is out of frame, with me figuring that in the latter portion of the scene, when she gets pretty still, we'd be able to use everything if we wanted to; with the more active first half, well, maybe we'd get lucky with a moment or two. But even if we didn't, I could still use it as long as I cut from Jimmy's close-up first, rather than from the master, because then there'd be no issue of matching action. In any case, all of this is beside the point, because I'm already reasonably certain of using the master shot in its entirety anyway. The infuriatingly linear and unfriendly continuity girl doesn't know this is what I'm thinking, and so blurts out in a disdainful way that half of what Barbara is about to do will be unusable, speaking to me as if speaking to a retarded child. I don't care so much about that, but Barbara hears it, and it's the last thing in the world I want—for my already troubled and exhausted actress to hear that half of what she's about to do is pointless. Especially when it's not really true. Every day now, I'm continually forced to waste precious time explaining to the continuity girl how I'm going to cover action that doesn't exactly match, and listen to her sigh and then roll her eyes, when she's the one who really doesn't understand. (*She would be replaced not too long after this, much to my relief.*) Now I've got to explain it to her *and* Barbara. I've got no time for this shit! Barbara slogs through the close-up listlessly, though there might be a usable moment or two near the latter portion of the scene, and we shut it down for the day. I find Jimmy alone in the other room, put my hand on his shoulder and lean down, and ask him if he's upset with me. He assures me he isn't, it's just everything coming down on him at once, his life, this part (which is a daunting one with or without any prep time), and once again, I take him at his word.

A little before we finished shooting, the word had come from Roy that Joan Jett had signed on the dotted line, but I was too tired and stressed out to be jubilant about it. The day has been so trying and joyless (with the exception of that one successful adjustment I made to the argument scene), all I can see is the downside: another actor I haven't met or rehearsed, whom I'm going to have to throw in front of a camera and pray she can hack it. The thing is, despite how all this sounds, it was actually a good day in terms of shooting, in that we got everything we needed, some of it quite good, and we are still right on schedule.

I decide to stay at the house, not wanting to risk being late and showing up frazzled and tired before we even begin. Denise and her assistant Ben Heyman are up on the top floor getting the set ready for the next day's shoot when I crawl down into the basement and stretch out across a small bed we used for Michael's bedroom the previous day. It's lumpy and uncomfortable, as if a dead body were stuffed inside it, but I'm too exhausted to care. The room is dark, and I'm lying there when it hits me: I've got to direct Joan Jett tomorrow.

FRIDAY 7/27. Morning of a beautiful day, weather wise. The first thing I do is, upon his arrival, I take Jimmy out back and ask him how his head is feeling. He says he's better, and looks it. I then tell him, "You know we've got Joan Jett coming in today. I'm not sure what we're going to be dealing with, but I just wanted to apologize in advance if I have to cater to her more than you. I don't want you to think I'm consciously neglecting you or anything." He instantly shakes this off and tells me not to worry about it. A little while later, I'm in the back seat of my car being interviewed by our two making-of documentarians when I spot a tiny, black-leather-and-boot-clad, short-cropped, dark-haired sparkplug of a woman striding past us along the sidewalk. "Joan! Joan!" I call out as I climb out of the car. I introduce myself as the director, then meet her long-time partner Kenny Laguna, an older, personable, redheaded guy, and another, younger, crew-cutted guy named Jon. I take Joan inside and introduce her to Jimmy and any other crew people who are nearby. Barbara's not due in till later. (*A pleasant aside: Before Ms. Jett's arrival, I'd gone to one of our younger female crew members, who'd been one of my students at SVA, and openly lesbian, and told her I needed someone to stay close to Ms. Jett all day and bring her anything she might ask for or need. With that, I instantly became the bestest teacher she ever had.*) My immediate sense is that Joan is very cool, very approachable, and ready and willing to jump in and get started. Some of my anxiety abates. We've got a tremendously busy day ahead of us if we're going to get everything I need to finish up at this location so that I can give the crew the entire weekend off and not drag them back in on Saturday. The truth is, I need the weekend off too. And I've got my heart set on staying on, if not ahead, of schedule. Fortunately, we're not shooting anything terribly emotional today, so it's already in my head to keep the takes to a minimum.

The first half of the day goes very well. The storyboards I drew up have been turning out to be a big help, we know exactly what we need to get, and I'm trying very hard not to be self-indulgent or indecisive. I want to keep things moving, keep the crew jumping. Roy has indicated that they'll like this, that a crew works better and maintains a better attitude if they feel like things are cooking, that we're getting the shots and staying on schedule. So far, that's what we've been doing. The scene we're shooting with Joan and Jimmy is funny on the page, and with her in the role and Jimmy's natural comic ability, it seems to me we've got a very good chance of it being even funnier on the screen. I've storyboarded the sequence (which involves Michael being handcuffed to the headboard with a drunken, libidinous Sherry straddled over him) so that most of it is conveyed with subjective POV shots à la *Silence of the Lambs*, with the camera either looking straight down at Michael or straight up at Sherry. But what I realize as my DP lies down on his back and shoots Joan's part of it is that she can get much closer to the camera lens than I'd anticipated, so he can move with her. I crouch next to the bed and watch the monitor while reading out Jimmy's off screen lines, squeezing her leg to cue her on timing, and I can tell instantly it's going to be fucking hilarious, especially when she threatens to heave right into the camera. It's also one of those moments when I actually feel like a director, being right in there, and sensing it working.

Just before lunch, both pairs of handcuffs break. Joan had warned us the moment she saw them that they were not the good kind. I'm told we have no backups. How this could be so eludes me, given they're such a prominent prop in the script. On top of this, one pair is black and the other is silver, and so it's not just a question of replacing two pairs, but two pairs of different colors. We're just lucky it happened right before lunch and not an hour or two earlier, or I don't know what we would have done. I get a little frantic about it and Brian Gunther, our line producer, calmly tells me he's on it. An hour later, he comes up to me smiling with a new pair of black handcuffs. What about the silver, I ask. "You

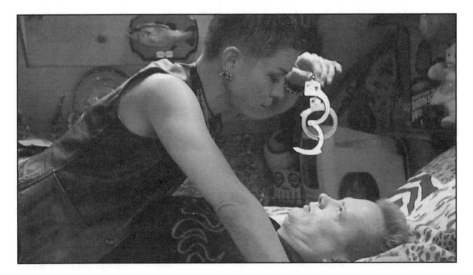

"You don't mind, do ya?" *Sherry* (Joan Jett) *in bed with Michael* (James Lorinz) *and a pair of handcuffs.*

needed a silver pair, too?" My look tells him all he needs to know. A second mad dash, and a number of silver pairs are procured. So, in the end, we lost no filming time because of the snafu, but it's still annoying to me that the art department didn't just have a few pairs as backup already on the set.

Where we do lose time is after lunch. At 5:00 P.M., the camera crew has the next setup prepared to go. Then I'm told that Barbara won't be ready for another half an hour. This stupefies me, since she's been at the location since 2:30. I want to rage out loud, but what good would it do? So I wait. And wait. The thought of the crew just sitting up there on the set doing nothing while the clock ticks gnaws at me, but I resist the increasingly urgent temptation to bust into the makeup room and tell them to hurry it up. Again, what good would it do? I know Terry's going as fast as he can, that it was the art department (again) not being on top of Barbara's wardrobe that's caused the delay. Denise is brilliant and, given the miniscule budget we've given her to work with, has done some marvelous things, especially in regard to set design. The main problem is, she's not with us full-time. Shortly before shooting was to begin, she informed us that her employers were not going to allow her the five-week leave of absence she'd requested, so she's still working there much of the time while trying to do her job for us. It's the worst possible situation, for her and us, and it leaves me torn between anger and sympathy, because as upset as I am that I feel we're being let down, I'm also left to wonder when the hell she sleeps. Every day, the actors come to me and ask me what they should be wearing, and in which scene. Suddenly I find myself trying to keep track of clothing continuity, along with all the other questions I'm constantly being peppered with. The other day, when we were getting set to shoot the scene in Lila's room, which takes place just after they've finished eating, Terry came to me in a frazzled state saying Denise (who wasn't on location) had called and instructed him to go out and get food for the half-eaten remnants of the meal that were to be left in the plates during the scene, that nothing in the refrigerator and cabinets chock-full of food right here in the house would do. He started to go off, saying he signed on to do makeup, now he's doing three jobs, et cetera. I praised him into submission, telling him he was doing a great job (which was the truth), that everybody liked him (also the truth), and that from now on any time he got such a command from Denise via a phone call he was to come to me first. I told him that when she's not physically present on location, as far as I'm concerned she doesn't exist. Therefore, the food in the house would do just fine. Go back and take care of the actors. He appeared relieved, thanked me, and went back to work.

When Barbara is finally ready, she looks very sexy and terrific, and we're off to the races. The setup sequence we've planned will have us bouncing back and forth between two or three different scenes, so we constantly have to keep track of the clothes. We're really pushing it, and I'm never calling for more than one or two takes before moving on. I keep looking at my watch, calculating the ratio of shots left to the time we've got left. I want to finish. I want to do what I said I would do. I'm sweating profusely and I've got a knot in my stomach, which grows increasingly tighter the later it gets. The actors, God bless them, never cost me a moment's delay. I'm particularly impressed by and grateful to Joan, who pretty much hits it every time, which is something, given we've had utterly no prep or rehearsal time together. Sometimes you just get lucky, and with her, we certainly did. Fortunately, there are no big emotional moments to film, so I'm reasonably comfortable shooting as few takes as we are doing.

Then, with only an hour left, thinking I'm barely going to be able to get the remaining shots I want to get, I'm struck by a thunderbolt of sickening realization: I've missed getting a crucial, in fact indispensable, shot when I should have gotten it earlier. After Sherry passes out on Michael's stomach, he looks up at the ceiling and utters, "I'm in hell." In the script, we dissolve to a shot of him asleep, then he wakes ιpon hearing something off screen, lifts his head from the pillow, and looks up to see Lila in the doorway. We got the shot of Lila in the doorway, but when we had Jimmy cuffed to the bed I forgot to get the shot of him asleep and then waking up. *And I've got to have it.* I can't link the two scenes without it. I start beating the Wiffle ball, which I've been squeezing and rolling in my hand all week, against my forehead, incensed with myself for having pulled such a moronic gaffe. How could I have missed it? And what about the goddamn continuity girl, who's given me nothing but grief all week, yet uttered not a peep about this? The only way I can figure to get it is to shoot a two-setup scene we're about to do in just one, and abandon one of my more cinematic storyboard shots (of Sherry's face over the side of the bed when she's threatening to puke in the foreground, with Lila visible in the background) and cover the action in a much more rudimentary way. On a shot of Lila saying one line in the doorway, Carman tweaks the lighting for what seems to me, given our situation, an inordinate amount of time, until I utter in despair, "James, it's just one line. *Please.*" Finally, we get it. Then we get the shot of Joan as Sherry hanging over the side of the bed holding the wastebasket beneath her face. Then Carman quickly sets up to get the shot of Michael waking. (Thank God I didn't send Jimmy home earlier when I thought I was finished with him.) We get that shot too. It's 9:45. We made it. Better a little overtime on the last day at a location then to bring the crew in and pay them for a whole day on Saturday for just a few shots. And now we can all take two days off. I feel like Mister Roberts, having gotten his crew a liberty. They deserve it. They've really been working their asses off.

I go downstairs and ask our sound man if the day was as action packed as I felt it was. I've never directed before, so I've got nothing to which I can make a comparison. "I'll tell you in a second," he says, and consults his clipboard. "We did twenty-two setups," he tells me. "Is that a lot?" I ask him. "Oh, yeah. Definitely." Thus I figure, in spite of the casting difficulties we've had, coupled with starting a day late and my inexperience, it was only in the last hour of the last day of the week that I abandoned trying to be creative and just covered the action. And we only missed getting one storyboarded shot I'd have like to have gotten. But we're on time, on schedule, and we've got what I think is a pretty substantial amount of good footage in the can. (*I'll learn later from Roy that in this initial three-and-a-half-day shooting period, we filmed twenty-two pages of script. What's up with that number?*) Not a bad week at all. Too bad there's still four more to go.

At 10:30, I'm told I can go, and Jimmy, Barbara, and I head off to Lenny's Clam Bar. Driving there, I lean my head out the window and start bellowing into the night like Jack Lemmon in *The Out-of-Towners*, "I got my week in, Howard Beach! How do you like that?! You're just a city! I'm a person, and persons are bigger than cities!" We sit outside at the restaurant, drink beer, eat baked clams and fried calamari and antipasto, and laugh our heads off like an air crew just returned from a deadly dangerous bombing mission. We made it back alive. This time.

CHAPTER NINE

RE
UP AGAINST THE FATES

When I enrolled in NYU's Film School in 1966, I assumed my destiny was to become a director. Three-and-a-half years later, after I'd finished coproducing and assistant-directing my first feature, *The Projectionist*, and the film's director, Harry Hurwitz, asked me what credit I wanted, adding that he was taking the producer, director, and screenwriter credits, I (a) realized that in the future I'd better get my credit guaranteed in writing up front, and (b) asked for the "Assistant Director" credit, because I *still* assumed, as I had upon entering film school, that directing was where my future lay. And after twenty-five years teaching filmmaking at the School of Visual Arts, I can tell you that 85 percent of the freshman students assume directing is the career they're heading for as well.

So, it came as something of a surprise to me, as the years went by, that I felt least comfortable in the director's role, and much happier and less pressured as either producer or screenwriter, or preferably both. I directed two features—*Burt's Bikers* and *Document of the Dead*—and I'm proud of them, but the experience was daunting. I never felt learned enough to communicate all the technical data to the crew, nor glib enough to sweep the actors into my vision of what the film was about. Rocco proved adept at dealing with the actors, and, with time, he'll be equally fluent with the crew. He's a natural director. I'm not.

THE INDIE PRODUCER'S GOAL

But I *am* a natural producer . . . in the off-Hollywood sense. Out there in LaLa Land, I wouldn't be. There, the relationship between producer and director is often adversarial. The producer is in charge, the director is a hired hand, and the producer can fire the director fairly easily. Hence, when you see a director also listed as producer—Kubrick, Pollack, Hitchcock, et cetera—it's not because he enjoys the paperwork, it's so he can control the production and, consequently, his own role in it.

My overriding vision of what a producer should be, bypassing the bookwork and managerial skills inherent in the job, is Richard

Rubinstein's definition in my film *Document of the Dead*: "We tend to operate in more of a European style in the way I produce and the way George directs, in that we tend to follow Sarris's auteur theory. I see my function as a producer in terms of providing George Romero with a brush, palette, and a canvas, and his creative control is absolute in terms of the film itself." Romero was fortunate to have had Rubinstein for a part of his career in that capacity, to watch over and protect him, to run interference and clear the playing field. And I'd like to think that, in the independent-film world, such a producer/director relationship is what it's all about. Of course, it doesn't often work that harmoniously on the indie scene, but then again, *Document* was meant to be a role model, and role models are difficult to live up to, particularly under duress.

I'm also a staunch believer in the climactic realization in *The Treasure of the Sierra Madre*, as it applies to the filmmaking experience. In that classic 1948 film directed by John Huston, the characters portrayed by Tim Holt and Walter Huston end up laughing their asses off about the ill-fated results of their quest for gold in the Mexican jungle. One of their party of three—played by Humphrey Bogart—was killed by bandits after shooting Holt, and the gold dust . . . it just blew away. All their energy and paranoia and dreams, all of it was gone in an instant. Yet in the depths of their disaster, they were able to acknowledge not only the fatalistic nature of their journey, but also that it wasn't just about the gold; it was about the adventure.

And so it is with our industry: Films seek their own level of excellence or failure, regardless of who is at the helm or what financial support they're given. We've seen Kubrick, Chaplin, and Scorsese create films that haven't risen to their normal level of excellence, yet their creative spirit going in must surely have been the same as always. Given, then, that a film's ultimate quality is not predicated solely on the talent involved, one would hope that the experience *itself* would be a rewarding one. *Something* wonderful has to come of all this concerted energy.

The short, frenetic life of a film production is, not surprisingly, a fertile ground for intimacy. I've heard this three-to-eight-week (for indie productions) period described as being akin to living an entire lifetime. Relationships spring up, peak and ebb, and former lovers gravitate toward new relationships, all on set. And why not? Creative, intelligent people, usually young and sweating and showing off their expertise, dominate filmmaking. Actors are needy, grips and stunt extras are buff. Directors are father figures. These are facts of film life. The only change

I've seen over a thirty-five-year period is that political correctness has crept in: "hitting on the chicks" is no longer a wise practice. One has to be more subtle in one's approach than in decades past, not to mention that one can no longer assume that just because a man and a woman are working together, they're looking for opposite-sex partners. But all that's just an incremental alteration. The hanky-panky endures. Such partnerings as I've described are usually positive, but the breakups can spew some negative energy around the set. (Check out François Truffaut's *Day for Night* [1974] and Tom DiCillo's *Living in Oblivion* [1995] for honest depictions of the graphic life of an indie-film production.)

So, even with a carefully chosen cast and crew, chemical problems will inevitably crop up. That's Murphy's Law at play, and it's never more virulent than on a film production. Nonetheless, a producer must *try* to handpick his or her players with regard to the well-being of the production. Everything a producer does should be directed toward the well-being of the production.

IN SEARCH OF THE ELUSIVE DREAM TEAM
To that end, I have always striven to build a cast and crew who will work well together. And it disappoints me no end to report that in the case of *The Sweet Life* I failed to pull that neat trick off. Roc tries to pacify me whenever the subject comes up, but nonetheless I feel obligated to shoulder the blame. It certainly wasn't anyone else's fault . . . except perhaps the "fates." Let me give you three examples.

The major problem was the DP and his department. Now, if you want the "fates" scenario, then you can start three months before filming began, when David S., the DP I knew would work wonderfully with Roc (I'd worked with David before, also with a first-time director, on *Street Trash*), was blocked because our art director, Denise LaBelle, had creative differences with him on a previous film. Denise was already on board—in fact, she was the first on board—and had been on board for over a month, contributing dazzling design concepts to the Business Plan you perused a few chapters ago. She had also—bless her—set the standard for key players' salaries at a mercifully low figure: Since she was the first on board, she was also the first I asked what she would want per week to do the film, and she delighted me with her request. I needed her in this regard so that, when negotiating other salaries, I could refer to hers as the ceiling.

And so I acquiesced. My DP of choice was no longer a candidate. Ironically, as shooting drew near, Denise informed me that her full-time employer, the Y&R Agency, wouldn't grant her the five weeks vacation time she requested in order to do the film, and that she'd have to be working part-time for us and part-time for them, a dreadful option. It was July 12 by then, which left me little time to find a new art director and break that person in. Besides, Denise had done so much work already, and was midway through transforming a house in Howard Beach into two apartments. I made the decision to let it ride. And so, in a way, I'd actually lost *both* of my prized people, because though Denise tried valiantly, she was just too dispersed.

Time was going by, but the DP situation was not yet worrisome. I next went for Igor S., the School of Visual Art's prized lighting teacher, who had shot many music videos and features and is considered a master of his field. However, he had recently sustained a broken collarbone and, after considering the assignment for several days, felt he just wouldn't be able to do the handheld shots, and that even the normal DP duties outside of holding the camera might be too much of a physical strain.

Eight weeks remained before shooting was set to commence, and now I could feel the pressure. I approached John S., an SVA graduate who'd been in the professional world for several years, a sweet and extremely competent guy, who certainly would work well with Roc. He'd shot digital video, and he currently worked for a fully equipped production house, so he would also have access to a vast resource of additional equipment for us, both in production and post. He signed on, and our problems in that area seemed to be over, and then, on June 6, stricken with guilt over leaving his day job at the height of the season, he penitently backed out.

Six weeks to go. Now Roc and I were desperately watching demo reels—actually tapes—of various cinematographers' work, and trying to make a decision based on these demos, which obviously represented their best moments excerpted from whole films they'd shot. One casts a DP the way one casts an actor. It doesn't end with the reel (or the head shot); you meet the prospective person, you scrutinize his résumé, and then you try to reach a few of the producers he has worked for, to see if he is good to work with, or if he was replaced halfway through production. But time was running out for us to do a thorough investigation of our candidates. Six weeks hardly left enough time for the chosen one to break the script down, book his equipment, and hire his crew—assistant cameramen, grips, gaffers—which is a DP's want and prerogative.

On June 13, we chose James Carman, who had shot a lot of PAL in Europe. That, plus portions of his reel, sold me. When he came in to meet us, he seemed a levelheaded, knowledgeable sort who clearly was connecting with Roc and putting up with his manic, cynical humor. We were both in agreement that, little as we knew about him, he appeared to be the right choice for the project. I asked to meet his crew and he said he'd have them call me, if possible.

A few of them did. And what I should have picked up on (but would it really have mattered this late in the game?) was that they were mostly foreign-born, and that some could barely speak English. Added to this, once filming started, they began dropping out a few days a week for other, higher-paying gigs—always dutifully replacing themselves. Still, this lack of easy communication in English, plus the transience of faces in the key tech roles, worked against any chance of camaraderie on the set. Very tragic indeed. For the most part, they worked hard; I had no trouble overall with their work ethics. But the sense of communal adventure I would have felt proud of having assembled just didn't materialize. Now, several months later, I speak to cast members who recall the shoot as one of the most congenial and professional they have ever been on, which should make me happy, but these are day players I'm speaking with—actors who came in for one day to do a supporting role—and they naturally would not have seen the larger, abiding sense of estrangement.

Not that there was ever any serious fighting among the crew; I gave them reasonably easy days, a comedy is a pleasant type of film to work on, and to be honest, work was scarce in 2001, so they knew they were fortunate to have scored any kind of gig at all. (In fact, in speaking with the crew recently to get them their tax information, I learned that few of them have had jobs since.) No, it wasn't a disaster . . . disasters are far worse, and I've fortunately never had to weather one. There was just no strong bonding as a team. It was just . . . cold.

A RISKY PRODUCTION DECISION

And that's only a part of how the communal endeavor went awry. Example number two begins almost four years ago. I had a student named Jon in my production class at SVA. I liked him because he was creative and outspoken. He had Attention Deficit Disorder and was a real pain in the ass, but still, I liked him, and I tried to be supportive of his talent and tolerant of his shenanigans. After his second year, he dropped out of school, and one summer day he called and asked if I had something he could do. He was going stir crazy, and anything would be great. Roc and I were in the middle of a screenwriting assignment for TNT, a screenplay based on the true story of a sociopathic Olympic swimmer who won the gold in Barcelona in '92. We'd done thirty hours of interviews, and had backed up most of them. I offered Jon the job of transcribing the final one we conducted, an hour-long phone interview with one of the swimmer's teammates. He jumped at the offer, came over and picked up the tape, and promptly disappeared off the face of the earth. I called his parents, his girlfriend, I called everyone he'd known at school. And finally, since this was the last interview we'd con-ducted and therefore one of the few tapes I hadn't backed up, and the script was due in two months, Roc and I were forced to improvise the voice of the interviewee.

Six months later, I get a call from Jon. "I bet you're mad at me," he offered. "Well," I said, dredging up an idea I'd found in the preface to a collection of Algernon Blackwood short stories, "they say every seven years we replace every molecule in our bodies. So . . . why don't you call me again in seven years."

"Really?" he had the audacity to ask.

"Really!" I replied. And that was that. For two weeks.

The phone rang and there was Jon on the other end. "Jon? What brings you back so soon?"

"I figured out how I can make it up to you."

"Okay . . ."

"My mother is getting divorced, and I can fix you up with her." I was speechless.

"She loves movies, she's a lot of fun. She's cute . . ."

"Ya know what," I finally responded, "I'm gonna go for it."

And I did. And she *was* cute, and endearingly eccentric, loved noth-ing more than to sit around and watch DVDs, loved food both cheap and fancy, loved to travel, didn't love hiking and camping out; good Lord, it was a match made in heaven. At the end of the evening, I told her to tell her son he could scratch off six years.

Now, where's this going, you ask? Well, six months into our lovely relationship, along came *The Sweet Life*, and Janet offered to do the catering and craft services. Have you all heard about never working with family or lovers on a film production? It's something worth seriously considering, and my motto in life has always been, "When you are warned, you must listen." So how come I didn't? Partially because the budget was painfully low; I was trying to come in under SAG's arbitrary

$200,000 ceiling requirement (which I'll discuss more thoroughly later). Partially because I thought she could do it, and it would be a useful way for me to find out about what was going on from the inside, since people didn't know we were dating. And partially because I found her personality so upbeat and quirky that I believed it would translate well onto set. The first people the actors encounter each morning as they arrive, tired and wary, are the makeup person and the craft-services person. And depending on how these two people interact with the actors, the day can start off on a positive note, or on a negative note, and what follows may have nothing to do with the director's skill, or the merits of the script, or all the talent involved—rather it would fall under the umbrella of that phenomenon known as "the magic between the frames." You'll never know whom to blame it on, but something just went wrong . . . You can see, therefore, that serious consideration should be given to the hiring of both those individuals.

So, I took a chance.

Don't you!

And then again, there are countless examples that fly in the face of such a pronouncement. How about Philip and Belinda Haas (*Angels and Insects*, *The Blood Oranges*, *Up at the Villa*)? Or Baz Luhrmann and his wife, art director/costume designer Catherine Martin (*Moulin Rouge*)? Or Arliss Howard and Debra Winger (*Big Bad Love*)? Burton and Taylor did a few successful ones together before they split. Then there were Alec Baldwin and Kim Basinger. Hmmm. Or Tom Cruise and Nicole Kidman. Hmmm . . . Well, you know what I'm driving at. Sometimes it works, but I wouldn't advise it. And I wasn't lucky with Janet. She became overwhelmed with the job, and started complaining a little too loudly. Some got a kick out of it. Others protested . . . to me. And while I can play the cipher with every actor and crew member—the cooler head prevails—I can't be quite so objective when it's my girlfriend. Personal emotions quickly came into play. And it led to some rough moments.

Example number three: The gruesome episode with The Name and No-Name resulted in new actors being drafted at the last minute, which had reverberations that were felt for weeks. I'd originally picked actors with Roc in preproduction during the casting sessions and then, when they came in to sign their contracts, I still rejected one or two because something in their natures just didn't seem right. I'd tried and tried to set things up comfortably for Roc. But the "fates" were against us, I suppose. The situation created by dropping these new actors suddenly into the mix called for his undivided attention, and made him seem isolated from the crew. It must have looked as if he'd formed a clique with the actors to the exclusion of everyone else, whereas the truth of the situation was that the rip in the chemistry, which had nicely evolved in pre-production rehearsals, needed to be repaired, and he was the only one who could do it.

An old friend of mine, Bruce Kirschenbaum, was about to produce his son Ari's first feature a few months after we wrapped. So I invited Ari and his friend Robbie onto our set as the "documentary filmmakers," so that they could not only get us some good, behind-the-scenes footage, but also so that they could see how a low-budget film was made, which would empower them to make their own decisions later. I covered this in the cast/crew agreements; by signing, they agreed to have their image in the "making of" documentary shot on set. (Joan Jett's agreement was amended to allow her to have approval over any footage of her that appeared in the documentary, but that was understandable.)

Ari and his father observed the cast and crew closely, and, toward the end of production, they approached several crew members and invited them to join their production. Interestingly, but not surprisingly, none of our camera crew was approached. Later I visited their production up in Greenwich, Connecticut, and damned if things weren't going far smoother than they had for us. Of course, we had shot in New York City, where 60 percent of our sound was problematic due to street noise, whereas Greenwich at night is so quiet you can hear a dollar bill drop! But beyond that, Bruce and Ari had the advantage of seeing which of our people were not only the most professional, but the most user-friendly. (Ari's film, shot in Super 16mm, is called *Fabled*. Keep an eye out for it.)

Oh, and I guess you're wondering how things eventually worked out for me and Janet. Well, after filming was over we patched things up, took a trip to Oaxaca, Mexico, flew back to the States and made a stopover in Las Vegas to visit Victoria Alexander (an old friend who appeared in *The Sweet Life* as one of the "bad dates"), spotted a little structure on Las Vegas Boulevard that looked like a Burger King but said "Drive Through and Say I Do" on its facade, did just that and got hitched by Reverend Chip Bendel while Victoria sat in the back seat snapping pictures, and then, not five minutes later, as I was driving my new wife to the Mandalay Casino to sample what I'd heard was an incredible food concession called "The Wall of Gelato," our car was rear-ended by a hit-and-run driver and I ended up lying on the pavement with whiplash and a cracked tooth. (Fortunately, four Swedish tourists in a neighboring SUV got the other car's license-plate number.) I looked up at the jovial Las Vegas cop who explained, "This happens fifty times a day; the driver of the other vehicle was drunk, and by the time we get him, he'll claim that his car was stolen that night and returned the next day, and you'll end up settling with his insurance company."

"That's fine," I said, "but what I really wanna know is, I just got married: Is this an omen or what . . . !?"

And despite the fact that she got mixed reviews during production, at the wrap party, when Rocco introduced and thanked the various members of the crew and cast, Janet received the biggest round of applause. Go figure.

CHAPTER TEN

THE BIG RED CIRCLE: FACING THE DAY YOU FEAR THE MOST

Remember how, in Forrest Gump, *the title character buys a shrimping boat in order to keep a promise he'd made to his dead friend Bubba? Gump has never shrimped before, but Bubba, an expert shrimper, has told him every-thing he knows about the craft. Armed with this knowledge, Gump heads out on the water and quickly learns, as he tells us in voice-over: "You know what? Shrimpin' is tough."*

So is filmmaking. Despite what Roy and I had initially thought about the script, in reality Sweet Life *was not a typical ultra-low-budget-first-time-director's project, where the number of characters and locations are kept to the barest of minimums. We had thirty speaking parts, and would be shooting on multiple exterior and interior locations in Queens, Manhattan, and New Jersey; three scenes set in crowded barrooms and dance clubs; and a climactic wedding reception set in a large hall with fifty or sixty extras.*

The wedding reception. That was the killer, the shooting day of which I was living in dread fear. In my perfect world it would have been the last thing we filmed. But, as things worked out, it had to be scheduled for the beginning of the second week of production. I took a red marker and circled the date on my calendar.

It loomed there, for me, like a date of execution.

TUESDAY 7/31. The day I've been dreading for weeks. We have two days in the reception hall to shoot the wedding sequence that climaxes the film. I only have the extras (about fifty or so) for the first day. That means we have to break down the shots so that we shoot everything we have to shoot toward the crowd today, and everything toward the head table tomorrow. If I miss something with the extras today, I won't be able to remedy the problem on Wednesday, and this weighs heavily on me. Also, we only have Joan Jett for the first day at the hall, so, if I want to keep her scene with Michael at the head table, I'll have to get that today too.

Of course, things go wrong from the start. We've planned to make the first shot of the day the wedding-photo zoom out, with Jimmy and

Robert and Barbara and Joan Jett (who, to my delight, has agreed to be clad in a bridesmaid's dress) and the other actors playing their immediate family posed outside on the front steps of the reception hall. This way we can get something in while they're finishing the big lighting setup inside. I go downstairs to check on the actors. Jimmy is looking dapper in a black tux. Then I see Barbara in the wedding dress she and Denise have selected for her, and my heart catches in my throat. Barbara told me on the phone that it was kind of cheesy and overdone, and I suppose it is, but she still looks beautiful in it, and when I tell her so she smiles and something radiant comes into her eyes. Though married, she's never had a wedding like this, with a gown and guests. It makes me happy we can give this to her, even if it's only make-believe.

Then I see Robert Mobley, who is playing Michael's brother, Frankie, walking around in his street clothes. I ask him why he's not already in his tuxedo, and he tells me it isn't here yet. Not here yet? I learn from Denise the tuxedo shop simply forgot to include it when they sent the other stuff over. Now someone is racing there to pick it up. I don't even dare ask where the place is. Already this morning, while devising the setup and shot list with Carman and our assistant director/production manager Glenys Eldred—most of it based on our belief we will have a Steadicam for today's shoot—Brian has told me no one bothered to tell the operator we're shooting in PAL, so he doesn't have the proper converter. Roy and Brian have made the call that no one can be spared to race back to the city and get one. Carman says that's ridiculous, there must be someone, it's only a $35 item, et cetera, and I agree with him. Half my day is planned around having a Steadicam! I offer my car up, and tell Brian to put *somebody* in it, and get the damn converter, or whatever the hell it is we're missing. Now I'm almost ready to start shooting and there's no tux for Robert. It's frustrating as hell, because I know it will put Carman in a foul mood. Every day he's ready to shoot before we are, and every day I hear about it from him, and rightfully so. That half hour or hour we lose because of this kind of stuff always catches up to us at the end of the day, when I'm forced to race like a madman to get all the shots I need. We simply can't afford overtime. I'm angry as hell but I hold it in, for the most part. By 10:30 or 11:00, Carman's ready to get the shot outside, but we're unable to get it till shortly before noon, when we're forced to rush it. The art department has neglected to provide prop wedding rings for Barbara and Robert, and so I beg a wedding band from my friend Rico Pagliei, to whom I've given a line in the picture, while my sister Terri

The wedding photo. From left to right: James Lorinz, Gary Cooper, Joan Porter Hollander, Robert Mobley, Barbara Sicuranza, Karissa McKinney, Joan Jett, and Tony Lover. *The flower girl is* Christine Houlis. *The photographer is* Larry Merz.

donates her band and engagement ring. During one take, Denise actually runs into the shot to fix someone's hair or flower or some such nonsense, and I bellow, "Get the hell out of my shot! What the fuck are you doing in my shot?!" We have to start again. We get one that looks acceptable to me, and move back inside. Denise comes up to me with a downcast expression, and I apologize for having snapped at her. Everyone's underpaid, so I'm always torn over how much I should complain when they screw up.

Once inside the hall, we put the camera up on the balcony and try to orchestrate some general crowd shots—first a wide establishing view, then Carman zooms in and just pans the extras, holding for a while on one or the other, moving on, et cetera. I have no megaphone and the place is huge, so I'm either running up and down the stairs from Carman and the camera to the set below, or yelling my lungs out from above to get somebody's attention. We get some good stuff, then move the camera to the opposite side of the balcony. But the view from there isn't quite as interesting as we thought it would be, though I think we get some usable stuff from the head table, especially when the makeshift wedding cake Ben Heyman has constructed collapses, and Carman catches Barbara's and Joan's laughing reactions. Then it occurs to me we should have gotten more from the first camera position, the clinking of glasses and calls for a toast, then the reaction to the toast. Let's move it back. I go downstairs and instruct the crowd on what I want them to do. I stay down there to orchestrate during the takes rather than run back upstairs to look at the monitor. I have to take it on faith we'll get good shots. (*We didn't, for the most part. Live and learn. I'll never take anything on faith in regard to camera work again.*) The extras do what I ask of them and seem to be having fun. It's 1:00 P.M. and time to call lunch, but I need just a little more before I can bring the camera down to the floor level, and Glenys asks the crew for fifteen minutes grace. They grant it, and we get the rest of what I think I need from that camera position, then call for lunch.

Of course, it isn't ready. The chef says, no, it wasn't supposed to be ready for one o'clock, he was told two. Brian produces the signed contract on which the time stated is clearly 1:00 P.M. The chef blanches and races to get the food out. I hear all this secondhand, because after everyone has filed out of the hall to go downstairs to eat, I've gone over to the far side of the cavernous room, taken a seat, and poured myself a drink of water. I sit there in the quiet for a few minutes, just pondering the day ahead, consumed with worry that we're not going to make it, I'm going to miss something, the shots aren't going to match. Jennifer Santucci, one of my students, who has volunteered to work on the film on days she doesn't have to be at her regular job, finds me and tells me everything is going fine. She's very sweet and very bright, and I can tell she's worried about me. I talk to her about the previous day's shoot (*an overnight at Fubar, one of our barroom locations*), how we got it in on time because I cut lines and setups on the fly, and for her to keep things like that in mind when she shoots her thesis film next year. Brian comes up and urges me to get some lunch. I go downstairs. I eat a little, then go from table to table, making sure everyone is okay, that I give a moment to every extra, just show my face, crack a joke, thank them for being there. The actors, too. Maybe it's just a hand on their shoulder, asking them how they're doing, just letting them know I'm there, I'm still aware of them, as distracted and frazzled as I might seem at times. It's so draining, this constant attention I feel I have to give to everyone. But it's also necessary and appropriate.

We go back to work and film Deborah's exit, a Steadicam shot that ends at Tick-Tick's table in the back. I've chosen a really marvelous young actress, Karissa McKinney, to play Deborah, and Carman is completely enamored of her face, of what it looks like on camera. In the scene as written, Tick-Tick's supposed to choke an old guy who insults

A tuxedoed Tick-Tick (Axel Engmark) *with a giddy Sherry* (Joan Jett) *on his lap.*

him, but we never found anybody right, so we've enlisted Larry Merz, whom Roy has hired as our still photographer for today's shoot, to assume the role of the choking victim, since he's thin and has a long neck, and it seems to both Roy and me that he'll look funny being strangled. We try it a couple of times, work out the technical gaffes, shadows and reflections, et cetera, finally get one we deem acceptable, and move on to Joan Jett's scene with Jimmy Lorinz at the head table, which will also involve the Steadicam. She exchanges some dialogue with Jimmy, is alerted to Tick-Tick's antics in the back, gets up and clomps over to her biker cohort, pulls him off Larry, and plops down into Tick-Tick's lap. Joan adds a piece of business, which I think is terrific, swinging her legs up onto the table to reveal the black combat boots she's wearing under her bridesmaid's dress. We need to change the line she was supposed to say to Tick-Tick—"Tick-Tick, man, let him go! The guy'll be dead soon anyway!"—because the victim is no longer elderly. Given Larry's slender frame and long neck, I suggest she say, "Hey, Tick-Tick, let him go! You look like you're choking a chicken!" but Joan is reluctant, saying she doesn't want to say anything that might make her look foolish. Apparently the phrase "choking a chicken" comes under this heading, but I'm left a little confused as to just exactly where the line is drawn, since she's already feigned nearly vomiting directly into the camera, done an incredible spread-legged pratfall off a bed, and is now clad in a bridesmaid's dress, which is falling off her, with combat boots. However, she's been so flawless, never missing a line or causing me a moment's delay, as well as being more accessible and friendly to the cast and crew than anyone could have dared to hope, that I have no intention of pushing her into doing anything she doesn't want to do. I put my arm around her and ask, "What happened to you? Did you do a film where you feel people lied to you and made you look bad?" She says *no*, she just thinks one always needs to be aware of that kind of thing. So I tell her to simply say, "Tick-Tick, let him go! The guy's turning blue!" which she agrees to, though I'm disappointed. I really feel the other line would've gotten a laugh, while this one probably won't. Again, we have to do it a couple of times to get it right, or at least close to right, since Roy rejects Carman's request to do it one more time. On the last take, Joan ad-libbed a bunch of lines, hoots, and hollers we can use for cutaways, and it will have to do. The clock is ticking, and I can feel Roy's quiet insistence like a brick-loaded backpack on my shoulders.

We start to shoot the scenes involving Michael's and Frankie's mother and father, Jean and Vinny, who are being played by Joan Porter Hollander and my film editor, Gary Cooper. Joan is not only dead-on perfect with the lines, she gives them a terrific spin, and I realize with a surge of relief and gratitude that I'm dealing with a seasoned pro. I'd never met the woman before this morning, they simply showed me a picture of her the night before, and I called her to hear what her voice sounded like. Her résumé included a lot of daytime dramas, which shoot at a pretty breakneck pace, with lots of dialogue to memorize in not a lot of time, so I rolled the dice with her. I couldn't rehearse her, just spoke with her for a bit and gave her an idea of the situation. Now here she is, delivering an absolutely wonderful performance, spitting her lines out with real feeling, and giving me alternate takes so I can have choices. Sometimes you just get lucky.

Sometimes you don't. We turn the camera on Gary, and, to my horror, find he can't remember or even say any of his lines. He'd been hilariously bitter in *Street Trash*, and Roy told me he used to be a comic or performer of some kind, so I find his inability to get anything right inexplicable. I will learn later that he's a diabetic, and hadn't eaten for hours sitting under those hot lights, and, as his blood sugar crashed, he grew more and more incoherent. The place goes dead silent as the throng of extras perceive the barely controlled state of hysteria that is beginning to overwhelm me. All I can think to do is to go into a close-up on him,

Michael and Frankie's mother (Joan Porter Hollander) *shakes a fist at her boorish husband* (Gary Cooper). *The director's mother can be seen over Cooper's right shoulder.*

put the script pages out of frame on the table in front of him, let him look down and read them, then lift his face and say them. But I grow dizzy as take after take it becomes clear he can't even do this. (*Though I don't remember doing it, my brother John will tell me a few days later that I was banging my head against the fireplace mantel in despair and frustration.*) Time is slipping away, and now Roy or Glenys or somebody tells me the grip electrics will not work beyond 7:00 P.M. I turn away at one point because tears are coming into my eyes. I just let the camera run and get as many takes as I can of Gary saying the lines, or attempting to say them, hoping I can get enough, maybe just the beginnings of lines, so that I can go to reaction cutaways in the editing room and have him loop the stuff he's missing later. My insides are clenched, and I double over at times, pressing my hand to my stomach as I look at my watch and the shot list. What's really tearing at me is that it's ultimately my fault, Gary's failure, because I didn't make enough effort to cast the role properly; that I took it on faith he could do it, without having him read for me beforehand; that I didn't take his diabetes into account when I made the call to shoot his stuff at the end of the day; that I am failing, utterly, in front of most of the people I know and care about, as well as others who have entrusted me with their money to make a movie. Roy asks me if I'm getting the stuff I'm supposed to shoot, with my brother and brother-in-law Chris holding Gary back from charging the head table, and I snap, "What the fuck do you *think* I'm doing?" then storm past him. God bless Johnny and Chris, because I get their little scene in two takes, and in that one, for whatever reason, Gary is actually good. We get Jimmy's exit, then my friend and former writing partner Rico Pagliei's line, then Joan Hollander's lines, of which she gives me great, varied readings. I yell *cut*, walk over to her, and kiss her hand (or was it her cheek?), the extras applaud, and I call it a wrap with five minutes to spare. Carman actually wants to keep shooting for that last five minutes, but Roy nixes this. I thank everyone, tell them to give themselves a big hand, and, looking at them now, I realize they've actually been having a pretty good time all day; that, to them, things appeared to run much more smoothly than they'd anticipated they would.

I go downstairs and sit down at the bottom of the steps. There aren't too many people down here, just Barbara and a few of her friends who'd served as extras. Terry the makeup artist and his sister, but they're out of sight behind some dividers. Maybe Jimmy and Robert, though I'm not sure. Barbara sees I'm in a bad way, comes over and sits down with me, and tries to tell me it's all good. But how can it all be good when, after this thing surfaces, all I'll be able to get a job writing or directing will be porn? And not even the good, stylish porn, the Michael Ninn porn; it'll be gaping-asshole porn shot in cheap motels along the Indiana Turnpike, starring dead-eyed truck-stop whores with flabby

Frankie and Michael's father (Gary Cooper) *being restrained by two wedding guests* (Chris Houlis and John Simonelli).

bellies and pimple-spotted buttocks. I can feel my eyes welling up again, and it's almost beyond my control. Tony Lover (of New York–based Liberty Studios, a provider of much advice and many lunches, who gave me a fun performance upstairs as Lila's father) comes over and tells me what a great family I have. I tell him he's right, I do have a great family. I think of my mother taking care of me when I was laid up for almost two months after knee surgery, and of how my brother John, and now my sister Terri and her husband Chris, have been out finding investors for our film, and putting up money themselves. I think of Roy, too, of all the work he's done to make this possible for me, and of how I'd cursed at him upstairs. A wave of guilt and shame sweeps over me, and I start blubbering, bury my face in my hands, and sob like a goddamn baby. When the flood of tears finally abates and I can breathe again, Jimmy Lorinz approaches and states adamantly that he and Barbara are getting me the hell out of there. They want to go back to Lenny's Clam Bar, where we'd had such a good time last Friday. I find Roy upstairs and apologize, and he tells me not to worry about it. In the parking lot, I tell Barbara to go with Jimmy in his car while I'll follow in mine. Somewhere along Cross Bay Boulevard, I start crying again, and it's ridiculous. If Otto Preminger were alive, he'd slap my face. I imagine him sputtering indignantly, like Tom Hanks in *A League of Their Own*, "Are you *crying?* There's no *crying in directing!*" I'm laughing at this image with tears streaming down my face, and at red lights, the people in cars opposite mine stare at me like I'm a lunatic, and it occurs to me that they're right, I *am* a lunatic. I must be. I'm a filmmaker.

Reading this now, I'd like to slap my own face. What the hell was I getting so damned emotional about? Why was I torturing myself so? Barbara told me that day I simply had my heart wrapped around this project, and that was certainly true. Some months removed from it now, other reasons become clearer to me. I've always believed, as many do, that no one who has had a generally happy and carefree life can ever develop into a meaningful artist of any kind; that the best and most worthwhile work comes only with a great deal of pain. A couple of sweeping generalizations, I know. Are they absolutely true? Of course not. On the other hand, are they true more often than not? You bet they are. Talk to some artists. Read about them. I've never encountered one who claimed it was effortless, or painless, or who wasn't consciously or unconsciously working out some thorny personal issues through their work. Which is why I think I was generating a lot of needless anguish in myself out of some subconscious certainty that nothing I was doing could be any good unless I suffered for it—a very stupid and self-destructive approach, as I look back on it now.

In any case, I got past it. At least I didn't fall apart until after we'd gotten everything we needed. And the following day, dealing only with my main actors and shooting simpler, more manageable scenes, would be a welcome and much needed respite. That was my plan, anyway. Can you hear God laughing?

WEDNESDAY 8/1. Second day at the reception hall. Luckily, the call time is noon, so I've been able to get a decent night's sleep and spend a quiet few hours at home before coming in. I'm still dazed and drained from yesterday's events, though, and after I arrive, I want nothing more than to sit and sip my coffee before easing into what I'm hoping and expecting to be a less trying day.

No such luck. Robert Mobley arrives, plops himself down in front of me, and launches into an increasingly agitated harangue regarding his experience of the previous day, the gist of it being that Barbara had been paying more attention to Jimmy all day than she had been to him, and had at one point said to Robert that she was marrying the wrong brother. Now, Jimmy had told me he was going to remain somewhat in character all day Tuesday, and so it was only natural, given the situation, that Michael would be cool to Lila. Knowing Barbara as I'm beginning to, it doesn't surprise me that the indifference Jimmy was directing toward her for most of the day served as a powerful magnet, perversely drawing her toward him, forcing her to find some way to win him back. As for telling Robert that she was marrying the wrong brother, well, as the writer of the script, I can say I agree with her, though I'd add that I don't believe either brother would be the right one; that both marriages would fail, but for different reasons. Still, Mobley doesn't want to hear that, and in truth he shouldn't have to, so I don't say it. "Yesterday was supposed to be my preparation for today," he continues. "I mean, this is my wedding day! And this girl is with me because she's crazy about me. I don't need to see her hanging all over him like that. I know they shot together all last week and did all kinds of love scenes because you're shooting out of sequence, so they've gotten close and all, and I've only just gotten here . . . ." He goes on about it, and though I'm not unsympathetic, I'm at a loss as to what I'm supposed to do about it. Can I go back in time and make last week unhappen? I'm sitting there, looking him in the eyes, trying to appear sincerely concerned, but all I'm thinking is, *Please, God, someone, anyone, stop this, I can't take it today, not today. Not after yesterday.* Jimmy arrives, gets a cup of coffee, and comes over, thinking we're having a friendly chat, but quickly picks up on what's really going on. He tries to be helpful, asks what he can do. I ask Robert if he wants me to talk to Barbara. He tells me no. So what *can* I do? He says he'd like to have his own room today, away from everybody else, like Joan Jett had on Tuesday. I think it's a childish request, and a grim harbinger of the day to come, but I tell him, fine, that I can do. At least it will get him away from me for a while. I call our assistant director/production manager Glenys Eldred over and tell her to give Robert the space we had Joan Jett in yesterday. She looks at me worriedly and I just shake my head, we'll talk about it later. Jimmy and I talk for a bit, trying to figure out how to deal with this, then Barbara arrives. I clue her in to what's going on, and chastise her for saying what she said to Robert about marrying the wrong brother. I tell her where he is, and that she better go find him and make nice with the guy before my head explodes.

While she's off doing that, Joe McGinty of *The Psychedelic Furs* arrives. He's a friend of Barbara's and her husband, Chris Stein, and he's agreed to come in and play our wedding musician, gratis, just as a favor. We place him on the balcony overlooking the reception hall, where he sets up a vintage seventies electronic organ. Then he dons a maroon velvet jacket and ruffled tuxedo shirt. I decide to hook the instrument up for sound so we can record it, and he asks me what he should play. I tell him he can't play anything we don't own the rights to, but that I'd like something with a wedding-reception, "Girl from Ipanema" feel to it. He presses some buttons and the instrument produces a percussive rhythm. It's a bit fast, and I ask him to slow it down a bit, which he does till I feel it sounds right. Then he just begins riffing on the keyboard, some melody of his own. I instruct him to just keep playing while we shoot him from an angle looking up from the floor level, first in a full shot, then zooming in for various closer framings. I stop him briefly, reset the camera in a close shot, and ask him to give me some reactions I can use for cutaways. We wrap it up, I thank him profusely, then urge him to get something to eat. Since he was just doing us a favor, it was important to me that I get his stuff out of the way first so that he wouldn't have to waste his entire day sitting around waiting.

We get Jimmy and Barbara and Robert and Karissa McKinney to the head table, and the first thing we shoot is Jimmy's and Karissa's scene. She's wonderful every time, and we get it with really no trouble at all. Then we set up a master shot of Jimmy, Robert, and Barbara. I don't like how it looks or feels, and, given how I've storyboarded the sequence, I don't plan on using much of it, but I need it in order to waste some takes.

Earlier, in addition to complaining about the previous day's events, Robert told me how he was planning to approach the scene, and it didn't jibe at all with how I think it should go. I refrained from sharing this with him, fearing that since he was already upset and somewhat frazzled, if I then rejected all his ideas in one fell swoop I would lose him entirely. He wants to play to the crowd for much of it, and to Lila, and as we rehearse it, I see him being very physical, turning away in frustration during Michael's toast and its follow-up. Today, fortunately, I feel I have some time, and so I begin taking masters, and after each one I walk up to the table, think for a while, rub my chin, and *change one thing*. I sense what appears to be my uncertainty creating a weird kind of tension on the set, but I can't tell anyone what I'm doing. I can see Glenys growing confused and a little concerned about the time I'm burning up, doing take after take. What I want is for Robert to play everything to Michael, that Lila and the crowd have absolutely nothing to do with it, that this is just between the two of them. I want him to be less physical, to appear to be holding a great deal of anger and rage just under the surface. So, I keep suggesting small changes, which start to add up, and by the time I'm ready to shoot the angles I'm really interested in getting, the scene is playing closer to how I think it should be played. We don't get there without some unpleasantness, though, as Robert complains repeatedly about the heat, and getting enough powder for his face. He comes close to really going off about it at one point (my sense is that he's feeling all his choices slipping away, and is growing increasingly disgruntled about it), and I go up to the table, put my hand on his arm and say, very gently, "Robert, do you want some touch-up? It's okay. Terry's right here. Terry, would you take care of Robert, please?" I do this after every take, just go up to the table and speak very softly. We're drawing close to dinner, and I make the call to save Robert's close-ups for after the break, to give him time to relax and retool. I'm also thinking I can put the air conditioners back on for the entirety of the break period and beyond, right up until I'm ready to call action for Robert's first take, so that it will be as comfortably cool as I can make it for him when we start shooting again.

We call for the break, and Glenys takes me aside, telling me we've really got to start moving if we're going to get everything in. I fill her in

Michael (James Lorinz) *and Frankie* (Robert Mobley) *confront each other at the wedding reception as a worried Lila* (Barbara Sicuranza) *looks on.*

on what I've been doing and why, and tell her that once we finish at the head table my belief is that we'll fly through the other two scenes we have planned for the evening, Michael and Lila's farewell in the hall, and the closing scene between Michael and Deborah outside on the steps. Both Jimmy and Barbara have told me the farewell scene is going to be great between them, and seeing how they're working together now I believe them. And the scene on the steps outside will be done with one setup, because having watched her work for two days I know Karissa's not going to cost me a moment's delay.

Dinner is good, and Robert sits with Brian and me, and I tell some stories about my brother. Just trying to be loose and friendly and not give any indication that I'm in any way troubled with anything he's doing. After dinner, we resume shooting at the head table. I continue the practice of going up to the table and touching Robert's arm and speaking quietly to him, and once he looks at me and says, "I'm fine. I'm not crazy." I get some nice close-ups of Barbara, then shoot Jimmy's exit. He's got a problem with his exit line and gesture—making a vaguely papal cross over the crowd while revisiting Frankie's earlier utterance, "Amen. Power to the people. Kumbaya" (*my little nod to Dick Diver in Fitzgerald's* Tender Is the Night, *which we would lose in the editing room*)—but gives me pretty much what I want, and we're out. I tell Robert he did a fine job, we got some good stuff, and that he's free to leave if he wants. He indicates that he would like to go if it's okay. I tell him goodnight and move on.

We set up in the hall and begin shooting. Jimmy does something marvelous during the scene, that actually gives me a chill. The last lines exchanged between Lila and Michael are:

LILA
You still haven't kissed the bride.

MICHAEL
Yes. I have.

Barbara takes his hand in hers and delivers her line, but then Jimmy takes a pause, leans in slightly as if to kiss her, and then delivers the line. It's a brilliant choice, and I go up close to him afterward and say, "That was *so* good." We start shooting Barbara's close-ups, and with each take she grows more and more emotional, until I'm hissing to Carman and his crew to just roll and keep shooting, we'll tail-slate it, just get the shot *now*. Tears are pouring down her cheeks, and when I say *cut*, she doubles over and staggers sobbing to the reception-hall door. I run to her and take her in my arms until she regains some

Michael (James Lorinz) *and Lila's sister Deborah* (Karissa McKinney) *outside Il Palazzo at Villa Russo in Howard Beach.*

semblance of control. We do Jimmy's close-ups, and then it's outside, for the film's final shots.

Carman has set up scaffolding across the street to get the camera up high. We'll shoot the final shot first, then go for the dialogue. I climb trepidatiously up the ladder and crawl out onto the platform. On the monitor the shot looks gorgeous, better than I could have imagined. The front of the hall has been lit dramatically, and the camera adds colors I'm not seeing with the naked eye. I've got a walkie-talkie, and I'm barking orders and requests over it as some neighborhood people gather below me to watch. We get the shot, and, as Jimmy and Karissa walk off, I couldn't be more thrilled. I tell Carman that, even if nothing else works, we've got one hell of a fine fade-out. He says he really likes this as the closing image of a movie, that it looks otherworldly, and I agree. I climb down and approach two neighborhood guys who are smiling, excited to be watching a movie shoot, even one as small as ours. I introduce myself as the director, tell them what a kick it is, that I say things into this walkie-talkie and people do them. Then we set up for the dialogue.

We've got maybe half an hour or less left (I've been told I need to finish sometime around 11:00 P.M.), and so have made the decision to just get it in one master two-shot. This backfires on me when the traffic going by never stops for more than thirty seconds or so. And it's not just

A pensive Michael (James Lorinz) *and subdued Deborah* (Karissa McKinney) *on the steps out-side the reception hall.*

cars, but trucks and buses, and hot rods with music blasting from expensive stereo systems. Then we're forced to wait when a garbage truck pulls up and begins emptying dumpsters. If I were shooting coverage from more than one angle, this wouldn't be such a big deal, since we'd eventually get all the lines clean in a combination of takes. But because I only have time for one setup, there won't be any place to cut. Now we're going to have to loop much of the scene, which is a shame because the live performances are just perfect. (I'm also operating under Roy's assessment that we can't afford to do much looping.) We go past eleven, hoping maybe the traffic will die down and we'll get one clean take, but it's no use. I finally call for a wrap, saying it's pointless to go on. I tell Jimmy and Karissa that they were great, that I'm the one who fucked up. Carman takes some stills as the crew begins breaking things down, and I walk off down the street, muttering to myself. A disappointingly sour conclusion to a day that had more than a good amount of sweet in it. What the hell . . .

CHAPTER ELEVEN

CIRCLING THE PERIMETER

Producing keeps me on the sidelines. In fact, when it comes time to organize the staff, the first thing I do is hire a dynamic, confident line producer who will represent me on set, taking care of the minute-to-minute crises, while I float around the perimeter, taking meetings, troubleshooting, visiting the location or set to see how things are going, keeping everyone calm, and doling out checks and producerly advice (and trying to keep my mitts away from the crafts services table).

Initially—in development and preproduction—I am in the direct center of the firestorm. In fact, Rocco was feeling guilty after three months of development had passed and I hadn't asked him to join in yet. But there was little he could do to help me budget the film beyond breaking it down for shooting days, and suggesting how he thought he'd be covering a scene, whether he needed a piece of special equipment like a Steadicam on a certain day, things like that.

In preproduction, I adjust the budget and assist in casting, hiring the crew, getting all agreements signed, finding locations, and supervising the breaking down of the script for shooting. I'm a compulsive list-maker, so I enjoyed it, and was aided by line producer Brian Gunther and assistant director/production manager Glenys Eldred. If there'd been more money in the budget, both of them would have come on earlier and lightened my load.

During production, my direct staff does the dirty work and keeps me constantly informed. Or, at least, that's the plan: it didn't work out that way at all during *The Sweet Life*. I didn't spend terribly much time on the set, but I ended up becoming the production still photographer (two days a week was all that took), recruiting extras (normally a full-time job, which no one had the time for, so I allowed it to be delegated to me), and before long I was even sharing the responsibility for driving the grip truck to the set each morning at some ungodly hour and then getting it back into a garage whenever the schedule stipulated its return. Truly the lowest rung on the production ladder. To have produced eight features and come to this: I appreciated the absurdity. And what I learned from it was that, at least during production, shooting in digital video did not lessen the need for a full crew.

I had arranged for fewer camera crew personnel than on a film feature, and this proved correct: since each DVCAM-PAL tape was three hours long, we really had no need for a camera loader, which would have been necessary if we were dealing with film rolls of approximately ten-minute lengths. I hired one less art-department member as well, and in this regard, I was off by one: a costume coordinator would have saved us considerable time. But it was in the production-assistant department that I was way off. I assumed we'd need only a handful, but twice that number would have been better, even if some were just standing around most of the time, waiting for instructions. I hadn't hired a PA driver for the grip truck, for instance, and at the end of a day, the crew felt too drained to trust themselves driving that huge vehicle back downtown, and since I had miscalculated in this regard, I felt it was just retribution that I be elected.

MY PERSONAL DEMONS

I'm an old hand at budgeting. The only new wrinkles were (1) digital video, which was a big one, and for that I relied more on my cinematographer and editor than I would have on Brian, and (2) SAG. All my professional life I've avoided dealing with the unions. They just scared the shit out of me. I felt that with them breathing down my neck, I would have no room to maneuver when things went awry during production. I even sacrificed a project here and there over the years rather than get embroiled with the unions. The understanding I had was that they hovered around the production every minute of the day looking for trouble, demanding copious reports that ate up valuable time, scrutinizing your books, supervising meals, overtime penalties, safety standards, contracts, et cetera.

I felt equal dread about completion-bond companies. A completion bond is an insurance policy that guarantees your film will be finished no matter what goes wrong. It initially costs about 6 percent of your budget, but a knowledgeable producer can wrest half of that money back at the end of production, provided nothing has gone amiss. It requires e-mailing or faxing bookkeeping notes to the bond company every evening, and if you begin to fall behind, they go on high alert, and if you fall more than a few days behind, they have been known to show up on the set threatening to take over the production. If a film is really in trouble, they may also impound the producer's salary to make up for the losses before venturing any of their own capital toward rescuing the production.

It happens a lot. It happened on *The Substitute*, a film Roc and I wrote, down in Florida. It nearly happened to Wes Craven on *The Swamp Thing*. The acidic waters of the swamps were eating the latex makeup off the stuntman playing the eponymous creature, so that every time he'd surface, the body suit would be dripping off him in pieces. The production began to fall behind schedule. One morning, Wes came out on the location, and there was someone he hadn't seen before lurking around the set, looking official. For a while, Wes tried to ignore the apparition, but finally he inquired who the man was, and was told it was a representative from the completion-bond company, waiting for Wes to fall any further behind schedule. Pretty creepy. Fortunately, Wes didn't lose any more time. But those are things I personally wouldn't be able to sanction. It's not just that I'm a control freak—which I am—but on independent films it's all about the director's vision. I don't like the notion of spending good money to buy a possible means of destroying that vision. A completion-bond company's delegated director will finish the film as quickly and cheaply as possible: no adherence to the style the director might have been trying to create; just get it in the can and get it over with.

So, a completion bond was not a consideration for *The Sweet Life*. I don't even know if a completion-bond company would get involved with a film whose budget was lower than $2 million. But perhaps they would. After all, SAG is now pursuing that kind of production so intently that they've created new contracts to make it feasible for producers like myself to give it a try. The writing is on the wall about the indie production tidal wave, and the unions don't want to lose all that business.

On *Street Trash* (1985), we put our casting ad in *Backstage*, honestly noting that the film was nonunion, but still SAG members sent their photos and résumés. Work is rarely plentiful in New York City, and the unions don't campaign aggressively on their members' behalf. So, with the tech unions, there is much moonlighting using fake monikers, and with SAG, there are more dangerous chances taken, since the actors' names and certainly their images will, most likely, eventually be visible on their union's radar. If the film turns out to be good, it may enhance an actor's career, and if it's a first-time offense, the actor may get docked five hundred dollars or more. In an actor's mind, I'm sure, it's a chance worth weighing, based on the size of the role and the caliber of the script. Second-time offenders are in much more serious trouble, and for third-timers, as I understand it, game's over.

We hired three SAG actors for *Street Trash*, and when the film was announced in the trade papers, they were nailed. I had put two paragraphs in their agreements: one stipulated that they knew our film was non-SAG, the other allowed that we would pay their fines if they were brought up before their union for a misdemeanor. The film did come out, and their names were in the ads and reviews, and all three had to go before a court of their peers and suffer the indignity of being berated, having to plead their case, and then being fined. I went in with one of them, and although the jury listened, the verdict clearly had been reached before the court was convened. The only surprises were: (a) that one of the actors, R. L. Ryan, was fined twice what the other two were fined, and, seeing as he was six-foot-two and four hundred pounds, I couldn't help but wonder if the fines were based on weight; and (b) that when another of the actors, who played a psychotic Vietnam vet in the film and was a bit on the edge in real life as well, leaped up and berated them back, the shocked and cowed SAG members were left speechless. He got fined anyway . . . by mail.

The experience left a bad taste in my mouth for what I perceived to be a kind of fascist mentality toward people who were barely surviving financially . . . after all, I never seriously believed these SAG actors were risking their union membership purely out of love for the artistic promise of *Street Trash*.

And so, wasn't I astonished to find that when we decided to try working with the actors' union on *The Sweet Life*, SAG proved remarkably easy to deal with. In fact, the union did me a favor by setting the bar for us, otherwise the budget easily could have drifted higher and higher, as budgets so often do. To qualify for their Limited-Exhibition Agreement, I had to bring the film in for under $200,000. (That did not include expenses involved with seeking distribution: screenings, festivals, hiring a publicist, preparing a distribution publicity packet, et cetera.) Their exact wording on the subject was thus: "The budget figures include any payment required during production but exclude deferrals and participation. Producer shall submit a fully detailed production budget, shooting schedule and shooting script to the Guild at least one (1) month prior to commencement of principal photography in order to permit verification. NOTE: In no event shall the budget including deferrals exceed $500,000. All deferrals must be reported to the Guild with the budget figures." So deferrals were excluded, as was, I found out by asking, costs incurred in seeking distribution. Fitting into that range, with those exclusions, was do-able.

When I submitted a budget of $198,000, however, SAG rejected it, saying that, in their experience, if a budget is that high, unforeseen contingencies will drive it over the $200,000 mark, so that by the time the film is in the can, the producer will find himself in a new contract range and have to renegotiate, and pay the actors a whole lot more money.

I went back to the drawing board and honed the budget down to $183,000, and the new figure still included a little cushion in each category. Creating hidden mini-contingencies is kind of like setting your watch five minutes ahead. You know it's fast, but it's still somehow reassuring to check the time when you're running close and to know that you've got five extra minutes. Same way with your ever-mutating budget. The categories may seem like they're firmly set in laser-jet ink, but they're really pulsating with hive life. If one department comes in on target, or low, another invariably swells and eats up the reserve. Your task becomes a balancing act. I try to pad each category by 10 percent, and to all the categories combined I add another 10 percent of actual "contingency" at the budget's tail end. Twenty percent total. This way you come out looking like a hero, as if you anticipated every unexpected dilemma. When the inevitable happens—if Murphy's Law delivers unto you a lacerating snafu that couldn't have been humanly anticipated—if you have that cushion, that hidden reserve to dip into, you'll emerge unscathed.

But perhaps you think it was laziness on my part to add on these mini-contingencies? That it was slacking off, not to have sat a little longer at my desk figuring every possible detail to the penny? Well, let me throw a few at you:

- One of the production cars breaks down and gets ticketed. It was my car, and I loaned it to the production, but after that, it was no longer trustworthy, so I opted for public transportation and taxis for Brian's assistant Doria, rather than rent a car to replace mine. (Most of her work, after all, is in the city.) Should I have budgeted one breakdown and all the concomitant costs, just to play the odds, or should I have "contingencied" it?
- Another: Roc wanted to use a Steadicam a few times. Our DP wanted it even more. I okayed three uses of it. But when the day of shooting arrived, our DP informed us that we had to rent an alternator to switch from NTSC to PAL on the Steadicam device. Not a big charge: $35 × 3. But he had neglected to mention it when he gave me his camera-package budget, and Brian and I, not being cinematographers, and not versed in digital video, weren't supposed to catch that oversight.
- Despite air conditioners in the house we used for the first week's shooting, the deadly hot summer, combined with our lights,

pushed temperatures inside to over a hundred degrees. The need for water rose dramatically. More than we'd budgeted for.

- The generator truck used diesel fuel instead of gasoline. Filling it was upwards of $200, which we had not anticipated.
- Robert Mobley approached me on the set and asked if he could have his hair stylist give him a trim, at a cost of a hundred and eighty-three bucks. As I mulled this over, he added that he knew we were working on an austerity budget, and if I thought it was too steep, he would go to a regular barber shop. On the one hand it *was* too much; on the other hand, he hadn't asked for any indulgences yet, and it's good policy to grant each key person at least one or two. Good for their morale, good for the generous image of the company. *And* it jockeys me into the position of not having to grant a possibly more painful expense later on. He got his designer sculpt.
- The extra PAs we hired, even though I'd contrived a way not to pay their salaries out of the budget (which I will explain shortly), still had to use public transportation each day, and be fed. One day we shot in Long Island and they had to use the railroad to get there and back, which was $50 more than we'd allowed in our "Transportation" budget category.
- In addition, Brian insisted on having $200 a day in his pocket, calling it "Petty Cash." After the production was over, he had to provide receipts to account for every petty expense (approximately $5,000), reorganizing it by category, and these hundreds of petty expenses were absorbed into their respective categories. Be aware: when your QuickBooks accounting record is prepared for tax purposes, the government is apt to become suspicious if you have a substantial "Petty Cash" category, and may decide to audit your books, which is something you'd like to avoid. So, these costs must be redistributed after the shoot back into the categories where they belong, hence eating into those "mini-contingencies."

DEALING WITH SAG REQUIREMENTS

How did I pare the budget down to $183,000? How might *you* do this? One way could be to shorten your mini-contingencies to 5 percent each but retain the 10 percent overall contingency at the end. But I think that may be putting you in harm's way. Another approach, which I implemented in this instance, and it's something anyone can do, is to get student PAs from a college that has a tax-exempt foundation (most do). Speak with the representative at the college's foundation office, arrange a deal whereby any of the students working on the production will be compensated through the foundation, then secure a donation to the foundation of the amount needed to pay however many students you hire. Our production assistants got $50 a day. For twenty-five shooting days, plus one week (five days) of preproduction, that's $1,500 per student. I arranged for a $5,000 donation to the Visual Arts Foundation at the School of Visual Arts, who paid my student workers accordingly. This was no longer considered part of our budget, since I didn't have to put this money in our account and later account for it. There were no points in the film given out for it, and no one needed to recoup it down the road.

SAG did require that a lot of paper work be filled out. My production manager had done this before, so she handled it under my supervision. I kept copies of everything before turning the work in, and sure enough, as I'd been warned, a few things were misplaced by SAG and I had to bring them copies. SAG sounds like a vast, well-staffed organization, and on some level it probably is, but in a department such as low-budget contracts, and in the paper chain all of our forms have to follow throughout the arcanum of the union, things disappear with some regularity. Paradoxically, this erratic behavior on the part of such a megalithic entity was reassuring to me. It made me feel more equal to dealing with them. I found I was allowed to bring things in later than their instructions indicated, and as long as I stayed in touch with them, and didn't let it slide too long, they were more than willing to work with me. Certainly, in all discussions we had, they would reiterate company policy, including warnings of what would happen if I went over budget, in a kind of robotic way. But in such dialogues, I felt my role was to remain cool and acknowledge everything politely, not to be argumentative. During production, when slight alterations in the rules became necessary, I found these same people, on a personal, case-by-case basis, to be more human and tolerant.

There were certain prerequisites for entering into a relationship with SAG. There had to be a copyright notice for the screenplay, which I hadn't anticipated, and time was short, so I hired the Federal Research Corporation in Washington, D.C. (202-783-2700), to rush the procedure through for me, which cost under two hundred dollars. They faxed me the copyright notice for SAG's files, and later mailed me the original.

SAG wanted either 40 percent of the total SAG actors' salaries, or the entire first week's SAG actors' salaries, put into escrow, which meant giving them a certified check for the amount. I was still raising money, and several thousand dollars was a formidable chunk to be tying up for the entire production. But there was no way around it. After the production, when they received their final paperwork and approved it, the money was promptly returned, and I felt like I'd invested in a Christmas Club at the bank. No interest, but my savings were returned just when I needed them.

We dealt with SAG East, at 1515 Broadway, where Nickelodeon and Paramount Pictures also reside. The Times Square area was someplace I occasionally found myself during the five weeks of shooting and afterward, and at such times I made it my business to drop in on my SAG representative even when nothing was due, to show pictures of the production, and discuss how we were doing. Personalizing business relationships is important. When a situation arises where they don't *have* to bend the rules, but doing so would get you out of a tight spot, if there is already a relationship, it might make them more amenable. It might not, but it's worth the time and legwork to establish the possibility. I drop in on, or call, all the equipment rental houses, the owners of locations, the investors, et cetera. I see it as part of my job, but I also enjoy it, which is one of the reasons I'm meant to be doing my job.

SAG had a minimum salary of one hundred dollars a day in their limited-exhibition contract. The remainder of what their members' regular salaries should have normally been was to be made up in a first position ahead of the investors if money was earned in distribution. I balked at their receiving money ahead of the film's backers, but it was that or nothing. And the total deferred sum wasn't too painful. Under twenty thousand dollars. In all dealings other than SAG, however, I endeavored to place any deferments behind the investors' recoupment position.

SAG never visited our set. They never called their actors to see how they were being treated. However, one of the SAG actors we used wrote the union a letter praising us for our kindness and consideration, and my SAG rep produced this letter from her file to show me. So, in terms of poor public relations, the things you do by two and two come back to haunt you one by one, and, conversely, the effort you expend to keep everyone happy can occasionally come back and be supportive when you least expect it.

As for the digital-video wrinkles in our production, you will find our editor, Gary Cooper, discussed at more length in the final chapters of this book, when we get to postproduction, though the editor ideally gets involved in preproduction, and has input into the script breakdown, the storyboarding, and even the way sound is recorded on set.

CHAPTER TWELVE

MAKING THE MISTAKE OF FEELING HAPPY AND OTHER CRISES

THURSDAY 8/2. A 10:00 A.M. call for a 4:00 P.M wrap. We're shooting the crucial Michael and Frankie lunch scene, where Frankie will indicate that he knows what's going on between Michael and Lila, but will not interfere. It's a solid four-page dialogue scene, full of subtext and hidden inferences, so Roy has scheduled it as the only thing we'll be shooting today, that I might have enough time to get it right without rushing it. It also serves as a break for the crew, who've been really busting their asses the last three days. Today will be just a half day, followed by a good meal here at the Indian Oven restaurant where the scene is set, then tomorrow we'll all have off, followed by a 6:00 P.M. call time on Saturday. I have the greatest hope that the day will go smoothly. Though the scene is emotionally complex, the way I intend to stage and shoot it couldn't be more simple. An OTS (over-the-shoulder shot) close-up and a tighter single close-up on each character, and a two-shot for only the opening few lines of the scene. My intention is that when I cut it, I want to isolate Michael and Frankie from each other in the frame once the subject of Lila comes up. Therefore, a master two-shot won't be necessary. Carman has suggested a dolly shot to open the scene, and I've told him if things go well and we're doing good on time he can have his dolly shot at the end of the day. Right now, I want to start with Robert's close-ups. Carman looks at me strangely and tells me I'm doing things backwards, that usually one goes for the master shot first. But what I'm finding is that the actors rarely give you much in the masters, they tend to save it for the close-ups (something I've always heard that's proven to be true), and since the masters always take the longest to get, by the time you're ready to shoot the close-ups, everybody's hot and tired and cranky. Why not get the close-ups first, while everybody's still fresh?

We do the setup, get the actors in place, and start shooting. The location is a good one, it looks nice on camera. Between the OTSs and single close-ups, we do six takes of Robert, and each one is usable. He rarely misses a line, and is giving me exactly what I want: a quietly confident reading full of hidden meaning.

"Maybe I made a mistake." *Frankie* (Robert Mobley) *at lunch with Michael, reconsidering his feelings about Lila.*

However, as soon as we turn the camera around to film Jimmy's OTSs and close-ups, Robert can't seem to remember his lines. We start again, Robert continues to freeze up, and finally I'm forced to let him read from the script pages. We're in an OTS shot, and so on the monitor one can see his head turning down to look at the script, which Glenys points out to me, thinking I'll call *cut*. But Robert's head comes back up for Jimmy's responses; I'm figuring some of those I might be able to use, so I let it run. We go in for the tighter single, and so it doesn't matter what Robert does anymore. I'm grateful to Jimmy for not making a stink, which he'd be justified in doing, but all Robert has really achieved is guaranteeing Jimmy will have more single close-ups than he will. It's a little before 2:00 P.M. when I call for the master, and since we've got time I tell Carman to go ahead and set up the dolly shot he wants. I decide to go for the whole scene in master, and by the fourth take or so, we get it. It's 2:45 P.M., and that's a wrap. The crew breaks down and then we have lunch.

Later, I drive out to see our editor, Gary Cooper, in Brooklyn. He expresses how bad he feels about his performance the other night, and I apologize for not taking his condition into account. We talk about how we can save the scene in cutting, and it doesn't seem like it will be as bad as I thought. I spend the evening in his editing room, looking at rough cuts of two scenes, the argument between Michael and Lila that precedes the massage scene, and the Miranda scene. We spend some time tweaking the latter, and it gets better, much better. I went back and forth on this scene, twice cutting it from the shooting schedule, and then finally filmed it only because I didn't have the heart to tell the actress we'd cast as Miranda that we'd decided not to do it. Now I'm glad we went for it. Gary, who is tough to please, tells me he loves the scene, that it's very subtle and funny, and seeing it now, I agree with him. Roseanne Petsako, who is playing Miranda, strikes just the right, sweet tone for the character, and does all kinds of wonderfully quirky physical things with her expression. And Jimmy's performance, his responses, are just dead-on right. We also work on the Michael and Lila argument scene, start to blend in close-ups, and I see that start to get better, too. I leave sometime after eleven, exhausted but also invigorated. Maybe we've actually got a movie. If only the shooting of it (which is so arduous and draining) could be over and I could just spend all my time in the editing room. That I found fun. No people to stroke or praise or appease or coddle or condemn. Just darkness and coffee and film.

SATURDAY 8/4. A 6:00 P.M. call time outside Roy's building on West 83rd, just off Amsterdam Avenue. I arrive, and before I can even put my bag down, I'm being pulled in three directions. First, I go with Ben Heyman, Denise LaBelle's assistant, to pick a motorcycle helmet for the scene we're shooting here, where Michael and the audience first meet Jett's character, Sherry. She is to toss him a helmet that is described in the script as looking like German war surplus, to which his response is, "Where are we going, Stalag 17?" After eight days of shooting, it's become clear to me I can't count on the necessary props being on the set without me calling someone in the art department and reminding them of what's needed beforehand. This is why, earlier in the day, I'd made phone calls to the actors to make sure they knew which clothes they needed for tonight's shoot. Then I called the art department and asked about the motorcycle helmets. Do they understand that I need one that looks like a WWII German army helmet? Or will I arrive on the set and get a blank stare? It's not made clear to me if they were already on it or not, but at least now, upon my arrival, I'm given two choices of German-type helmets, one black and one khaki. We decide on the black. It's surprisingly heavy, and I worry about Jimmy getting hurt when it's tossed to him. I give myself a mental note to remind him to be careful, and to try and make sure Joan hurls it to him round side first. Then I check the motorcycle out, an old Triumph, and it's good, I like it, it looks beat up and lived in, so to speak. I was adamant that we not have a Japanese bike, it just didn't seem right for Sherry, and I worried that Jett might have been unwilling to climb aboard one. She has a lot of biker fans who'd be alienated at seeing her on anything other than a Harley, I think, but we couldn't get one, so it seems like a Triumph should be acceptable. Didn't Brando ride a Triumph in *The Wild One*?

I approve the bike and the helmet, then move on to James Carman to talk about how we should shoot the scene. I explain that this is Jett's intro in the film, and I want to do something interesting visually. I suggest a dolly shot (which I know will make Carman—whom I've taken to calling Salvador Dolly in response to his daily requests to put the camera on tracks—happy) starting on Jimmy coming out of his building and walking toward us as we dolly back to bring the motorcycle's handlebar and mirror into the frame, with Joan's face reflected in the mirror. Thus in one shot we can introduce her, the bike, and Jimmy's facial response to them both. Carman likes the idea, adds the notion that we might dolly back even further when Jimmy walks around the side of the bike, and do the whole thing as a master shot, and I say make it so.

Joan arrives a little early, and I see her in the car going over her lines. Then it's upstairs to Roy's apartment to get into costume and make-up, and sometime after 7:30 P.M., we're ready to start trying to get it. We

An unnerved Michael (James Lorinz) meets Lila's roommate Sherry (Joan Jett, in the mirror) for the first time.

rehearse the dolly shot a few times to work out the focus problems, and to position Joan in such a way as to pick her up properly in the mirror. With all the Saturday-night traffic and crowd noise, I resign myself to getting nothing usable sound-wise. However, when I watch the takes on the monitor as we're shooting them, the background is very alive and real, and adds something to the scene I'm very excited about. We're racing the light now, and we go for Joan's single first; I feel I can live without a single of Jimmy, since by this point in the picture we've seen him quite a bit, but it's Jett's first appearance and I want a usable single of her. We get it, then hurriedly change the setup for Jimmy's single. It's getting dark fast now, though, and I don't think any of the takes we get of Jimmy will even come close to matching. I'll simply have to cut between the master and Joan's single. Luckily, Jimmy's performance and reactions in the master are quite good, so I think this will work out okay.

I hop in my car with some crew members and head off cross-town to the next location. Despite the fact that I wasn't able to shoot anywhere near the coverage I would have liked to have gotten, there was something very New York about the experience, and I find I feel happy and energized. This is a grievous mistake on my part, one that flies completely in opposition to the overruling beliefs I hold about life, which serve as the themes of *The Sweet Life*: good news brings retribution; no good deed goes unpunished; and lastly, Mack Sledge's haunting final lines in *Tender Mercies*, "I don't trust happiness. Never did. Never will."

We get to Fubar and begin setting up outside. When the location was suggested to me as one we could use for the exterior of Lila and Sherry's building (Fubar is part of a larger apartment building, and the stoop can be framed so as to keep the Fubar signs out of the shot), I told Brian and Roy that I hated it; hated the street, hated the stoop, everything. But they'd been having a hard time finding a decent brownstone exterior we could use, and said they could get this easy, since the two guys who own Fubar also own the building. Since they'd gotten me so many other great locations (Il Palazzo at Villa Russo, The Indian Oven, the apartment sets that were built in Janet's house, and the interior of Fubar itself), I felt I shouldn't balk at this compromise and said, fine, I don't like it, but I'll make it work. We decide to cover Michael's and Sherry's stagger home in a long dolly shot, and begin to set the tracks.

Now Brian comes to me in an agitated state. Prior to tonight's shoot, I'd been told that we were going 6:00 P.M. to 6:00 A.M. Then, today, Roy had informed me that he'd told Jett's people we would be finished with her no later than 3:00 A.M. Now Brian pulls me up the sidewalk and says we only have a couple of hours. I look at my watch. It's 10:00 P.M. What the fuck does that mean, a couple of hours? First it's 6:00 A.M., then it's 3:00 A.M., now it's midnight? What the fuck is going on? Trouble with one of the owners, he tells me. I bark at him to find out precisely what a couple of hours means, then stalk away from him. I'm fuming, thinking it's hard enough to get everything we need when things go right and we have enough time. What in hell am I supposed to do now? I go to Carman and tell him what I've been told, and I feel like an idiot. After a while, Brian comes back to me and says we can go to 2:30 A.M. Okay. That I can live with. Let's roll.

We rehearse the scene a couple of times, trying to work out focus, set the marks, and adjust the lights. The street is very busy, the bar is open, there's noise and cars and people constantly. When we try to keep people from walking through or ask them to cross the street, some comply while others tell us to go fuck ourselves. One of the bar owners (the one creating all the problems, I assume) insists we remove a light from the top of the stoop, one that Carman burned up at least fifteen or twenty minutes setting up properly, then repairing after it died. We get one take in when Brian tells me we have to stop shooting, we've lost the location. In addition to that, the generator truck has gone down. The generator problem we could surmount, but not the loss of the location. I snap at Brian, "Why don't you just stick a fucking knife in my heart!" *(Poor Brian, having always to deal with my operatic emotional outbursts.)* It's over. I'm humiliated.

Jimmy and Joan Jett are down the street, waiting for me to call action. Barbara has arrived and gotten into costume and makeup. She's standing there on the sidewalk, a slightly confused expression on her face, uncertain as to what's just occurred. And I'm sitting on an apple box in the middle of 50th Street, revealed for all to see as what I am: a rank amateur. I've dragged my actors and crew down here on a Saturday night for nothing, to a location I loathed and only accepted because I was told we could get it, that it would be easy. And now I've missed my day, I've fallen behind. Even if we can reschedule, it means paying Joan for another day, no small thing on our miniscule budget. It's a clusterfuck, a balls-out clusterfuck. I should go up the street and talk to Joan and Jimmy and Barbara, but I can't face them. Roy and Brian go, at least I see them all together. After awhile, Joan comes over and puts her hand on my shoulder. Tells me it's cool, things go wrong, she's fine, she's here to work, don't worry about her, we'll get it. I tell her she's been wonderful, but I can't really look her in the face. Barbara leaves with Jimmy, and now I feel really alone. I talk with Roy for a bit, as well as our students Jennifer Santucci and Alex Serpico. I talk about the evening's events, trying to spin it into a learning experience, at least for them. Driving home to New Jersey, I'm numb, and thinking only that if I'm going to finish this thing on time and on budget, I must remember never to allow myself to feel happy again.

MONDAY 8/6. Another one of these pain-in-the-ass 4:00 A.M. to 12:00 noon shifts at Fubar. (We still have permission to shoot inside the place, though I've been edgy about it all the time since the Saturday-night debacle.) Of course, 4:00 A.M. means 3:00 A.M. for me and Brian and much of the crew. I napped in the afternoon, then slept for about two hours from 11:30 P.M. to 1:30 A.M. At least I think I slept; I dreamed, so I must have. I arrive at 3:00 A.M. on the dot. Brian and Glenys and Carman almost immediately corral me to talk about this morning's shoot, though I'm able to get some coffee first. I'm still in a foul mood over Saturday's failures, so, when they start pushing me about getting a short, one-line scene involving Michael coming to the bar in search of Lila and being told she's left with Frankie, in addition to the day's primary focus, Lila's introduction in the film, which involves twenty extras, moving shots, and lots of coverage, I tell them calmly I'm not going to worry about it. They start in again, and I repeat my earlier response: I'm not going to worry about it. They must force me to say this three or four times, until they're just staring at me blankly. I simply will not rush Lila's intro. It's one of the most important scenes in the film, it follows two or three rather static scenes, and needs to be as visually dynamic and energetic as I can make it. I ask Carman if we can build a dolly track that follows along the length of the bar and then curves around the end, so that we can put the camera on wheels and get some sweeping moving shots, and also roll quickly from setup to setup. He says, yes, we have curved tracks, it's do-able.

While he and his crew begin on that, Brian asks me to take a walk with him. We go around the corner, and he asks me if I don't want to work with him anymore. I tell him that that's not the case at all, that I'm well aware he does a hundred things a day right for me that I never hear about, that I'm screwing up as much as anybody else, if not more, and things seem settled.

I go back and check the set. The tracks are down, and it's just as I'd envisioned it. We can get most of the coverage we need this way, just rolling from setup to setup. I ditch my idea of pushing in from the entrance onto Lila arm-wrestling as her introduction, and instead we go for a shot that starts with her hidden by the roaring crowd at the bar, then tracks right to reveal her and her opponent, moving back and forth on them till she prevails and then shouts her first line, "Fuckin' A! When you fuck with me you are fuckin' with the best!" Then it's Frankie and Michael's entrance. I've placed my friend Rich Van Zandt and two of his buddies at the bar so that they'll be right next to Frankie when he reaches the counter. They have just the right look, since they're precisely the kind of guys who'd be hanging out at Lila's joint and palling around with Frankie. As the morning progresses, we're getting most of what I think I need, but it's slow. There are lots of moving shots, and choreographing of extras. The latter takes some time because everyone is half asleep, so much prodding must be done to liven them up.

At around 8:30 A.M., Glenys and Brian take me aside and tell me I need to be wrapped up by 10:00. I'm taken aback by this, since I've been told lunch is at 9:00. How in hell am I supposed to break at 9:00 for thirty or forty minutes and then finish all I have to do by 10:00? We're supposed to be cleaned up and gone by 12:00 (that's my understanding), so in my head I've been figuring I could go at least till 11:00 or 11:15. Why wasn't I told this before? Why are they springing it on me now? They don't want to rock the boat with the owners, is the most I can glean

Frankie (Robert Mobley), *Lila* (Barbara Sicuranza), *and Michael* (James Lorinz) *at Fubar.*

from them. But after Saturday, I'm in no mental state to deal with it. We're out of sight from the crew, but I'm shouting at them both in my frustration. I walk away and resume shooting till 9:00, then break for lunch. I tell them during the break there's no way I can get all my shots by ten. We somewhat loosely agree on 10:30 or 10:40, but in my head I'm already ignoring it, knowing it's unrealistic. When we start shooting again, I decide to not go for the business of Michael spotting the spider tattoo on Lila's back when she leans over the bar to kiss Frankie. It's not something I want to lose, but it's two setups and I don't feel I have the time anymore. I'm also thinking I can get it tomorrow, maybe. With it removed, we finish by eleven, and I'm annoyed that I've been made to feel I'm late when all I've done is come in within the parameters of my original plan. And just as I suspected, even if the wrap time hadn't been altered, we didn't have time to do the small scene I'd refused to worry about earlier. Again, we can get it tomorrow. The scenes we're shooting on Tuesday don't involve any movement, it'll all be on the sticks, we'll go fast. Today's stuff couldn't be rushed.

TUESDAY 8/7. Roy called me last night and told me Glenys was threatening to leave the project, that she felt I'd undermined her on the set and that she'd lost control of the crew. Neither Roy nor I believe the project can survive her leaving in midstream, and so I spend a very fitful and sleepless night. What we're always fighting, on top of everything else, is that we can't go past the 26th, because SVA must have the equipment back by then, so it's not like we can shut down for a couple of days and replace her. We have to keep going. I never have any power in any situation, because I can't fire anybody, none of the department heads anyway, and they know it. Certainly Glenys does. So, I'm seething with resentment and sick with worry as I drive into Manhattan to face her and, somehow, keep her from quitting. Roy has charged me with this duty, telling me I must do whatever is necessary to change her mind, that he's tried everything he knows to do and she's remained intractable; that the entire project hangs in the balance. I think like a writer and try to see her as a character in a script. What makes her tick? What button can I push to get her to stay? It occurs to me then that, apart from her filmmaking career, she is also some kind of homeopathic New Age–type healer, a CranioSacral therapist, and I clutch at this straw like the drowning man I am. I call Roy from the car and tell him the only chance I've got is to make her fear for my physical and emotional well-being. I must take her aside and have a nervous breakdown in front of her. That, insane as it sounds, is my plan. "Do you think you can pull it off?" he asks me. I respond that I've been on the verge of a nervous breakdown since we started shooting (and actually did crack after the first day at the wedding reception hall), so it's not like I'd have to fake it.

When I arrive on the set at 3:00 A.M., I'm a depressed zombie, so out of it that I actually try to kiss Terry, our makeup artist, on the cheek to say good morning. He was turned away from me, I saw long hair, and thought he was one of the girls. He pulls away from me, freaked out. "Rocco, what the hell are you doing?" I look at him, jarred from my trance, and stutter out an apology. "Terry, man, I don't know where I am yet." Glenys is about to go out for coffee, and I suggest I go with her. I take her around the corner and let loose all the emotions I'm usually trying to keep in check. Within moments, I'm sobbing uncontrollably in her arms, snot dripping from my nose, body shaking. And it works. She says she'll try to make a go of it.

We then go back and have a great day. We actually build a scene from nothing, using only the description on the day's shooting list— "Lila becomes disgruntled with her job"—as a guide. I place Barbara at the beer taps, then start adding elements. Two extras in front of her, snapping their fingers for more shots. Another extra, blowing cigarette smoke at her. Others, yelling at her from off-screen for service. The other bartender moving past her from behind and bumping into her, causing her to spill the drink she's pouring. Me screaming for a Bass ale, and the spigot (which I'd found to be malfunctioning before we started shooting) just spewing foam and air. Barbara plays it terrifically, growing more and more angry and frustrated. It's all done in one stationary shot, with all of us making noise, and it works better than I could have hoped. We set up for another beat in Lila's disgruntlement, which I've storyboarded simply as someone reaching across the bar to paw her. It doesn't work here though, because Barbara has to stand too far back from the counter for the reach-over to look plausible. So, again, we build a scene from nothing, placing two male extras at the bar and having Barbara lean across the counter in between them to hand an off-screen customer (me) a drink. I tell Barbara not to let go of the glass, that I'm going to ask her what's in it. *Is it vodka? No, it's gin. I asked for vodka. No, you asked for gin.* This way she has to remain extended over the bar with her breasts vulnerable to groping. I instruct one of the extras I've placed at the bar to reach over and squeeze her tit. The guy's name is Reed, he's a bartender at Fubar where we're shooting, and, I learn later, he is also an actor. We rehearse it once or twice, and then he makes a suggestion:

Why not let him stroke her face first, which she wouldn't be threatened by, then the breast grab? It makes sense to me, so I tell him to go for it. We shoot it, and it does work better. And Barbara's response is terrific, as she curses and swipes a drink violently off the bar and into Reed's lap. Since I was actually playing in the scene, I wasn't able to be watching it on the monitor, so I turn to Carman for affirmation that it worked as well as I think it did. He purses his lips and says he thinks we should go again, that Barbara should have thrown the drink in the mauler's face. I tell him to rewind the tape and let me look at it. We watch it, and I decide to leave it as is; that throwing it in the guy's face is what they do in every movie ever made, and that the way Barbara has just done it feels much more real. I forgo the other two beats I had planned for Lila's disgruntlement, believing I've got enough with the two pieces we've just shot.

Next we shoot the "Michael's Women" sequence in the back room. First off is Margaret Gavin, as the girl who can see Michael's soul through the palm of his hand. She's a very serious and intense actress, but surprises Jimmy and me by knowing as much about the *Odd Couple* TV series as we do. I've come up with some physical business for her scene (which is just a one-line take into the camera) that isn't in the script. I have Jimmy positioned out of frame and put his hand in both of hers. My thinking is that she should deliver her line—"I can see your soul . . . through the palm of your hand"—and that Jimmy should then try to pull his hand from her grasp while she holds on tight. It's dark in the back room, and I sit near the camera and speak very softly to her throughout the takes. (Later, Jimmy will describe me as George Cukor revisited.) She's not as good here as she was in the audition, where she really infused the line with authentic emotion and intensity, even going so far as to conjure tears in her eyes, and this disappoints me. But it's a very simple shot, so I just keep having her do it over and over again, until finally, on the last take, she really hits it. And the hand business is really funny. I can use it or not, since I can cut out right after she delivers the line, but I can decide about that later, in the editing room. At least I have it now as a choice. Ellie Mae McNulty, a British actress, is next, playing the girl who likes to be choked when she climaxes. As written, the character was supposed to be flouncy and scary and large-breasted, but as I thought about it that seemed like too obvious a way to go, and so not very funny. When Ellie Mae came in to read for another part, she was so sweet and giggly and youthful-looking, it struck me that if she were to deliver that line, it might really play. I do the same thing with her that I did with Margaret: I sit next to the camera and address her very softly, telling her what I want, what to try, what poses to strike. She gives me a whole selection of varied readings, so many I'm not sure how I'll choose one, but it's a nice problem to have. We then bring Victoria Alexander in to play herself, the woman who is being stalked psychically. I ask her to deliver the monologue as written, then to ad-lib and keep going, so I have something to cover Michael's voice-over. At first, she's wooden on the monologue and marvelously alive on the ad-libs. I keep having her do it till we strike some kind of balance, and then we're out. We have lunch, and then we shoot all the stuff we didn't get to yesterday; the one-line scene with Carly (Lila's fellow bartender, played by Kristabelle McDermott), and Michael's casting an unnerved glance at Lila's spider tattoo as she leans over the bar to kiss Frankie. We wrap early, and everybody is happy, most important, Glenys. She believes that my changing the "vibration" I'm putting out had a positive effect on the whole crew. Yes, I tell her, that must be it. The truth is, I just got lucky. It was a light day and the actors really delivered. Later, talking to Gary Cooper on the phone, I tell him the horrific lengths to which I had to go to keep Glenys from walking. He laughs his head off at my debasement and tells me, "Rocco, you are such a *whore!*"

CHAPTER THIRTEEN

HOGS, HEIFERS, AND GUERRILLAS: THE LOCATIONS ISSUE

Despite everything you do in preproduction, despite every minute spent, each of which saves an hour of headache in production, despite all that labor, what can still go wrong *will* go wrong. Filmmakers are meant to be tested on the anvil of pain. Maybe that's why I do a film only once a decade. I'd much rather be spending my time ferreting out new restaurants with challenging chocolate-mousse recipes . . .

Locations, for instance, can be a nightmare. They can be frustrating to find, lock down, and keep available until needed. Even if the finding and booking goes smoothly, there can be unforeseen complications since they were not constructed to accommodate the specific needs of film shoots. Hence, the great reliance on sets built in studios where all elements are under the filmmakers' control.

On the other hand, a location can be as mood-inducing as the cinematography, and as much a character as any of the performers. I took my cue from *Dawn of the Dead*, which was filmed predominantly in a mall-under-construction outside Pittsburgh. This fabulous location was obtained at no cost other than electricity, insurance, and compensation for the night watchman—by giving the mall's owners points in the production. I had a similar plan in mind when I wrote and produced *Street Trash*: the director's father owned a collision yard on the Brooklyn-Queens border. We not only filmed there for three months, but cannibalized car stalls to build our makeup, wardrobe, and camera rooms, and even a standing set.

THE LITTLE LOCATION THAT WOULDN'T
In the previous chapter, Roc mentioned the Indian restaurant scene. That took a half a day to shoot, but several of us spent months searching for a suitable place that would give us a suitable price. In fact, successful location hunting was one of the tasks that eluded us far too often on *The Sweet Life*. First Denise had one she was pursuing, then Ben had one, then someone else, and always it was lurking in the back

of my mind, worrying me while I went about other things. Shooting began on July 25 and still we didn't have one. Finally, August 2 drew near, and no one's leads had come through, and I had always liked the food at the Indian Oven, one block from my apartment building, so I walked in and started negotiating.

New York and L.A. are not the greatest places to secure locations either for free or cheaply; the business populace is hip to the copious fees film companies will pay to use their property. The Indian Oven had recently allowed a commercial to be shot there for $2,500, but somehow they understood that mine was not that kind of production. So, they asked for $500, which was within my range. Since I truly felt that it was one of the finest restaurants on the Upper West Side, I asked if they could also give us a decent price to cater lunch, and that was arranged as well. The scene was an important one, emotionally complex, so I had scheduled a very light day. In fact, it was the only scene scheduled for that day. If it proved troublesome, we had the time to work it out, but I doubted it would go the distance. And I figured the crew would enjoy such a double treat: an early day plus a delicious Indian repast.

And indeed, they did, until several of them started feeling sick, and then my benevolent idea seemed to be backfiring. (Glenys's bellyache persisted, and I'm sure it was instrumental in making her feel like quitting four days later, which led to some hasty after-hours strategizing with Roc, since at that juncture, after the fiasco with The Name and No-Name, I felt we couldn't weather another major loss.) Making matters worse, a crew member's wallet was stolen, and it seemed clear that one of the kitchen employees did it, but there was nothing I could do about it. The best of intentions, gone to earth. Then again, there was a way to look at all this as a glass half full: If I had scheduled another scene for the afternoon, we probably would have had to cancel it due to food poisoning.

SHOOTING AT A SCHOOL

Roc and I both teach at the School of Visual Arts. I'm completing my twenty-fifth and final year as I write this tome. Reeves Lehmann, the film department chairman and my old friend (he shot *Document of the Dead* for me), who has done more for SVA's film department than the two chairs before him combined, had been very supportive of our endeavor. He understood, as the school's administration should have, that if we succeeded they succeeded, both financially (I'd offered them a healthy percentage of the producer's net) and through positive publicity. Moreover, we were shooting during the summer, when the school is not operating at full capacity. In fact, there were almost no student shoots at all, much to the bafflement of the production office staff.

And yet, the school's lawyer hardballed me on just about every contract point, reducing the amount of resources we could take advantage of while we were there to the point that, after the third time the contract came back with items crossed off or compromised, I said to Reeves, "You see the clause down at the bottom about the percentage the school is getting? You can cross that off, too." He laughed, but I was serious, and they got less than I'd originally offered.

One afternoon we were shooting an office scene, representing Jimmy/Michael's day job for a film magazine. Since I own the country's oldest film publication, *Films in Review*, and there would be no legal problems, Denise made huge blowups of back-issue covers and hung them around Reeves's office. It was a small office. We had our eyes on a larger one, but, for no good reason, the school wouldn't let us use any offices at all, so Reeves volunteered his. Mind you, during the school year, when I'm teaching, if students want an office to shoot in—any office—with a week's notice, they've got it.

The result was a cramped space in which there was no room for camera movement, and I could tell Rocco was unhappy about it. *How could I tell?* Was it that unspoken sixth sense that develops between writing partners over decades of working together? Not really. He was just walking around openly complaining to anyone within earshot. And I couldn't blame him. We'd been looking forward to these three days as a sanctuary from the inclement winds that buffet indie productions. And yet, we were treated like hostile invaders, with no one save Reeves willing to bend very much to cut us a break. A shame. But not unusual. It is not a given that using a friend's apartment, or home, or place of work, will go smoothly. Unless one is in the industry, he cannot fully imagine the imposition of a crew invading his turf.

And lest I complain too greatly, let me add that it was by no means a washout at the school: we got good material, and for three luxurious days we didn't have to load our equipment back in the truck each night and unload it the following morning. It sat locked in an unused room on the school's fourth floor, saving us valuable time.

A BAR WITH HEADROOM

The Biker Bar was our most difficult location to secure. Rocco had his heart set on Hogs and Heifers, an uptown, East Side version of the raucous downtown venue. The centerpiece was a clog dance on the bar, featuring the characters of Sherry (Joan Jett) and Becky, a tough-as-nails bartender. So, we needed a heavy, wide, extended bar with enough headroom to allow people to get up on it and cavort. Fewer bars in New York fit that description then you might think.

We visited the H&H on 95th Street and First Avenue and it was pretty dead, which seemed good for us. But our attempts at negotiations got us nowhere. My regular (nonentertainment) lawyer, who represents restaurants in the meat district and elsewhere around the city, and who knew the owner of Hogs and Heifers well, couldn't get her to come around. We located other places and visited them, but something physical about each place wasn't right, or the price was too high.

This search went on for two months. Now, suddenly, the shoot was upon us. Brian was stressed out; he had been losing sleep trying to solve the problem. Then he mentioned it to Denise, and within the two days remaining before the shoot, she secured a terrific joint for us—Don Hill's on the Lower West Side, it's eponymous owner a friendly, easygoing guy who stayed out of our way and let us do anything we wanted to with the place. It cost us a grand, exactly the price I had allotted, and as far as Brian was concerned, Denise could do no wrong. She ended up coming through for us again with the Russian dance club Neva, which we also used for our wrap party.

For Don Hill's, a location in our fourth week, I had the unenviable task of filling the place with bikers and other appropriate types, both women and men, but I'd already used up most of my reservoir of friends and acquaintances on the wedding sequence, which led off the second week. I called people as far away as Woodstock (two hours from New York City), and they came, and most of them didn't make it into the final film, which was painful for me, after making them go out of their way. But most of them had a good time. Joan Jett's hit "Fetish" was playing on the sound system, as it will be in the final cut, and she got up and danced to it on the bar, so all those one-day visiting extras were privy to a spectacular performance. I saw no one who wasn't having a good time for two-thirds of the day. As time wore on, film-set boredom set in, and for those who weren't finally used, it must have seemed like a vast waste of time even with the free food and entertainment. The following day, I called as many as I could and thanked them for showing up and being so tolerant.

A STOLEN LOCATION

It's infamously hard to get approval to shoot in the subways in New York. The city doesn't want people down there, getting in trouble. There's a lot of dangerous electrical current in the darkness.

I visited the location of *The Taking of Pelham One Two Three* back in '73, while Robert Shaw was filming his character's death by suicide on the third rail. An entire subway station had been commandeered by the film company. A subway car sat idly at their disposal. Shaw had completed a second take just before I was shown into his improvised dressing room. He looked up at me and, it being the first time we'd met, I was startled by how old he looked. Attempting to be tactful, I remarked that he was looking tired. He scowled at me, and the makeup artist urged him to get the makeup off before it began to stain his face. I didn't realize they had put some sort of chemically unstable appliance on him that appeared to shrivel as the current coursed through his body. The first take, he explained, had been pure acting without the aid of the makeup. He had persuaded them to let him try it once that way, likening it to Barrymore's purely histrionic transformation in the silent *Dr. Jekyll and Mr. Hyde*. The stuff looked pretty gruesome and artificial, and as near as I can figure after watching the finished film, it was the first take they used.

Nowadays, an indie film might get access to the Transit Museum, to use a nonfunctioning subway car, though I'm hearing even that is becoming difficult. But to get into the actual subway, your best option is to go without permission (you can supply the synonym) and "steal" the shot. Tripods are a no-no, and will invite a ticket and the possible confiscation of your equipment.

Guerrilla shoots are a romantically viewed tradition. Larry Cohen made his career on them, and talks with much pride on the DVD commentary track of his film *Black Caesar* about how he and his cameraman stole all those incredible city-street shots, with bystanders thinking Fred Williamson had actually been shot and was bleeding to death. Sho Kosugi explained to me that when the City of Houston refused to give him a permit for a dangerous stunt, he simply stole it on one of the city's bridges. He did a back flip out of the rear seat of a convertible car, over the top of the truck in back, and landed on the car behind the truck, while a camera car alongside caught the action. It was one of the most dangerous stunts I'd ever seen in a motion picture, and since they stole it, they had to have been totally uninsured.

So, when we considered the options for our subway shoot—a simple scene in which Michael's character interacts with a pathetic bag lady in a deserted station, followed by his ride in the subway car—we decided to take our chances, though we did rent a second, cheaper camera just in case we got caught and it was impounded. We also put together our lightest crew—maybe six people, in two cars—and went out to the farther reaches of the subway lines in Brooklyn, hoping that the cops wouldn't frequent those stations in the mid-to-late evening hours. The second camera cost us $225 for the day, and the shoot went without difficulties. I wasn't there—the producer was considered expendable for a guerrilla shoot like this—but I sat at home anxiously awaiting a phone call informing me of the outcome. There *was* a close encounter with the men in blue, I was told, but otherwise the shoot went smoothly, and the day wrapped up well before the twelve-hour limit.

A CONSPIRACY OF COOLER HEADS

Then there are the locations that don't present many problems . . . except those that the cast and crew impose upon them. Case in point: we had a Week Three Monday call at 4:00 A.M. at Fubar. I arrived in the morning around 8:30, having missed two-thirds of the shoot, and I immediately sensed things weren't going well. Doria, Brian's assistant, was out sick, and Brian was complaining of a bad cold. This, added to Glenys's ongoing malaise from the Indian meal, resulted in a simmering air of discontent that was hard to miss. Roc was missing it, however, since he was pissed and only saw what he perceived to be the production team conspiring against him . . . and they were, out of fear of losing Fubar over one more infraction in the mind of the co-owner who cost us our Saturday night. It had become tentative and unpleasant there, and originally Fubar was supposed to be one of our sure things. The only amusement of the morning occurred when Mobley asked if his hair stylist could receive a credit on the film.

Eleven hours later, the shit hit the fan. Brian called and told me Glenys was going to quit. I called Glenys and found her intractable in her resolve. It pissed me off: The woman is a professional; how difficult could it be to endure another few days and see if things turn around? I should have known better than to trust someone who, with her husband, owns the largest cricket farm on the East Coast. But, *the film is everything* to the producer and the director, and this problem had to be resolved if humanly possible. My personal feelings had to take a back seat.

I brought all my seductive forces to bear—humor, cajoling, sympathizing, practical reason—and she threw up a wall of resistance. But, when the call was over, I'd got her lingering at least to the end of the week out of professional courtesy until I could replace her. I called Roc and laid it on him. It's not just *my* job to keep the members of our team calm, it's his as well. A director, among many things, must be a psychologist, and when he doesn't do his job properly in relation to the cast or crew—like Sam Peckinpah, infamously, or, in my experience, Harry Hurwitz on location with *The Comeback Trail* (a film I associate-produced in 1971), where the gaffer, pissed at Harry for keeping all of us overtime in a fake western town outside Sante Fe, short-circuited the entire location and part of the city as well, forcing us to call it a day—a viral form of ill-will results, and the film suffers in more of those subtle ways that you can't quite put your finger on, but the end result is that it's not as good a film as it could have been.

Much to his credit, and it's one of those unsung acts of heroism of which the critics will be utterly unaware, Roc pulled the sinking situation out of the fire. His bravura breakdown in Glenys's arms worked, she was recruited back into the fold, and that second day at Fubar, our last at the location, went smoothly. The fever had broken . . . the ill-will dissipated.

(A few days earlier, Roc had relayed to me his quick take on averting another such problem, this time with our makeup person: "Terry was giving me trouble, but I praised him into submission." At the risk of incurring *your* ill-will, I reiterate: *the film is everything* for the producer and director . . . and sometimes that means biting the bullet and holding tough—as with The Name and No-Name, and sometimes that means the cooler head must take precedence over pride, as with Glenys and Terry and a hundred other little skirmishes during the production.)

And I was just kidding about the crickets being indicators of human untrustworthiness. That's all I need are the insect-rights activists coming after me.

A BENEFIT OF FRIENDS

I arrived again that second morning at FUBAR around 8:30, and just missed my old friend Victoria's performance. Victoria had flown in from Las Vegas for the day to play herself as an insane date who blithely terrorizes the camera /Michael's point of view. Seventeen years ago, she had been funny in a cameo in *Street Trash*, screaming shrilly as her screen husband was pulled out of a car window by a malevolent wino and smashed through the front windshield.

Victoria was sitting at the bar when I got there, her scene completed. Out of the limelight, she chatted animatedly with those nearest her. And yet, she was the focal point of the entire place, which is three rooms long, with forty ostensibly busy people. Later, when I asked Barbara Sicuranza how she liked Victoria, thinking she would have gravitated toward her since her husband has an astral-projection-friendly Web site, she looked at me and said, "She scared me!"

Whenever I take a moment to reflect on the production, I smile at having been able to bring some of my friends and some of my *Street Trash* alumni into it with me. Those few things are about all that's really personal to me about the film. One takes one's pleasures where one can. When it comes down to it, I did this film for Roc. It's well directed, and he should get plenty of job offers as a result, or at least a few. Me, I'm seventeen years his senior, and I've had a bellyful of this misbegotten industry. My plan for the future is to pull a "B. Traven"[1] and disappear into the underbrush. Thanks to cyberspace, I can still write screenplays with my partner regardless of what little jungle cranny I might be occupying. We never really sat in a room and wrote together anyway; that's how our partnership has lasted as long as it has.

---

[1] B. Traven—the mysterious author of *The Treasure of the Sierra Madre* among many other novels about Mexico. A recluse, he may or may not have shown up on the location shoot of *Treasure*, passing himself off as someone else, though John Huston suspected it was him. No one even knew what he looked like . . .

CHAPTER FOURTEEN

RS
SCHOOL DAYS

WEDNESDAY/THURSDAY/FRIDAY 8/8–8/10. Three days of shooting at the School of Visual Arts. I've been looking forward to this as a relief from the problems we've been encountering on the other locations, whether it be noise or troublesome owners. Here I feel I'll have some control. We're scheduled to shoot the movie-theater scene first, in room 502, an eighty-seat screening room that will double nicely, I think, since the whole scene will be covered in a pretty tight two-shot of Michael and Lila. Carman has requested a fog machine to make the projector light really show up. The school doesn't have one, or just maybe refuses to give it to us. Carman arranges a deal for a fog machine from Hotlights, and it is picked up and brought over while the lighting is being set up. After it arrives, he fires it up and fills the place with the billowing white vapor. We kill the lights and start the projector to test the effect, and on the monitor, it does look great. We're just getting ready to go when a fire alarm goes off. The film department chairman Reeves Lehmann is in the room with us when this happens, and, like us, assumes the fog has triggered it. We're waving placards around, trying to dissipate the mist while I resign myself to losing the visual punch it lent the image, though I find it hard to believe the fog vapors could be the cause of the alarm. This is, after all, a film school, and someone must have used a fog machine in here at some time or another. A minute or two later, my suspicions are confirmed when Glenys rushes in and tells us there actually *is* a fire in the building and that we have to evacuate. We hurry down the stairs and outside, and all I'm thinking is that, once again, something I thought was going to be easy (in this case, filming at the school) has proven otherwise, this time before I've even begun. I stand on the sidewalk with visions of the building (and the equipment inside, and thus our project) going up in flames.

Fortunately, this darkest of scenarios doesn't come to pass, and, within ten minutes, we're allowed back into the building. Some work was being done in the elevator shaft, a little smoke was created by the welding or whatever it was they were doing, and that set the alarms off. We go back up to 502 and start shooting the scene. But we keep being interrupted by the noise of desks and chairs being thrashed about in other rooms and dragged down the staircases. I ask if someone is building a goddamn railroad, and Glenys and Roy go to see if they can kill the noise. We work things out by sending PAs with walkie-talkies to the rooms where work is being done and having them ask the maintenance men to hold off smashing things while we're getting takes. They comply, but only (I believe) because Reeves is in the building, backing us up. If he weren't here today, I'm sure we'd be screwed. We shoot the scene in the two-shot as I'd planned, but since we don't need to change setups, I decide to push in for single close-ups, too, and have the extra coverage. Since Michael and Lila are at odds during the scene, it might make sense to be able to separate them in the frame, and cut back and forth. (*This is how we ended up cutting the scene, and it allowed Gary to create some comically effective moments by altering the timing and rhythm of the actors' deliveries.*)

We finish and head upstairs to shoot a scene in Reeves's office. It's not very big, and a bitch to light. One of the many things I've learned over the last few weeks is that the smaller the space, the longer it takes to light, so that scenes you think are simple, just people talking to each other over a desk or some such thing, take forever (or what seems like forever when you're in there, sweating) to get right. Reeves is playing Michael's editor, the one who gives him the advice that sends him

"Where's the color?" *A bored Lila* (Barbara Sicuranza) *with Michael* (James Lorinz) *at an arthouse revival of* La Dolce Vita.

spiraling off into what will eventually turn out to be emotional destruction. He requested a part, and this one seemed right for him. He's not an actor, but he questions me like one, discussing who his character is, what his and Michael's relationship is like, asking for line changes, et cetera.

We cut a lot and simplify the scene to make it feel more conversational. Jimmy feels he should have some business, be fiddling with something when Jeff (Reeves's character) enters, and we cast about looking for something appropriate—a stapler or Rolodex, or maybe a stress ball. Reeves says he used to have one, but that it's disappeared. I then suggest a Wiffle ball, and Jimmy jumps for that. (I've been carrying a Wiffle ball around with me during the shoot, rolling it in my hand, flipping it, et cetera. It's my director's affectation, like George Romero's scarf and yo-yo.) It actually has resonance in the script, in that one of Michael's last utterances to his brother in the film is a vehement declaration at the wedding that "This isn't a game of Wiffle ball, Frankie." Reeves amuses me greatly during filming by responding to Michael's line about getting to his work later with a clearly unintentionally menacing ad-lib, "You'll get to it . . . ." A little of the old marine coming out there (Reeves was a marine and served in Vietnam), and I laugh, thinking it sounds like he's going to smash Michael's face into the desk.

It takes a while, but we get the scene, and then move to a larger office space on the second floor. I'd been told we weren't allowed to

Michael's boss (Reeves Lehmann) *advises Michael* (James Lorinz) *to try being Lila's friend. An apparently prescient Janet Leigh looks to be screaming horrifically in response.*

shoot there, but Denise LaBelle talked to the woman working there, and she gave the okay. But it doesn't turn out to be much of a favor, since the woman retreats to a rear office and refuses to be quiet during takes. It's only a two-line scene, but she continues chattering on the phone behind the closed door no matter how politely we entreat her. This is the kind of thing I can't stand: Do me a favor or don't do me a favor, but don't do it only halfway and then make me feel like I'm bothering you. We finish and wrap hours early, and it's another good day, all in all.

Thursday morning we're shooting the playground scene, where Frankie and Michael sit talking on a bench while Frankie's daughter plays on the monkey bars. Roy has gotten permission for us to shoot at a playground just a block from SVA, so in that regard it's convenient. It's also located way off the street, out behind a complex of buildings, so I'm thinking we should have an easy time getting usable sound. But when I see it, I don't like it very much, mostly because there are no monkey bars. There are things she can hang from, though, and they'll have to do. I've cast my brother John's daughter Diana to play Frankie's kid, since the lines the character utters in the scene were originally spoken in real life by Diana. She's cute and low-key, and looks younger than she is, so it should play.

We're in the middle of a scorching heat wave (one of the reasons we're all grateful to be shooting mostly inside SVA this week, where it's air-conditioned), and the temperature when we get to the location in the morning is in the mid-Nineties. The area is pretty well shaded, and this affords us some small comfort throughout the shoot. (By the time we finish, around 1:00 P.M., the mercury is over a hundred degrees, easy.) We set up to get Michael and Frankie's dialogue on the bench. I've planned things so that Diana will never be in the same shot with Jimmy and Robert, so that she (and I) won't have the added pressure of worrying about her screwing up entire master takes. We'll get her stuff in singles, and she can just keep doing it till she gets it right.

Just as I'm ready to roll, a mechanical buzzing fills the air. A work crew is standing atop some walls not too far from us, trimming tree branches. We send a crew member who speaks Spanish to go negotiate with them, see if they'll at least stop during takes. I'm beginning to believe that no landscaping or garbage pickup is done in this town unless I'm in the vicinity, ready to call *action!* We work out a deal and begin shooting. I'm keeping things simple, three setups; a master two-shot, then two angled two-shots, one toward Jimmy and the other toward Robert. We finish with the bench stuff by 11:00 or 11:30 A.M.,

Frankie's daughter (Diana Simonelli).

and I tell Robert he's free to go. (*An amusing side note: Robert and Denise spent a good deal of time figuring out what Frankie should be wearing in this scene. They finally settled on shorts, a pullover top with a collar, a Yankees cap, and sneakers. Robert suggested Topsiders, but Denise nixed it. When my brother [whom the character of Frankie is loosely based on] showed up with his daughter, he was wearing shorts, a pullover top with a collar, a Yankees cap, and Topsiders. I told Robert his footwear instincts were right, and we marveled at how on the nose they've hit it. We made sure we got a photo of the two of them together, dressed so similarly.*)

We set up for Diana's shots, the first being one of her going down the slide. She can't seem to go down smoothly, the slide surface has gotten damp, and she's wearing shorts, which means her skin is sticking, too. Can't anything be easy? We put her on a piece of cloth, and then dust the slide with baby powder, which, fortunately, our makeup artist Terry has in his kit. She's able to slide easily now, and we get the necessary shots, both wide and close. Now we have to get her hanging from the bars, but the sun is climbing higher, so we have to set up shades to try and keep the lighting consistent. We also have to cool the handles she's hanging from with ice water, because the sun has made them too hot to touch. It takes longer than I would have liked to get what we need, because her eye line is never quite right; she keeps looking at me instead of where she should be looking, so finally I just move away from the monitor and stand where she should be looking, and that's how we get it.

"How come you've got your hand on my chest? Maybe you like it there." *Michael* (James Lorinz) *taunts a pair of homophobic bar patrons* (Robert Amore and Michael J. Meyers).

We break for lunch, though I'm able to only eat a few bites because I have to audition actors for the role of the ER doctor in the scene we're shooting tomorrow. We'd cast someone, but the actor dropped out, and now it's the day before and I still haven't seen anyone I like. I see a woman, then a man, but neither one works for me. Glenys has someone she knows coming around later, and I'm praying the guy will work out, because I'm running out of time and options. We finish setting up for the bathroom scene, where Michael gets beat up by two gay bashers. It's another one of these tight sets where the lighting has to be continually tweaked, and the actors have to hit and stay on their marks just right, and cables keep turning up in the frame . . . a nightmare. But the lighting looks good, a cold dim blue, which creates just the right ominous tone. We've actually brought in a stunt coordinator, and he helps us work out the angles the punches need to be thrown from to look real, as well as some other blocking. We're in there a while, trying to get things right, and as we creep up on 6:00 P.M., I'm told classes will be filing in on the floor where we're shooting. I hadn't anticipated this, and suddenly I'm up against the clock trying to get my shots in. On the last beating take, Jimmy is struck on the back of the head in precisely the same spot Barbara nailed him when we were shooting the massage scene. All I can think is, thank goodness it didn't happen till the last take, because Jimmy is pretty much finished after that. We push in for close-ups on the gay bashers, and I can hear a commotion out in the hall. (Later I'll learn it was Glenys having an altercation with a disagreeable teacher who didn't want to hear we were getting our last shot and would be done in a matter of minutes. He had to make a big show in front of his students, this despite the fact that he'd arrived late for his own class.) We get the last close-up and get the hell out, once again early. I'm not done, though. I run upstairs to audition the actor Glenys has brought in, Robert McKay. He's African-American, about six foot four, with a resonant, Shakespearean voice. I listen to him read the scene once, then tell Glenys to give him a script and a call sheet for tomorrow, because he's got it. Now I can go home and relax a little tonight.

Friday begins with the Scandinavian Institute classroom scene. I have no extras. Great. I decide to shoot the classroom the way we shot the reception hall, and hide half of it from view. I use five crew members for extras, and this looks like it will work on-screen. Doris Hicks, an Austrian actress who looks like a Teutonic Michelle Pfeiffer, is playing the instructor, and I'm using her German accent and language skills to kick the scene up a notch, telling her that her character is the kind of woman who can speak English, but reverts back to her native tongue when she gets angry. I rewrote the scene after I cast her, so that when Lila comes in late, she is berated by the teacher in German, which she doesn't understand. I'm able to take my time and do a good number of takes, especially of the opening dolly shot, and have fun with it. We're

Lila's terrifyingly Teutonic anatomy teacher (Doris Hicks).

all laughing a lot and having a good time. And the bit with Lila opening her desk and puking into it works just as I'd envisioned it in the storyboards. We couldn't find desks that opened, so Denise's assistant Ben Heyman built some for me, and it does the job. Doris does well in the scene, and looks great on camera. Now all we need to find is a dissection video gruesome enough to trigger Lila's nausea. But I can worry about that later.

After the break, we're up on the sixth floor to shoot the emergency room scene. They've constructed a curtained-off cubicle for me, but when Carman saw it earlier, he requested we turn the furniture and props toward the blue curtain, as opposed to the white wall. I said fine, not realizing what I was doing. What I should have done was told them to reposition the curtains so that they covered the walls, and left the other side, where we'd be placing the camera, open to the rest of the room. Instead, I've trapped us in another tiny space. I'll kick myself later for this. Not that we don't get the scene properly, with lots of coverage, but it just would've gone so much quicker and easier the other way. It would've been cooler, too, since the curtains went from ceiling to floor and really trapped the body heat. Stupid on my part, but what can I do but say that next time (if there ever is a next time) I'll remember and do it right. The scene is very funny for the most part, and all day Jimmy and Barbara and McKay and I have been laughing while they run the lines.

"I'm so sorry." *A tearful Lila* (Barbara Sicuranza) *ends her relationship with Michael* (James Lorinz).

The thing is, though, the scene turns very dark in its latter half, an odd and hopefully powerful shift. McKay appears nervous and keeps flubbing his lines, and so I have to go many takes with him. It's no disaster, since we have time today, but, given the discomfort inside the cubicle, it's a little trying. Still, he gives me some great line readings. When we get to the climax of the scene and are shooting Barbara's close-ups, she absolutely blows me away with authenticity of her emotions. On the last take, she does something extraordinary when, with tears in her eyes, she leans in toward Jimmy, forcing the camera to follow and bring Jimmy's face into the frame. She utters a plaintive "I'm so sorry," then turns and exits. The camera pans with her partway out and then holds so that I can end the scene on an empty frame with Jimmy calling from off screen, "Lila! Don't go!" It gives me chills. Afterward, Barbara is outside, still broken up and wiping her eyes, and I'm dancing with joy.

CHAPTER FIFTEEN

THE GOOD, THE BAD, AND THE UGLY

By this time, about midway through our shooting schedule, I was beginning to get the hang of things, to feel a little less panic-stricken every time I walked on the set. Up to this point, what had helped a great deal in overcoming my insecurities and lack of experience had been the fact that I had never come to the set unprepared. I'd spent the last two weeks before production began storyboarding the entire script, drawing by hand virtually every shot that would end up appearing in the final film. In other words— and these are words many of you may have become familiar with while watching the HBO series Project Greenlight—I always had a shot list. I always had at least a general idea, and often a very specific one, of just how many setups we would need to make our day. I cannot emphasize the importance of such planning enough, especially on a low-budget shoot. Big-budget Hollywood movies shoot perhaps one page of script per day, two at most. I had twenty-five days to shoot 102 pages of script. You do the math.

So, when I hear Project Greenlight's Stolen Summer director of photography Pete Jones say, "Shot lists are for wimps," or director Jim Jarmusch talking very casually with Elvis Mitchell on the Independent Film Channel about eschewing boards and shot lists, I bristle a bit. Because they're propagating the dubious and, I believe, dangerous notion that a shot you storyboard and plan out beforehand is inherently of less artistic value than a shot you just "think up" on the set. All I can tell you is that not having a shot list before you step on a set is low-budget-filmmaking suicide. A military commander doesn't marshal his troops to the battlefield without a plan; a batter doesn't step up to the plate without one; and neither should you. (And let me tell you, as producer, Roy would not have let me go forward without boards and setup lists.) Because no one is saying you can't change the plan if you see something that sparks in you a great idea. No one is saying you can't just "think up" a shot and get it. But you can't count on that happening every day. Some days you're going to be exhausted and devoid of inspiration, and what will happen then is worse than just not getting an artistic shot; what you'll do is miss getting a crucial shot you need to make a scene cut together, but you won't realize it till later, after you've

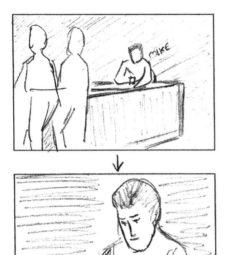

CAMERA DOLLIES IN

↓

ON MICHAEL

HE LOOKS UP

MIKE
"HEY! IS IT YOUR BIRTHDAY?"

DUANE
"DO WE KNOW YOU?"

finished shooting, and you're in the editing room wondering how in hell you could have been so stupid. And you're not Woody Allen or Stanley Kubrick, you're not working with the support of a major studio and a major studio budget, with the ability to go back and gather your crew and cast together again for reshoots. On The Sweet Life, once we were done with a location, there was no going back. They were gone from us forever. If I didn't get what I needed the days we were there, there was no fixing it later. This made boards and shot lists indispensable.

In any case, I was feeling better and the shoot was going better. So I think this is a good place to speed things up and look at just three more days, which I've dubbed (for reasons that will become obvious) the Good, the Bad, and the Ugly.

THE GOOD

SATURDAY 8/11. Great Neck, Long Island. An all-day shoot at my brother's business offices, JSO. We're set to shoot the latter portions of a sequence that begins with a walk and talk outside a restaurant where Frankie has just concluded a business lunch to find Michael waiting outside, eager to speak with him after spending all of the previous evening talking with Lila and learning from her that Frankie has ended their relationship. (We'll get the first, exterior part of the walk-and-talk at a later date on Bedford Street in the Village.) Today we'll pick up the sequence from Michael's and Frankie's entrance into the lobby, through their exit from the elevator on an upper floor, track with them down the hall to the door of JSO (which is doubling for Frankie's company), then pick them up again inside the office to the point where Michael makes the announcement that he's not gay and has the concluding confrontation with one of Frankie's coworkers, an angry lesbian. Roy has warned me he thinks the day will go long, and has already okayed me to go overtime if I have to. But the location is one of our better ones, reasonably quiet and spacious, and, to my relief, we have enough extras to make the place look appropriately populated. This was my greatest concern up until last night, when Roy told me he'd contacted Donna Drake, who is on the board of the Long Island TV-Film Foundation, and procured a half-dozen or so extras, who, together with the friends we've rounded up, should do the trick. I'm shooting the last part of the sequence first, Michael's announcement and the lesbian's testy response. I figure that's the most elaborate part of what we've got scheduled today, the section where I'll need to get the most coverage, so let's get it out of the way first. While we're doing that, some of the crew can be prelighting and setting up the dolly tracks out in the hallway. This way we can jump right into that portion of the sequence very quickly after we finish the confrontation and hopefully get it in before lunch. Then we'll shoot Frankie's and Michael's entrance into the office and their dialogue prior to Michael's announcement. I'm thinking we'll need two separate dolly shots to cover that, one in the outer office, then another once they come into the main area. We'll shoot the shortest part of the sequence, down in the lobby, last. For Michael's announcement and the confrontation, we set up a master shot of sorts, which encompasses Frankie at his desk and five extras placed from one end of the frame to the other. Michael will enter and play out the entire scene with his back to the camera. This is why I call it a master shot "of sorts," since I know I won't use a lot of it with Jimmy not facing the camera, but it's the only way I can get the whole scene in one shot. I'm certain I can use the beginning and end, the end especially, since I plan to have Linda Wahl (the actress playing the angry lesbian) step up into at least a medium close-up and deliver her most pungent dialogue after Michael is dragged out of frame by Frankie.

We do a number of takes to get Jimmy's and Linda's placement right, and to collect a variety of readings from Linda. They're all slightly different and all wonderful, very energetic and aggressive, and just what I wanted. When she moves up into the medium close-up, it creates

A disgruntled lesbian in Frankie's office (Linda Wahl) *sternly admonishes an off-screen Michael.*

exactly the effect I thought it would—it makes her look suddenly big and scary. A great place to cut out of at the end. Having got that, we go for coverage, turning the camera like a compass, first on Robert as Frankie, then on Linda and the other extras one by one. We turn around and point the camera at Jimmy and get all of his dialogue and reactions, which as usual are terrific and funny. He alters a line slightly and makes it better, by changing "I've got nothing against gays" to "I've got nothing against the gay *people*," a reading that more believably triggers Linda's character's wrath. So far, it's all gone well and I'm certain we've gotten good stuff.

We go out into the hallway and do seven takes of the dolly shot to get one that's usable. It's clear to me after the first take that we're starting with the camera too close to the elevator, so that when Jimmy and Robert come out we're unable to move back quickly enough to keep them both in the frame. I suggest moving the camera's start point back a bit, but, for whatever aesthetic reason, Carman rejects it, or simply ignores it. However, after the third take, I simply command it (something I should've done after the first take).

There are other offices in the building, and even though it's Saturday, a few of them are open for business, so people are coming and going through the hall. I assume we're safe as long as we're shooting inside my brother's offices, but I'm certain no one's ever gotten permission from the building's owners and/or landlord for us to be shooting here, which means I'm nervous anywhere outside them and eager to get a decent take and get the equipment back inside before somebody gets annoyed and makes a phone call and gets us booted and who knows what else. Soon as Jimmy and Robert get the lines right and I see they've both stayed within the frame, I wrap the scene and go back inside. Maybe we could've gotten it better with a few more takes, but what we got will have to do. I can't face losing another location in the middle of shooting. There's still time before lunch for the crew to start setting up the tracks inside JSO, and I've also realized that we don't need two dolly shots to cover the remaining dialogue, so I drop the one I'd planned for the outer office and decide to pick up Michael and Frankie as they emerge from it into the main office. We'll set up the dolly, break for lunch, then we can start right back in again after we finish eating. Barring any unforeseen problems, and despite Roy's intuition (usually an accurate barometer) that the day would go long, I'm beginning to think I'll be able to wrap early and avoid overtime for the crew.

Which is what we do. We go seven takes for the dolly shot into the office, and the last two are both good. Carman and the crew head downstairs to prepare the next setup, and when I get down there myself I see that he's got them laying down tracks for the dolly. The lobby is very small and so tracks seem pretty ridiculous to me. Plus, to use them we'd have to shoot toward the street, which won't match with the tail end of the walk-and-talk we'll be shooting next week on Bedford Street in the Village. Carman tries to convince me, but I say no, this is silly, it's only a few steps from the door to the elevator, just put the camera on the sticks in the corner here and pan with the actors as they enter. "Would it kill us to have a *pan* in the picture, James?" I ask. We put the camera on the tripod, do a few takes to make sure we have the scene (a short one, only a few lines), and I call it a wrap.

THE BAD

MONDAY 8/20. More Sunday afternoon and evening panic sweats preceding today's shoot at a restaurant and nightclub called Neva on Seventh Ave. South downtown. We're shooting the scene following the one where Michael takes Lila to see *La Dolce Vita*, in which she, in turn, drags him to a loud and crowded dance club. As of yesterday afternoon, we had only two extras confirmed, or so I'd been told. Hence, the panic

Michael (James Lorinz) and Lila (Barbara Sicuranza) on the dance floor. Lila dances; Michael winces.

sweats. And phone calls. Between all of our efforts, we scared up maybe twelve or fourteen bodies, enough of them attractive women so that I think we can pull it off if I keep the place dark and the shots reasonably tight. We set the extras around Barbara, darken the room, get the lights flashing, and start them all dancing to see what it looks like on the monitor, and I see to my relief it looks fine, very dynamic and lively and crowded. I go for a medium two-shot master on Barbara and Jimmy, doing the first one with the music playing, just to give Barbara and the extras a chance to get the rhythm set in their minds and bodies. From this point on, I only have the music playing before the shot to get everyone started, then kill it for the slate and the actual take. We get two-shots and OTSs of Barbara and Jimmy, and I can tell right off that the scene is going to work well when we get it in its final form, that it will be very close to what I had in my head when I wrote it (and in some ways better, because of the actors), visual and funny. As I've been doing more and more as the shoot has progressed (time permitting, of course), I get a lot of coverage and takes, and am being more demanding and specific about getting what I want in terms of bits and physical business. I wish I'd been this way earlier, especially when we were shooting the massage scene; that I'd been adamant and precise, and compelled the actors to give me more of what I wanted in all the shots. That was my failing, not theirs, and I'll have to face it later in the editing room. But I'm not going to let it happen again, if I can help it.

And so I bounce Jimmy around the dance floor from two different angles through a number of takes until I feel I've got enough to create the effect I want for when he ventures out from the bar to where Barbara is dancing at the heart of the crowd. When I feel I've got the scene covered to my satisfaction, I tell Carman to go handheld, let the music blast, and shoot Barbara and the dancers any way he wants for as much as he wants. I'll probably only use a few seconds of this footage, but we're doing great on time and I like to give him these little gifts when I can. And I love being able to look forward to a wealth of choices later on when I'm cutting. He shoots till he gets too tired to carry the camera anymore, and I wrap the scene.

By the original schedule, that would have been a wrap for the day. But Roy has suggested we use the bar downstairs to try and reshoot Frankie's introductory scene (#006 in the screenplay), which we initially shot in Fubar some weeks before. No one seems to like that footage very much, and I'm worried about it too. So, having this location available, along with a free half a day, we've decided to try it again, with a different actress playing the waitress. My plan was to get the dance scene in before lunch, with enough time before the break to get the set downstairs lit and ready to go, so we can dive right in and begin shooting right after we finish eating. This I managed to do.

But when I'm ready to go, I'm told that the shirt the art department has brought to the set for Robert is not the right one. And so we waste more than an hour waiting for it to be located and then transported downtown to the location. I spend that hour fuming in silence. And it costs me later, because by the time we are able to begin shooting, I've got to rush, and I don't get nearly the amount of coverage I need, and I'm not able to stay on top of what's actually going on in the scene because I'm so consumed with just getting enough shots before we get kicked out of the location, and it turns into a total fucking waste of time and effort. Twice now I've shot this scene, and twice I've fucked it up. I can't begin to describe how frustrated and angry I am, to have been given this opportunity to rectify an earlier misstep, and to blow it again? Fuck, fuck, fuck! (*In the end, we made do with the earlier footage, which wasn't so bad as I'd originally thought.*)

Then, upstairs, I spy Robert leaving and perceive he's upset, too. I catch him outside and ask him if he's alright. He tells me he's bummed out, he feels he wasn't focused at all when we were shooting the scene, that he's cursed, he must be, because things always seem to go wrong when he's on the set; that he wanted to be good in this role, and he feels he hasn't been. (*Not true; his performance in the film is consistent and effective.*) I tell him that nothing that went wrong today was his fault, that it's my responsibility to get what's needed on the screen, and if it's not there it's my failing, not his. I think he hears me, but I can tell he's still upset when he leaves, and my anger at the failure of the costume department increases, because for lack of having the right shirt on the set—which should be an absolute no-brainer, we take Polaroids of every costume used in every scene for that very purpose—for lack of a shirt, I've not only wasted a half day of shooting without solving the problem I was trying to solve, but now one of my main actors, who is supposed to be playing a supremely confident and self-assured individual, is beating the shit out of himself and in a completely undermined state of mind. A shirt. A fucking shirt.

THE UGLY

SATURDAY 8/25. Last night of shooting. We're at the east end of 82nd Street, right up against the river walk, in front of One Gracie Terrace, where Roy's brother Lewis lives. This will serve as the exterior for Frankie's apartment building. We're set to shoot the dramatic confrontation between the brothers that takes place at the end of the second act, after Michael has learned that Lila has gone back to Frankie. People keep asking me if I'm excited to be finished, and I keep telling them I'm *not* finished, I still have to shoot this scene; things can still go wrong.

And of course they do, right off the bat. Jimmy shows up in a terribly depressed state over things in his private life that have gone on today prior to his arrival on the set. Not that I worry over getting a performance from him; he invariably turns it on for me when the camera is rolling. But I'm concerned for him on a personal level. I'm not sure what's going to happen to him when this is over and he doesn't have an acting gig to come to every day. And Robert wants to talk about the scene. He and Jimmy and I go in my car for some quiet and privacy, as well as a little warmth. It's a cool night, and though I'm perfectly comfortable, just about everybody else, the actors most of all, will complain of being cold throughout the evening. Robert begins by asking about a particular line he feels troubled about saying. I tell him, fine, lose it. What else? He now begins to convey some confusion about the scene. Has he actually asked Lila to marry him already before he comes out to confront Michael? It doesn't seem to him like he would have, that they've only just gotten back together, or something like that. He thinks he should produce an engagement-ring box at the end of the scene to show to Michael, a suggestion with which I'm not very enamored. And why do I go up on the river walk, he asks, instead of just turning and going back inside? I want to say, "Because then I don't have a scene," but by this point in the shoot, I know I have to be gentle and reasonable and explain to Robert in great and logical detail why I want a scene a particular way, and I begin to try and do this. But Jimmy, who in my estimation (and at my request) has been enormously patient and restrained throughout the shoot in regard to Robert's constant questioning and need to be fussed over, can apparently take no more and launches in that a discussion like this should have happened weeks ago and not tonight, moments before we're going to film the scene, and that he has no intentions of changing anything he plans to do. Robert gets angry, and suddenly I feel like a dad in the front seat, threatening the unruly children in back to not force me to come back there. "Guys," I say, "calm down. We're just talking. Okay? We're just talking." I tell Robert that Frankie has been with Lila all night, and that, in fact,

Frankie has been thinking about her and musing on being with her since the moment, weeks or months ago (in the time context of the script), when he first gleaned she had gotten involved with Michael. Then, after we get out of the car and Jimmy goes off, I explain further that Frankie is the kind of secure and confident guy who visualizes a thing before it happens, so that even if he hasn't asked Lila to marry him before he comes down to face Michael, once the decision to do so has been made in his head, as far as he's concerned it's a foregone conclusion. We don't need something so literal and on the nose as a ring box to make things clear to the audience. I also tell him not to be too annoyed with Jimmy, that the guy is in a bad place emotionally, and that that's probably why he snapped. I'm annoyed too, but comfort myself with the rationalization that we're about to shoot an argument, so that if the actors are really at odds with each other, it will work for the scene. That's what I have to hope anyway.

We go to the set and begin to block the action for camera. We've got a Steadicam, which I hadn't planned on having, but at nearly the last minute, Roy okayed the expense, for which I was grateful. The shot will begin on the entrance to Frankie's building, he'll come out and see Michael standing at the steps to the river walk, head over to him, and begin the dialogue. I'm having a problem with Michael being so far away, but I need to bring the scene over there to get the visual thing I want. I see that the building's two doormen have signed releases to appear as extras, so I decide to give one some business that will solve all my problems. I tell Robert to come out and ask the doorman to camera right, "Where's my brother?" Then I tell the doorman to point up toward the river walk. This I'm thinking will fill in all the blanks for the audience. The transition will go right from Michael at Fubar being told by Carly that Lila left earlier with his brother, to Frankie exiting the lobby, querying the doorman, and being directed to Michael's location. Clearly, Michael has been inside, been stopped from going up, and has walked off fuming, waiting for his brother to come down. Now we can Steadicam with Frankie over to Michael, then follow them both up onto the river walk, where we have space and interesting city backdrops.

Once again, Robert conveys confusion about why he goes up on the river walk. Another lengthy explanation ensues. This argument, I tell him, is not one to decide anything. The issue—Lila—has already been decided. She is with you now. You've won. But you also know that now that she is back with you, sooner or later you'll have to face your brother, and that it's not going to be pretty. This is then just an unpleasant task, something to be avoided as long as possible. You wouldn't turn and go back inside, because you wouldn't want to take the chance he'd follow you and make a scene in the lobby in front of the doormen and your neighbors, or, worse, try to force his way upstairs. I quote Robert Towne, who believes the truth only comes out in anger, and that it shouldn't come too easily or it doesn't feel real. You don't want to say the things you know you'll say to him if he continues to press you, so you walk away from him, up onto the river walk, away from the building. But he won't let go, won't let up, so you finally turn and give him both barrels. This appears to make sense to him, but it frustrates me that I have to so extensively explain it to him. I am not an obscure writer, and it seems to me that everything I've said should be clear just from reading the script.

I warn them both that I'm going to cover this scene a lot, so be prepared to do a lot of takes. We do a couple of run-throughs to work out the Steadicam moves, then we start shooting the scene. As I've learned from the previous two Steadicam shoots we've done, the first few takes will always have problems. Tonight is no exception. Shadow issues, framing issues, movement issues (on one take Robert stops unexpectedly, and the operator nearly collides with him), et cetera. By the third or fourth go-round, we know what we're doing, so it's just a matter of getting good performances. I never get one take that's really good all the way through to the end of the scene, but that's okay. All I really need is for it to be good up to the point the actors hit their stationary marks and the argument kicks in to high gear, because at that point I'm certain I'll be cutting between OTSs and close-ups. So, I stop before Robert and Jimmy get too burned out. Robert has the lion's share of the dialogue from the point where they stop and face each other on the river walk, so I shoot his OTSs and single close-ups first. He's solid through six or seven combined takes, giving me some varied readings from which to make choices.

Then I turn the camera around to get Jimmy's OTSs and single close-ups. And again, as when we shot the lunch scene at the Indian Oven Restaurant, suddenly Robert can't remember his lines. I don't mean skipping a word or flubbing a line here or there—I'm talking about completely breaking down and stopping. These are the very last shots I need to wrap the entire movie, I'm intent on finishing by 2:00 A.M. so we don't have to keep shooting after the dinner break, and so I'm raging inside but trying not to show it. Jimmy comes over to me and says to tell

Last night of the Sweet Life *shoot: Michael* (James Lorinz) *and Frankie* (Robert Mobley) *regard each other tensely.*

Robert not to stop no matter how many lines he misses, that he'll react to nothing if he has to. I go to Robert and put my hand on his shoulder and tell him, "Look, man, don't sweat it. If you miss a line, just take a beat and keep going. We'll get it in another take. It's no big deal." We go for another take, and once again, he breaks down completely and stops. Jimmy is fuming but, thankfully, he doesn't do anything except turn away. I can see Robert waiting for me to come up to him and stroke him as I've done after virtually every take tonight. All I can think of to do is ignore him—turn my back on him and refrain from approaching him, as a means of indicating my displeasure. Finally getting the message that I'm not going to humor him, he walks off and takes a moment. Then he returns and we go again.

And with that he starts to get the lines right. I get the takes I need and call it a wrap. Jimmy walks off without a word. Robert sits down on a stool, looking unnerved. I want to get past this without having to talk about it, since we're done and it doesn't matter anymore anyway, so I feel I need to say something positive to Robert in order to give him an out. I go up to him and say, "Hey, man, we did it. We shot a movie. Isn't it great?" Just to indicate I'm happy and that we should all move past it. I grab a sandwich and walk up the street to the corner to have a moment alone. Jimmy comes up. I thank him for not erupting earlier, which allowed me to finish shooting the scene without any ugly verbal confrontations. He shrugs dejectedly and tells me he's just going to sneak off, he doesn't want to go back to the set and talk to anyone. He's afraid of what might happen, and I agree with his reasoning, so I say good night and tell him I'll see him tomorrow night at the wrap party.

He leaves, and I head back toward the set. I go up on the river walk and stand at the railing, looking across the dark water, thinking: I've just wrapped my first movie. I made it through. I'm a director now. I'm just trying to savor this unequivocal moment in my life when Robert approaches me.

And this, folks, is where it gets ugly, so I'm going to fade to black and say only that he and I had a difference of opinion in regard to this final evening's events and the film shoot in general. Life is like that, it has a Rashomon quality. Everybody has their own point of view and it's usually self-justifying. All that matters to me now is that Mobley's performance in the film works. The rest, as the saying goes, is sound and fury, signifying nothing. Just keep in mind that when you make your film, you're going to be dealing with a lot of different people, each with their own temperament, their own idiosyncrasies and insecurities. There will be times when Sartre's axiom that "Hell is other people" will seem like the truest words ever spoken. When those times come (and I assure you, they will), you've got to try and keep the big picture in mind, remember what should be most important to you, and that's finishing your movie. Everything you do, everything you say, and everything you refrain from doing or saying at the cost of your pride and your digestion, must be geared toward that singular goal. I once heard a man explain his philosophy of life as follows: "Steal, steal, steal— and if they catch you, look 'em in the eye like you love 'em forever and tell 'em you didn't do it." No one is going to give you your film. You're going to have to fight for it. You're going to have to steal it. To get our film completed, I lied to people, manipulated them, sacrificed my pride, and vitiated myself on an almost daily basis. And I don't apologize or make excuses for any of it. Rather, I take pride in what I did, and what Roy did, to keep the project on track. We finished on time and under budget. The actors' performances are pretty damn good across the board. And the script made it to the screen uncorrupted.

The rest, whatever that may turn out to be, is gravy.

CHAPTER SIXTEEN

THE EDITING ROOM: WHERE IT BEGINS AGAIN

A movie is made not one time, but three. The first time is when the script is being written. That's the time when anything is possible and everything goes off without a hitch. It's your universe and you have complete control. The shots are all beautiful and the characters do whatever you want them to, and speak their lines exactly as you wish. Not that you can't or won't encounter problems in the writing process, but hey, that's why they put erasers on pencils, and delete buttons on computer keyboards. Scratch it out, take a walk and think of something else. It's that simple.

The second time is when you shoot the movie. And, as you've learned if you've read this far, that's when everything begins to seem less possible and almost nothing goes off without a hitch. Equipment fails and personalities clash. The actors don't always want to do or say things just as you wish. And you become less concerned with all the shots being beautiful and more frantic about just getting enough shots to cover the scene. Why? Because *time*—or, more precisely, the lack of it—has now become the most pressing issue you have to deal with, the dragon you must slay every single day if your movie is to reach completion. There is no eraser, no delete button. You can't just take a walk and think of something else. The clock is ticking, the money is running out. If you don't get the scene today, *right now*, you're screwed.

The third time the movie gets made is in postproduction, when you go into the editing room with the footage you have managed to accumulate, and begin trying to cut it together. A relief at first, at least from the daily pressures of shooting, of people coming at you endlessly with questions and complaints, and the stress of worrying whether or not you're going to survive it all and at the very least get the movie in the can. But then you start to look at the footage, and all you can see is where you fell short, missed opportunities, or simply fucked up. You stare at the screen and ask yourself the same question, over and over again—*What on earth was I thinking?*

Why didn't I instruct the actors to do or say things differently?

Why didn't I tell the DP to change the framing?

Why didn't I get another angle, or a close-up, or a better master?

How am I going to get any of these shots to match up?

What on earth was I thinking?

If you're lucky and have chosen well, you've got a skilled editor to help you make sense of it all. Me, I had Gary Cooper, an indisputably talented cutter and a paradox as a human being, in that he can edit film but not himself. Whatever he thinks about you or the footage you've gathered travels instantaneously from his brain to his mouth and issues forth unchecked, without mercy or a speck of sugarcoating. Gary wouldn't sugarcoat a doughnut if he worked for Krispy Kreme, and it has nothing to do with his being a diabetic. But this is actually a good thing, because what you need in the editing room more than tact is ruthlessness and objectivity. Someone who, unlike you, has not suffered getting every shot, who is seeing it all for the first time and reacting to it with only one thing in mind: How can I use these shots to tell the story?

Tell the Story. It was a mantra he repeated endlessly, the way a Christian zealot proclaims that God Is Love, or a chef that Presentation Is Everything. And that was okay by me, because in effect it mirrored the way I write, certainly the way I'd written and directed *The Sweet Life*. No flash, no unnecessary sideshows; just characters and emotions and humor in service of a clear narrative where each scene (hopefully) pulls you forward into the next. Most of all, I wanted the focus to stay always on the characters and the story rather than on *me*, on what I was doing as director. Sure, I wanted aesthetically pleasing shots and camera moves, but not to a degree where the audience would become more consciously aware of what I was doing with the camera than what was going on with the characters. In recent years, I think too many movies coming out of both Hollywood and the independent scene have become too much about style over content, rather than style *in service* of content; more about breathlessly fast-paced cutting and fancy camera moves than about telling the story. Watch some of these films and you can almost hear the director screaming like a child perched on a diving board trying to get his parents' attention, *"Look at me! Look at what I'm doing with the camera!"* I, on the other hand, didn't want the audience to know I existed, if I could help it. Call me old-fashioned, retro, whatever. But that was my goal. *Tell the story.*

It's a weird feeling, going into the editing room and not being completely sure what you've got. Sure, you were there on the set every day, you watched every take of every scene. But then you were surrounded by people and distracted by the inexorable demands of getting your shots and making your days. I believe that, when all is said and done, the director's primary function above all others is to keep the whole picture in mind. Movies are made in tiny increments, individual scenes, individual shots, individual *moments*, and they are filmed, with rare exceptions, out of sequence. You may have to film the climax of your story very early in the shoot. (We did.) You may have to shoot the beginning last. And you won't know until you get in the editing room whether or not you succeeded in keeping the whole picture in mind, if all these individual pearls you've gathered will string together in any dramatically cogent way.

This is where the ruthless objectivity of your film editor really comes in handy. You've finished the arduous process of shooting a movie. Perhaps, like me, you wrote the script, and then directed it. You know the characters inside and out. Hell, you created them. Everything makes sense—to you. But will it make sense to others? Will they feel what you think they should be feeling at particular points in the story? They, unlike you, have not created this world and these characters. They know only what the images and the dialogue tell them. Anyone who works with computers knows the phrase, "Garbage in, garbage out." In other words, when a computer malfunctions, it is almost never the fault of the machine, but rather, the programmer. He's given it the wrong commands, or insufficient data. It's pretty much the same with audiences. You can't make them feel something just because you want them to, or think it's what they should be feeling. You can't fight their reaction. You have to reprogram.

What this all boils down to is, your editor is your first audience, and if you respect his opinion (and why would you have hired him if you didn't?), you have to remain open to altering things based on his reaction to the material. The worst thing you can do is fall so in love with what you've shot that you cease to be objective. As a teacher, I see the painful results of this all the time. Students struggle so much to get their films shot, and, in every frame, they see how much they worked and sweated to get those images in the can. So, they refuse to cut anything. And their films suffer for it. The audience doesn't know how long it took you to get a particular shot or how hard you worked to film a particular scene. *And they don't care.* All they're concerned with, all they want you as a filmmaker to do, is this: *Tell the story.*

Perhaps you're familiar with the James Cameron–written-and-directed film *The Abyss*. The story centers around the crew of an underwater oil rig that's enlisted by the military to assist in the recovery of a downed American nuclear submarine before the Russians can get to it. (The film was made in the late eighties, before the collapse of the Soviet Union, when the Russians were still our enemies.) Following the arrival of a Navy SEAL team, a storm erupts up top, and the inhabitants of the oil rig find themselves unable to communicate with the outside world, which is teetering on the brink of total war. All they can do is follow the last orders they received and continue with the recovery mission, during the course of which they discover a vast and wondrous alien base constructed by and populated with water-loving extraterrestrials. Thus discovered, the ETs decide to take a hand in what is going on above, and, with their amazing alien technology, create giant tidal waves and send them roaring toward all the great coastal cities. The waves crest at the shoreline, soaring hundreds of feet above the terrified city dwellers, all of whom are certain they are about to die—

And then the waves stop. Freeze in mid-air as if Moses has just raised his mighty staff. The tiny humans stare in awe at this miraculous occurrence, and the alien message becomes clear: Cut the shit, or we *will* wipe you out.

Now, those of you who only saw *The Abyss* in theaters when it was released, or perhaps on cable the first time it was run, are probably saying, "Rocco, what the hell are you talking about? There was no tidal-wave sequence in that movie."

Well, you're right, there wasn't. Not in the version of the movie you saw. But it was written, and it was shot. (And it can be seen today on special editions of the laser disc and DVD releases.) Much time and money and man-hours were spent designing and creating the sequence, probably as much as has been spent making any number of other *complete* films. It was a scene Cameron loved, one he'd dreamed of making since he'd first imagined it back in high school, one he felt sure would blow audiences away.

And he cut it. Why?

Because he realized it wasn't *telling the story*. And the story was down below, with the oil riggers and the Navy SEALs, with Ed Harris and Mary Elizabeth Mastrantonio and Michael Biehn, and not up top with a bunch of strangers standing on a beach gaping at a frozen tidal wave. Who cares whether or not those millions in the cities facing destruction get wiped out by an alien-conjured wall of water? We don't know them. But we've spent time with Ed Harris, we know Ed Harris. We *care* about Ed Harris.

Tell the story.

For another example of an accomplished filmmaker spending untold amounts of time, money, and effort shooting a sequence he was desperately in love with and then ended up cutting, look at the original theatrical version of *Apocalypse Now*, then watch the recently released *Apocalypse Now Redux*, which restores a number of cut scenes, most notably a twenty-minute-long section involving a French plantation that stops the movie cold. Why do I feel that way about the sequence? Because, for me, the story is about Willard's journey upriver, toward the mysterious Colonel Kurtz. That's the central purpose, the goal that keeps pulling us forward in the narrative. The plantation sequence is elaborate, beautifully photographed, and not uninteresting. But it feels like a whole other film, separate from the main story. Coppola's instincts were correct when he cut it, as painful as it might have been for him to do so. It wasn't telling the story. Watch both versions and see if you don't feel the same.

Was I facing such painful editing decisions with *The Sweet Life*? Well, first we had to finish a rough assembly of all the scenes and see what we had. Gary and I were working on a computer program called Final Cut Pro, which speeds up the editing process quite a bit from what it used to be, back when we were cutting actual celluloid film on Steenbeck tables. It also meant we were coming closer to a fine cut on the first pass than we would have the old way.

My first concern was pacing. The theory goes that each page of script should end up equaling about a minute of screen time. The script was 102 pages. So, I was looking for the film, when assembled, to time out at or about 102 minutes. (At the start of the editing process, Gary told me he thought the film should be 89 minutes, that no comedy should be longer than 89 minutes. I told him he was crazy, the script was lean at 102 pages, I hadn't shot any extraneous material, there was no way we were coming in at 89.) The first rough cut came in at 95. This was reassuring. It meant I hadn't directed things at too slow a pace, and wouldn't be facing the predicament many filmmakers face, having to cut things not because they're bad but simply because the picture is running too long.

Roy came in and we watched the whole thing from beginning to end. Roy's response was important to me, because he'd rarely been on the set when we were shooting and had chosen to not look at most of the raw footage. His reaction would be fresh.

When it was over, he seemed pleased and relieved. Apparently, it was not a piece of shit. The four main performances were all good. The narrative was clear and the story made sense. We wouldn't need to juggle scenes or alter in any dramatic way what we thought the story meant. He only had two problems with the picture as it now stood. One was a lull in energy he'd perceived during a long dialogue scene between Michael and Lila about a half hour in. I had been concerned about the picture slowing down too much at this point even before we'd screened it for Roy, but it was a tough scene to cut inside of without losing important expository information. Eventually, I figured out a way to trim about forty seconds from within the scene, and that seemed to do the trick.

The other scene Roy found problematic and suggested cutting altogether was the next-to-last scene in the picture, the final scene between Michael and Lila. I'd already clashed rather heatedly with Gary over this scene, which meant a lot to me. Lila has left Michael and returned to his brother Frankie. They've gotten married and, worse, have forced Michael to be best man. At the wedding reception, he makes a disastrous toast, which creates havoc amongst his family. He leaves the party in chaos, and Lila runs after him, catching him in the outer hall. This was a scene I'd written to play off the audience's expectations of the genre, to make them think that maybe Lila has changed her mind and is going to run off in her wedding gown with Michael, à la *The Graduate*. But nothing of the kind ensues. It just turns into a bittersweet farewell.

LILA

Michael, please, wait!

She grabs his arm to stop him. He turns and looks at her rather emptily.

LILA (contd.)

Michael, I know you're hurting, but you
don't understand . . . !

MICHAEL

I understand perfectly. The better man
won.

LILA

No, he didn't. (He looks at her) I thought
I wasn't good enough for Frankie. But
you're the one I really wasn't good enough

```
for. (Off Michael's emotional expression)
God . . . you're so much smarter than me.
You must know it.


                    MICHAEL
I'm not smart. I'm stupid. Very, very
stupid.


They look at each other for a moment. She takes his
hand in hers.


                    LILA
You still haven't kissed the bride.


                    MICHAEL
Yes, I have.


He squeezes her hand, then lets it go and walks away.
```

I thought this was some decent writing. And Barbara, when we shot it, oh God, was she in the moment. Jimmy did marvelous things, too, but in retrospect he played it a little harder and more unforgiving than I should have let him, though at the time it made sense. This is the worst day of Michael's life, he's hurt and he's angry, how magnanimous could he be expected to be? So the scene was playing a tad more bitter than sweet, especially at the end when Jimmy chose to lean forward as if about to kiss Lila but instead uttered his final line to her, "Yes, I have," then walked out, leaving her there crushed and waiting for a kiss that would never come. But was it too bitter?

Gary thought so, and gave me no end of shit about it. His main objection was that it made Michael unsympathetic at the very moment we should be feeling something *for* him. But I couldn't imagine cutting it. Wouldn't the audience need this one last scene between the two? Wouldn't they demand it—feel gypped without it?

Roy's objection differed some from Gary's. He thought that by allowing Michael to, in effect, "nail" Lila, the scene was letting Michael off the hook emotionally by giving him this petty little victory and thus invalidating the entire film. "Rocco, I just don't believe this is what you *meant*." He also believed the scene that followed, the last scene in the picture, would play better if we cut the farewell scene.

I was devastated. This was one of the most important scenes in the picture as far as I was concerned. It seemed crucial to me. Barbara's performance was spectacular. How on earth could I possibly cut it?

With the flick of a button on a computer keyboard, that's how. We took it out, looked at it again, and they were right—the film did play better without it. What the hell. You'll see it as a deleted scene on the DVD.

The other grievous cut we were forced to make was necessitated, at first, by technical mishaps. Translation: the shot was no good and the scene looked like shit, underlit and out of focus. It was another one of my favorite scenes in the script, the first walk-and-talk scene between Michael and Frankie, and it came five or six minutes into the film. The two brothers have just left a bar and are walking at night along a city street, smoking cigars and talking about women. I couldn't see how we could do without it. It not only had some of what I thought were the funniest lines in the picture ("The last woman I dated told me she wasn't ready for a physical relationship—and this was *after* we'd had sex"), but it was also when we first learn about Lila.

> FRANKIE
> Let's hit Fubar for a few pops, I told
> Lila we'd swing by tonight.

> MICHAEL
> Lila, which one is she?

> FRANKIE
> You remember, we met her that night a
> month or so back. The bartender. She works
> there.

> MICHAEL
> Right, the one with the nose ring, the
> tattoo and the rap sheet.

> FRANKIE
> I know, she's a little wilder than I usu-
> ally go for, but she just has something
> that keeps drawing me back.

                    MICHAEL
        Yeah. It's called a vagina.

                    FRANKIE
        You're just jealous because you know she's
        the kind of woman you could never handle.

                    MICHAEL
        You're right, I'd be afraid to enter her
        body because it might take hostage negoti-
        ations to get back out.

Like I said, some pretty funny lines. And important establishing information about Lila. It killed me to cut it. But the scene played in one long continuous take, and the shot, as previously stated, was no good; it had to go.

How had the shot gotten so screwed up? What went wrong?

Well, as simple as the scene appears—two guys walking along a city street at night talking—for an ultra-low–budget production like ours it presented a number of problems we obviously didn't transcend, the main one being we didn't have enough lights to properly illuminate the length of sidewalk we needed to cover the scene, no matter how slowly the actors ambled. Thus the under-lighting. And because the scene was underlit, apparently neither my director of photography nor the Steadicam operator could discern that the shot was also out of focus. Imagine my reaction when I got into the editing room and looked at all eight takes of the scene and found every one of them to be soft. A scene I felt sure we could not do without. How the fuck were we going to make it work?

Gary did as much as he could do with the computer program to lighten the image and then sharpen it, while I suggested cutting the beginning and then most of the second half of the scene. He did, and we looked at it again. It was definitely better, but was it good enough?

In the end, as much as it hurt, I made the call to cut it. I reasoned that if the scene came later, say an hour or so into the film, I might have chanced it. But I didn't believe we could survive showing the audience such a poorly shot scene so early in the film, that it would cast a nega-tive shadow over everything that followed. And after the pain subsided and I regained some objectivity, I realized the scene hadn't been as necessary as I'd thought. That it was actually better to let Lila introduce herself, so to speak, and to convey to us the kind of rough-and-tumble chick she is through her actions, as opposed to having the brothers tell us about her in the walk-and-talk. And with the scene excised, the pacing of the first act improved perceivably. Roy believed, and I'd come to agree with him, that the moment the picture really takes off is when we first meet Lila at Fubar. The sooner we got there, the better.

So it goes. Another deleted scene for the DVD.

We made a few other minor alterations and trims, linked it all up, and looked at it again. Want to guess how long it timed out?

You got it: eighty-nine minutes. (We would ultimately trim it down to eighty-three minutes, not including the title and credit sequences.)

Chalk one up for Gary.

CHAPTER SEVENTEEN

RE
PREPARING FOR LAUNCH

Now deep into our postproduction period, the months have rolled by, and the warmest winter I can remember has given way to a benign spring. James Earl Jones was presented with a plaque for his humanitarian work, inscribed to James Earl Ray. Tonya Harding chased Paula Jones around the boxing ring. INS student visas for Mohamed Atta and Marwan al-Shehhi arrived at the flight-training school in Florida six months to the day after they took out the twin towers. Mistakes were made on near-cosmic levels by people who should have known far better, and the little evils we perpetrated on *The Sweet Life* seem endearing by comparison.

What we've been doing since August 26 is: editing on Final Cut Pro, filming pickup shots (fronts of buildings, POV shots, beauty shots of New York City); getting the score composed—including two songs composed and sung by Kenny Laguna and Joan Jett; screening the unfinished film for graphic-design students in Denise LaBelle's class at the School of Visual Arts so that poster-art concepts can be developed for the marketing packet; taking care of the first annual accounting, including W-2s, and issuing tax documents to the investors; and writing this book.

Still ahead of us in postproduction are: sound-effects editing; recording the voice-overs; ADR work during which actors dub themselves for better line readings or to remove location noise; laying in the music; compiling and creating the titles; doing the final mix of all the soundtracks—music, voices, and effects—onto M&E tracks; and the rendering of the final product onto the various video formats needed to expose it to the world.

Then comes yet another stage, the final stage: "seeking distribution." This entails the judicial placement of the film into festivals to see what kind of a buzz we get and, based on those reactions, deciding on a plan of distribution. Rocco wants a theatrical release, no matter how limited. And this can be easily accomplished, even if test screenings such as festivals don't seem to warrant it. Our Limited Exhibition Agreement with SAG sets the parameters for theatrical distribution: "Non-theatrical exhibition for non-paying audiences, semi-theatrical exhibition before film societies and limited run exhibition in showcase theaters, i.e., runs of up to two (2) weeks in "art houses" and small-audience theaters, specializing in new creative films, of the type listed below:

Film Forum, New York, NY
Roxie Cinema, San Francisco, CA
Biograph Theater, Washington, DC
Brattle Theater, Boston, MA
The Music Box, Chicago, IL
Nuart Theater, Los Angeles, CA
Nickelodeon, Santa Cruz, CA
Fulton Theater, Pittsburgh, PA
U.C. Cinema, Berkeley, CA

These are not the only theaters available to us, but they signal the type of venue in which we would be able to show the film while staying within the limitations of the SAG parameters. These and others like them suit my plan, which is to show *The Sweet Life* theatrically in the digital domain, which is no longer a problem in theaters like these. However if, for example, we were to get the kind of festival response that merited a larger company's interest in us, well, then I might consider doing a 35mm blowup, letting the distributor go wider with the film, and renegotiating our agreement with SAG, which would mean more money for them, which, they have told me, they would not be opposed to. And why should they be?

I want to emphasize, though, that I don't see the wisdom of opening this film any wider than in a few small houses. I'm open to persuasion, but it doesn't seem economically sound. When we were putting *Street Trash* into the marketplace, we had two strong bids: Vestron Video and De Laurentiis. De Laurentiis wanted to make a thousand prints and open it wide. This would have meant $2 million just for the 35mm prints, and a few million more for advertising. Since we were unrated, and most local newspapers would refuse to run ads, and most local TV stations would refuse to run spots, we would inevitably lose this money, and the losses would be cross-collateralized into video, which is where we stood to make money. Under this game plan, our revenue would be eaten away to compensate for our theatrical losses.

Vestron Video, spearheaded by the much more hip thinking of David Whitten, one of the industry's stellar promotional minds, suggested we strike only ten prints, and move them around the country, playing midnight shows in theaters where the featured film of the week would pay for the ads, and along the bottom it would read "*Street Trash*, Friday and Saturday at Midnight." (In New York City, at the 8th Street Playhouse, Warner Bros. and *Full Metal Jacket* paid for our ads.) No money would be wasted, later to come back and drain our video profits. Whom do you think we went with?

And that's what I see as the game plan here. Theatrical release is a bottomless pit if one isn't careful. Ted Bonnitt was innovative with his *Mau Mau Sex Sex*, released in 2001—read his interview for insights into how to market digital video without blowing your budget.

The securing-distribution phase also means foreign territories. I'm not in favor of giving the world to one distributor. If that distributor chooses to screw you, you're screwed worldwide. If, on the other hand, you sell your domestic rights and then wait to see how it opens here, and if it performs well in this country, you are then in a better position to sell abroad, territory by territory. There are a number of formulas that work in favor of not letting all your territories go to one distributor.

FOREIGN REPRESENTATION

If you decide to separate your territories, the chances are you'll need a foreign sales agent, who will take 20 percent of your sales or more, plus expenses off the top. He represents several films at once, sometimes even twenty or more, and because of this, and because he is familiar with the workings of the foreign markets, he will have more clout. If you go to Cannes (a marketing convention masquerading as a film festival), or MIFED in Milan, or the AFM in Santa Monica, with only one film under your arm, you're at the mercy of the predators. Thousands of films are being peddled. Why should foreign distributors give you anything but a minimum bid? If you ask too high, they have hundreds of other films to choose from; they won't go home empty-handed. But if a buyer tries to lowball your sales agent, he's gambling on losing twenty films or more, not to mention the sales agent's good will down the line.

A foreign sales agent will need all the ammo you can supply him with, which is why, in my securing-distribution budgets, I include not only a category for stills and written publicity material, but for a trailer as well. A professional company may charge you $10,000–$14,000 to do a two-and-a-half minute trailer for your film. You may want to have a go at it yourself, but remember, they've been doing it for a long time and have a good understanding of the marketplace. A foreign buyer might not have time to see more than a few minutes of your film—there are simultaneous screenings going on constantly and it is in the distributor's best interest to see snippets of several than to sit through one in its entirety. But later, when they visit your suite, they can look at publicity packets and watch on the TV monitor the trailers for the films your agent is representing. The trailer we prepared for *Street Trash* cost us ten grand with a professional company (we talked them down from twelve). I had written a three-page script, which I thought was great, but when they presented their own, I had to agree that they had a better handle on what trailers are supposed to communicate to an audience in exactly that amount of time. Also, different countries respond to different aspects of a film, and they had all that worked out. So, my script was thrown out, and theirs was used. Having the trailer made a huge difference.

In 1986, I went to Cannes with Howard G., my foreign sales agent on *Street Trash*. He was representing twenty-nine films, and I was shocked to find that I was the only producer who showed up. This was very good; I was able to keep him focused on my film. And when he got bids—$35,000 from England, for example—I was able to discuss it with him. "Was it a good bid?" "Yes." "How good?" "Not great, but good." "Hmmm." My entertainment lawyer had advised me that features such as mine were going for no less than thirty grand, so I knew I wasn't under the minimum. However, I decided to hold off. Had he been alone, Howard might have gone for it; after all, it *was* a decent bid, and he wanted to maximize his time, and he had a relationship with that particular distributor to keep up. They'd done business in the past. But he acquiesced to my decision.

Activity goes on at Cannes for two weeks. I was there for the second week. The days went by. The British distributor peeked into Howard's suite again, and raised the bid to $40,000. I said I'd think about it. He looked at me suspiciously. At a party the next night, slightly inebriated, he came up to us and barked, "Who's biddin' . . . ?!" We played dumb, and actually there were no other bids, but I just felt like this guy would go higher, and Howard was casual about it; he played it the way I wanted.

I also ran into Sean Cunningham (the creator of the *Friday the 13th* franchise) at that party. He was pitching a package of unproduced titles to which he was attached, with the help of a venerable foreign sales agent, one whom I'd gone to with *Street Trash* but who'd passed on it (he wished me well but just didn't feel confident to handle that kind of aggressive genre material). Sean gave me a piece of advice, which I pass on to you, concerning investors: "You have to decide how much time to spend on each film you produce. My feeling is, if you can get your investors out, that's when you move on to another project." I liked that advice. It's not to say that you don't continue to keep on top of sales, continue to monitor the progress of the film, and endeavor to get the investors a profit. But if you've gotten them to the point that they're no longer at risk, they'll probably reinvest in your next project, and they'll probably double their original investment. At the point that you've gotten them out, you can stop spending all of your time on that film, and start spending more time on your next project.

Sure enough, on the last day of the market, the British distributor returned and upped his bid to $42,500. I went for it. My trip to Cannes, including hotel, food, entertainment, everything, was about $2,500. The additional money I made off that one sale far more than covered my expenses.

And we sold Scandinavia on that trip, too, for a whopping $75,000. The buyer brought his family to Howard's suite and they quietly watched all of his trailers; but when the *Street Trash* trailer came on, his kids started laughing and shouting at the special makeup effects, and he observed them carefully. He left without a committal, but later returned and bid about twenty thousand more than my lawyer had advised me to expect. He really wanted the film, and it was his kids' reactions to the trailer that did it.

I recommend that if you get a foreign sales agent, you go along for the first year to each market, and *learn*.

After the first year, it didn't pay to fly to each marketing convention and put myself up. Most of the larger territories had been sold, though on a few the advances hadn't been collected yet. And so, I stopped following Howard around. And that's when he started cheating us. A student came into my SVA class in the fall of '87 and said he'd seen *Street Trash* playing all over Italy under a different title. Howard's quarterly financial statements claimed that Italy hadn't paid their advance yet, and my deal with Howard stipulated that until a country paid their advance, they weren't to be given the film elements from which to strike their masters. I called him on it, and on several other territories that had never come in, and in the end, the executive producer, and I, and the director, flew out to L.A. for a tense confrontation with him.

We got some money on that trip, but not the bulk of it. In the year that followed, I was contacted by a Los Angeles district attorney. Seems Howard had been cheating bigger fish than us, and they were willing to take it to court. I testified along with several other individuals and companies as to Howard's shady business practices, and together we sent him to prison. But I never recovered the money he'd swindled us out of. All I had was the satisfaction of seeing him not get away with it. So here's some more advice: Don't trust these guys too far. They know you've only got one film to peddle, and limited funds to peddle it with, and that you're not going to be able to monitor carefully what they do. At the very least, insist contractually that they can't close a deal without your okay, even if it means reaching you by phone from whatever country they're in. They'll moan that a deal could be killed within an hour if they can't reach you. Too bad. Retain that power, or you're asking to get screwed.

Foreign sales agents are like actors, and DPs, and editors. You've got to interview as many of them as you can, to see which ones genuinely respond to your product, and which ones you connect with. And then you've got to find out whom else they've represented, and check on their credentials.

ONGOING EXPENSES AND PUBLICITY

If you don't sell world rights to one company, you will be expected to store your materials—negative, track elements, et cetera—on your own dime. This is fair, but it has to be built into your budget. As does yearly accounting and tax preparation for your investors. It may seem a bit annoying, but in the long run, it will pay off. The foreign deals I've made on my films were for five to seven years. Those original deals terminated long ago, and I've resold the rights again and again to various territories, and while the money never equals the original advances when the film was first being released, DVD is a good market, foreign TV is a healthy market, and new media are being invented all the time.

There's more to consider in this final phase. Distributors will never promise to push *you* along with your film. If they see the virtue in it, if the director is a newcomer and a social phenomenon, like Spike Lee was, then maybe they will. But they will retain the right to decide for themselves how they promote the film, and that shouldn't be good enough for you, since really it's *your career* that's at stake here as well. So, you should budget for a publicist for at least the month preceding and following the film's opening, and possibly for the video release as well. Publicists have good media contacts, and can get you exposure on TV and in the press, so that the public, and the industry, identifies you with your film. It will lead to more work. It can cost anywhere from $2,000–$10,000 but I believe it's essential if you're planning out the arc of your future in the industry.

In the final chapters, we've compiled several interviews with cutting-edge filmmakers who are exploring the filmmaking process, and the marketplace, in often-shocking new departures from traditional patterns. Roc and I may integrate parts of these new pioneers' work into our own game plan for *The Sweet Life*, or we may evolve something completely new, but since the deadline for delivering our manuscript to the publisher precludes us from letting you share the last leg of our journey with us (at least in these pages), consider these remaining chapters a taste of what's out there . . . for us, and for all of you, in the years to come.

P.S. You can track The Sweet Life's *progress through the distribution and release phases online at* www.TheSweetLifeMovie.com.

CHAPTER EIGHTEEN

AN INTERVIEW WITH TED BONNITT

Ted Bonnitt created something of an indie sensation last year with the self-produced, self-distributed, and practically self-exhibited feature documentary Mau Mau Sex Sex, *a loving, witty tribute both to the days of grind-house exploitation films, and to two of the elder statesmen who pioneered the genre—Dan Sonney and Dave Friedman. It was a particular pleasure for me to see his film get out there, since I've known Ted for a long, long time. The interview, conducted in front of a class of thesis students at the School of Visual Arts, started with a request for the filmmaker's background. It's important to see the whole arc of a career for it to be meaningful.—RF*

TED BONNITT: I've always had a dual love of radio and film. I went to film school. But at the same time, I was also doing radio when radio was still cool. I did FM progressive free-form radio, like college radio is to some degree today. And frankly, it was a lot easier to get into the radio business than it was to get into the film business. Bottom line is, I'm a storyteller. And it was easier to tell stories on the radio, obviously, on my own, than it was assembling a crew and a budget to shoot a movie. I've always been an independent in the sense of working alone and outside of boundaries. Never was much of a corporate person.

I do have a day job. I have a production company in Los Angeles. I produce radio commercials for movies. So, I have a marketing background. And I'm from New York, where I did marketing also. I went to Los Angeles eight years ago to get into the entertainment business because storytelling is best told in an entertaining fashion. In news, you have to pretend you don't have a point of view, which is nonsense if you listen to the news. But you have to pretend you don't, and I just felt the entertainment-oriented storytelling form is a lot more honest. But it was a problem, making a movie, not only because of the budgetary concerns but of the difficulties getting it out there . . . how do you distribute it? You have to depend on other people in the business that take advantage of people like us.

So, I waited a long time, and I also, honestly, didn't feel I was ready to tell long-form stories. For many years, I felt I needed to live life. I've taken a lot of adventures and studied a lot of arcane subjects and have graduated from telling five-second radio to thirty-second radio to five-minute radio to one-hour radio. I've done some TV. I did an A&E TV special. But I felt that feature length was such a responsibility that I needed to walk a little bit of a life before undertaking such a project, and I ended up walking for about two decades. Consequently, I don't particularly subscribe to Hollywood's obsession with youth. When you're eighteen to twenty-five, what do you really have to talk about other than your upbringing, which is the "coming of age" story, which is so popular in Hollywood because most Hollywood customers are eighteen to twenty-five.

But still it was more of an accessibility issue for me, and what's so exciting about where indie filmmakers are at now is that they're at a threshold of more opportunity in the motion-picture business than ever before. To get out there and tell your own story, your way, with your own tools, outside of the system and the constraints that have in the past dictated one's creative direction. . . . I wish I'd had an iMac and a DV camera when I was sixteen. I think the future now is so revolutionary that even the IFP and the film organizations, and the filmmaker magazines, all these things are somewhat out of touch about the essence of indie DV moviemaking. I think they tend to dwell on their own "indie scene" star system, and I think they're pretty clueless about indie DV. If I had my druthers, I would go to the high schools and get people on board before they're institutionalized in their thinking and tell them it's all new for you to figure out in terms of decentralizing the media, in terms of the democratization of technology, which is a fancy way of saying you can buy a computer for fifteen hundred bucks and make a movie. This was unheard of ten years ago.

I went out and bought—four years ago, for $15,000—a production and postproduction facility. Ten years ago, you would have been talking $150,000 if you were lucky, just to get started. It's radically changed, and of course it makes it a little more difficult for the indies as well, because it's raising the bar. There's a glut. Everyone can produce now, so in a sense the creative bar has to rise above this enormous clutter of mostly bad movies. On the other hand, standards are getting higher. You can go out and buy an $800 Pro Tools system and create professional-quality sound, you can do color correction in Final Cut Pro 3. There's no excuse for bad-looking video or poor sound anymore, particularly sound, which is far more important than picture when it comes to the marketplace. Remember, never use your camera mike, ever. No matter how convenient it feels or how spontaneous it feels.

So, the bar is rising for the indies, but the opportunities are exponentially greater, even than in the romantic early days of motion pictures. They always said there would be five hundred channels, that was the hype ten to fifteen years ago, and you could look at that physically as five hundred stages that needed to be filled with content. And, to a large degree, that's where it is now, whereas in the seventies, it was terribly tight. There were three TV networks and a handful or so of struggling movie studios. And that gave birth to an independent revolution. Coppola and all these people came out of it and there was a renaissance in film. And when things like that happen, it breeds opportunity. Chaos breeds opportunity. And right now, the industry is completely upside down. In Hollywood, recording studios are going out of business because people can now produce radio commercials at home on a Mac instead of paying $300 an hour through the studio.

ROY FRUMKES: *What was the genesis of* Mau Mau Sex Sex?

TB: I felt that documentaries, personally, was the way to go because I have a journalism background and I'm more comfortable telling a nonfiction story. Just to test my skills as a director and to test the technology.

I had no idea how I was going to make this thing. I priced it out for 35mm and it was like four or five hundred thousand. Which, in the documentary-film business, is just slash your wrists, don't even bother, you'll never make your money back. They say don't make a movie unless you make it with somebody else's money, but that's a trick—to get to that point, and that's why I did this with my own money . . . to get to that point.

A friend of mine, Eddie Muller, wrote a book called *Grind House*, which is a study of exploitation films, the underbelly of Hollywood, the dark side, where guys working outside the studio system, as *we* are, made a living selling movies that people wanted to see. It happened to be adult themes, which by today's standards are very tame. *Reefer Madness* was a famous one . . . drugs, sex, whatever appealed to people, that's what these guys did. And they were road show, carney guys. A whole other aspect of filmmaking. Eddie wrote about the genre and all the guys who made it, who were called "the forty thieves," and of these, two were Dan Sonney and David Friedman. In honor of his book, they showed one of David Friedman's movies, *She Freak*, and I thought, what a racketeer this guy is.

I like elders. I think they're wonderful. And I liked David Friedman a lot. I read his autobiography, which was laugh-out-loud funny, and I knew I could use clips from their movies because they were available. I could save money that way . . . so it started to become a good business venture. And don't let anybody tell you differently, moviemaking is a business first and an art second, and there's a good reason for that: because you want to protect your artistic vision so that it doesn't get trampled, ripped off, or twisted beyond what you wanted it to be because of financial considerations. So, I'm a producer by trade, to protect my writer/director avocation. Otherwise, I'll fail and never be able to make another movie again, and there goes my art. There's nothing wrong with calling your movie a product once you make it and package it. You have to think that way; otherwise you're not going to make any money. And it's not just about money, but getting it to people because you're storytellers, right? You want people to see what you do. In a busy world, how am I going to motivate you to get off your butt and take five hours of your life to spend ten dollars to go to a movie theater? I better meet you halfway by making it interesting. That's pragmatism and that's business. And that's not bad, that's smart. It's not a compromise, it's a challenge, and it's a good thing to know.

I met Dave Friedman and talked to him and he said he'd do it because he liked my angle on it—which is about their lives and who they are. But his partner Dan Sonney sounded like a real nasty bastard, and I was afraid to meet him, though I knew he had to be in the movie, too. A year later, as fate would have it, he found me. A friend was living down the street and said Dan Sonney was her landlord. I loved him at first sight. He was just a real lovable character . . . a rascal. And he was looking for something to do.

Now I was on the spot: I had to make a movie and I didn't have the money to do it. I walked by a Circuit City and saw a display of these DV cameras that were brand new at the time—this is '98—and I think . . . are these things for real? The salesman said "yeah, but you don't want this. What you want, we don't sell. C'mere, c'mere, c'mere." He was like a drug dealer, and he takes me to the back of Circuit City, opens up this briefcase, pulls out a brochure and says, "Look at this." It was the Canon XL1.

So I did research on the Web and I talked to experts in the business and they said you can't do a movie with it, it's a toy, and I said I don't know. I looked at it as a genie bottle and I bought it for $8,000 on my credit card, along with all the bells and whistles, and started shooting with it. I shot the movie in five days with Dan and Dave, and it cost ten dollars an hour in videotape. I shot seventeen hours for under $200. I had a feature in the can, but I didn't have any way of editing it. Adobe Premiere had 4.0 out, but it couldn't handle more than ten-minute timelines. I bought a video hard drive and put it in my G3, and it didn't work, and the hard drive guys blamed Apple, and Apple blamed Premiere, and it was . . . I just shipped it all back, got my money back, went to Jazzfest in New Orleans, and waited for the technology.

And sure enough, soon after, Final Cut Pro magically appeared at a trade show in Las Vegas and I bought it on the spot, took it home and booted it up and edited the movie, and it worked flawlessly. Before I bought Final Cut, I went to the Avid Web sites and asked the Avid editors—which was the standard in Hollywood—can you use Final Cut Pro, is it real? And they were like, "How dare you even come to our Web site and ask us about such crap!" And you know, a year later I went to the Web site and they're like, "Well, I'm selling my Avid, I'm getting Final Cut!" Many of the trailers you see in the movie houses now are being cut on Final Cut.

And so, we were just riding the technology wave, which took another two years to develop how we were to get into theaters. Essentially, we ended up shooting this thing, producing it and up-resing it to Digi-beta and doing a full-color correction and a full Pro Tools sound mix on a higher-end system, and what you see on the big screen originated on a Mac. At one point, I had five postproduction rooms going. Eddie was using Photoshop for the stills we used, getting them together. Keith Robinson, our executive producer, a great film editor (*When We Were Kings*) and mad-genius tech guru that got all twenty-plus computer programs talking to each other was doing color correction, another editor was on an Avid cutting in the film clips. In the next three rooms, I had the dialogue editor, sound mixer, and music mixer. In a sixth room, I had an audio engineer building radio PSAs for a client who was paying for all of it. It was really a funky month. And when we were done, we had a Digi-beta master, fully color-corrected and looking pretty damn good. It cost about fifty thousand to produce out of pocket. I made a lot of deals. And I paid for it all the way along, so I wasn't in debt and I owned it outright, including the rights to the motion-picture clips. The image quality of DV at the time may not have been good enough for fiction, but it was good enough for nonfiction, mainly because reality television has blurred broadcast standards. Also, basic cable channels don't pay much for programming anymore, and that's why you sometimes hear blown-out audio and poor video on channels like Discovery and TLC. So, the standards are lower and you can be a player for next to nothing. And that's how we made it, at 10 percent of what it would have cost me on film, all in one technological jump.

It was finished in April 2000. And if I did the same project today, two years later, it would cost me maybe a little less because I wouldn't buy a camera. I wouldn't shoot with a Canon XL1 anymore. We didn't have any idea that this was going to show in twenty U.S. cities theatrically. If I was going to do another movie, I would use a newer camera, like the Sony DV-Cam, which has higher res, and costs about $15,000, but I'd rent it, so it would cost me far less. The reason I would use that camera is because it has a true 16:9 aspect ratio—the chips are shaped like 16:9—as opposed to NTSC, which is 4:3, like pre-fifties moviemaking and the television box. I thought the end product was going to be TV, so I didn't worry about it. The XL1 will shoot 16:9, but it's actually a software codec that distorts the image. And you don't want to do that, to use filters or marry yourself to any kind of treatment that you're going to be stuck with in postproduction. Shoot it raw, because the tools in the postproduction realm are so great now, you can do anything you want later, at your will.

The second part of this story is what you do now that you've made a movie. I thought, oh wow, it was brutal and it nearly killed me but I got over the finish line and collapsed for three months and waited for the world to descend on me with laurels and distribution deals, and nothing happened at all. It was that sickening quiet of, "Now what? I've got to get it up again and get out there!?" I didn't have an agent, and I don't have an agent now.

The interesting thing is that it was so new, what we did, that I believe that it may have appeared heretical to even the independent-film establishment. Or that what we were doing was not yet valid in their world. People don't like change. It's human nature. And I don't know why it is, but we have been pretty much ignored by all the independent-film organizations and media except the IFP East, which I have respect for because they do the IFFM market here, which is a wonderful debutante ball for the independent. And it did do well for us. That was practical, they give you back something. But most of these organizations are precious, self-absorbed, "Quentin Tarantino wannabes," which offer no relevancy whatsoever to what we were attempting. They have created, as a credit to their success—the Sundance festival included—a brand name called "independent filmmaking," which ten years ago meant something, but today means nothing in terms of the reality of the term as applied to the DV guerilla. Unless you have an agent or a distribution deal ahead of time, the odds are that you're not going to get into Sundance. You're not going to get into a meaningful festival . . . which you can count on one hand, by the way. You can discard three thousand other festivals, if you plan to use them for business as they are willing to use you.

RF: *What are the five that matter?*

TB: I'd say Sundance, of course, matters, but paradoxically it's often irrelevant. I've been there eight years in a row, I was just there again, and everybody's in there with a movie from HBO, BBC, Artisan, or Miramax. I mean, what does this have to do with independents like us? Nothing. And the documentary festival slots that *are* open to individuals . . . you've either got to have the luck of a lottery winner to get in there, if you don't have an agent, or you've got to have a very politically correct and preferably humorless story to tell. Misery and plight are a plus for documentarians.

Slamdance is even harder to get into because they don't have ten venues, they have two, and the submissions have gone up from hundreds a year to thousands, because of the glut of DV. What are your odds? And the truly frustrating part of all that, if you look at the track record, is that a majority of the ones that get in never see the light of day. *Happy, Texas* was an example of a delightful and accessible film that never saw the proper light of day at the box office, but was the big hit at the Sundance festival. My buddy was in it, and I tried to get him to go the following year with a sandwich board saying "I was a Sundance darling last year and all I got was this lousy sandwich board." He wouldn't do it.

There's also Toronto and Berlin, but Toronto rejected us and Berlin doesn't really do documentaries. But I was in the IDFA in Amsterdam, which is a documentary festival, and we were one of only a handful or so of American movies out of four hundred films invited. That was great, and I made deals overseas through their market. Go to festivals that have markets, that do something for you as a filmmaker in return for exploiting your product for no money. Don't go just because they'll accept you, because nearly all festivals are barely hanging on themselves and are basically a failed business model, and you won't see a dime from it.

As an illustration of what I'm talking about, I submitted the movie to the North Lake Tahoe International Film Festival. Do you know where North Lake Tahoe is? It's the quiet side of Lake Tahoe. I had family up there so I thought it would be cool before we got into theaters to have them see our movie. I sent my $40 submission fee with the movie. We didn't make it in, of course, that's how incredibly important that festival is. The interesting thing was that I had sent them an additional five dollars to have them return my tape. It confirmed my suspicions—they watched about ten minutes of the movie, and mailed it back, without bothering to rewind the tape—and pocketed my forty bucks! Here's what I think goes on: You have well-intentioned dilettantes in these small towns who love movies. The National Endowment for the Arts budget has been so strangled by Congress that there is little funding for arts in small towns anymore, and since motion pictures are the popular art of our time and actually sell tickets, everyone wants to throw a film festival. So how do you do it? The festival organizers go to the hotels on the off season, in the summer up in the mountains, and say, "I'll fill up your hotel rooms," and go to the restaurateurs and say, "I'll sell your meals," just give me some seed money to run some ads in *Moviemaker*, *Filmmaker*, and *IDA* magazine. We'll call it the "International Film Festival." The festival programmers, who barely eat off the $40 admission fees and meager sponsorships, then send a letter to applicants announcing that they have been honored with an "official invitation" to come at their own expense and pay for those hotel rooms and meals so they can watch the festival pocket the film's box-office sales off the artist's sweat and labor. And not give the filmmaker a dime back, or bring any press in that will offer momentum. Or attract any buyers, because the festival is completely insignificant and no distributors will attend. Do you think they'd even send you a list of press who attended? Forget about it. There's no gain for you, only a cost, because you'll never be able to go to North Lake Tahoe and open your picture in a movie theater. If the festival shows your movie, they'll shoot your publicity wad and you'll have to buy ads to get whatever audience is left in that town that will buy tickets. Bottom line: They're costing you money, so don't go. That is, unless you don't care and you'll do anything to have people see your movie, which I have had filmmakers tell me all the time.

I go to festivals where we are invited. I went to three of them in the United States and did it for timing purposes. I go to festivals where they have a market in place, where they tell you who comes to the screenings, and if they're interested in talking to you. Go to those; they're good, like the IFDA in Amsterdam. I got a five-page lead list of thirty buyers who watched my movie, and, as a result, I sold rights over the Internet from Poland to Portugal, on my own. I never made one phone call, it was via free e-mail. We made the deal, e-mailed attached contracts to each other. My lawyer looks it over, we make the deal, it's done. You can do that with the Internet, you can now market your movie globally on the Internet for no money whatsoever.

When you're making a movie and you want to get it out there, in this day and age, in this transitional period, you still need to get into movie theaters, in my opinion. But we didn't have any money to open a picture. So what we did is we created a buzz on the Internet. We got listings everywhere we could. It doesn't hurt to have the word "sex" twice in your title because it really draws a lot of people from day one. Like a thousand people a day, even though 97 percent of them in the early days were looking for action, not independent film. But still, we had a lot of buzz, so essentially, what we looked at—and I say "we" as a fancy word for me because it was pretty much me the whole time as a one-man-band thing . . . what we did was take advantage of this new virtual reality that exists in our world. There is a virtual reality and then there's the real world. We didn't have that twenty years ago, but now we do. The Internet is a world upon itself . . . you can go anywhere instantaneously and talk to everybody worldwide. You can use that as a promotional, viral marketing plan.

So, we created a buzz. We have had nearly a half-million people watch our trailer on iFilm. That's huge. Where can you buy that kind of publicity? We would build this kind of buzz to get into the theaters, and then theaters like the Cinema Village would book it. You create a virtual groundswell in the root system of the virtual world, and then pop up in theaters for one week at a time all over America, and that's how you make the transition from virtual to reality for that brief moment in history. Think about it, because these are the tools at hand now that are really remarkably powerful and cost-efficient.

RF: *What are the costs involved in doing this by yourself?*

TB: Well, my lost wages, taking two years off of my day job. But while I would say that making a movie is one of the most difficult tasks that I've ever taken on, it only accounts for about 30 percent of my effort into this project. The publicity, marketing, and distribution accounted for 70 percent. And probably that works for the money, too. It cost about sixty thousand to sell it. So, I put about a hundred and ten grand in. But that's still pretty damn good. To get, in the end, twenty major U.S. cities, a good *New York Times* review, which books you all over the country, and great reviews in a lot of other cities. And now your little desktop video is a feature movie. You go to Google and put in *Mau Mau Sex Sex* in quotes, so it's a specific search, and you'll get, depending on when you do it, anywhere from 400 to 1,500 specific entries. And they're quality entries. It would have cost you a fortune five years ago to accomplish this. We went to the IFFM, and the buyers were there, and I drank in my fifteen minutes of "don't make a deal until you talk to me" come-ons. If we hadn't gotten into the IFFM, it probably wouldn't have mattered anyway. To be honest, we still would have done what we did and been as successful, because prior to the IFFM, our first show was in Los Angeles at the American Cinematheque's Egyptian Theater, which is sort of the New York's Ziegfeld Theater in a way of comparative quality venues. We had a relationship with them because Eddie Muller, who wrote *Mau Mau* with me, curates the film noir series there every year. So, we had an invitation to show it. Important: Work with theaters that have publicity in-house and calendar houses, which are theaters that send show schedules to subscribers, because it's all built-in publicity. You don't have to buy as many ads. It's a great way to get the audience without great expense.

But we ran a little quarter-page in the *LA Weekly*. I didn't know what was going to happen. It was a Wednesday night at 7:30, basically a cast-and-crew premiere screening. A hundred of us came into a six-hundred-seat theater and found that we'd filled the house with walkups! It's a documentary, and documentaries are not supposed to be that popular. But, again, it's all in the artwork and making sure you package it interestingly to people. I'm working on something now about medicine men, Indian medicine men, and I'm thinking about calling it *Medicine Men, Sex Sex.* Just kidding, but adding the word "sex" twice in any title certainly helps!

Packaging is all-important. Before we ever showed in any theater, I had everything packaged. I had a soundtrack album. I had the poster. I had the VHS. So, the screening at the Cinematheque was really a test market. We had about five hundred paid admissions: they paid to park, and they paid to see the movie, and after the movie they came out and stood in line and paid forty bucks to take home the "Mau Mau Wow Wow Pack," which included the poster, hat, VHS, and soundtrack. And I realized this was sticking to the wall when I went home with a lot of cash.

I wanted to go to New York with the film, but I thought the intermediate step was to go to San Francisco with a successful Hollywood showing under our belt, because its subject should do well there. Then I would book New York with that leverage behind it. So, I called theaters that had video projection. I realized that no one was going to pay an advance to distribute it and I wasn't going to pay sixty thousand dollars for a film transfer . . . they look like crap anyway. I wanted to keep it in its native format. I did some research on the Internet, and asked around, and found theaters that had video projection. It's still very new, but there were a few in San Francisco, so I called Mill Valley and Berkeley and the Roxie Cinema, and they said, "Okay, sounds interesting, just send us a screener cassette." I sent them a dub with the packaging, so they knew we were on the marketing ball. And I wrote a letter saying that I had press kits, publicity photos, posters, trailers ready to go, and they called back and said, "Great, we'll book it," and I got a standard booking deal, 35 percent of the gate. And then I got a letter from the IFFM that we were invited to debut there, so I had to pull the bookings, because you don't go into a market with used goods. Ironically, my problem was that everyone wanted to book it, and they were all pissed off at me because I told them I had to hold off. And Dave Friedman, one of the old guys, who you'll meet in the movie, said, "Well, if they like it in January, they'll like it in October." And they did.

I had three distribution offers that didn't offer any money up front, yet insisted I do a 35mm blowup, and promised me ten cities and home video out of it. I said to all of them, "So, what you're saying, basically, is you're offering to lose my shirt for me." And they said, "Yeah, that's the business," and I said, "Thanks, but no thanks."

I did hire a publicity agent in New York, because it was just too big a town to do it on your own. The theater guys know where all the deals are, and they turned me on to a guy who charged 15 percent of what the big PR agencies charge. He did six months of big-city publicity for fifteen hundred dollars, with no additional expenses tagged on, and delivered an Elvis Mitchell and David Kerr *New York Times* review and feature story on the day we opened, a *Daily News* feature Thursday, a review Friday on opening, *Time Out*, *Village Voice*, a massive spread in the *Newark Star Ledger*, original art in the *New Yorker* . . . We had huge press for that amount.

You do need to make a 35mm trailer, because a lot of these theaters are opening a smaller room with a video projector, or they'll hook up the video projector just for the run of your movie, so if you hand them a video trailer it'll never get run for the mass audience you need to reach. You need to spend the money on a film transfer for the trailer but you can get that done cheap. We had trailers running in twelve cities, and that's how we built much of our business. However, we did show the movie in theaters across the country on DVD—a first. And not one customer complained.

And I found that distributors are not crooks, necessarily. I actually have a lot more respect for them, having gone through this process, because it's a nickel-and-dime cutthroat business and there's so little money it, the reason they're taking everything is because it's the only way they can stay in business. A lot of filmmakers come up to me and ask if I would distribute their movie for them. I wouldn't dare. I don't have that kind of time or money. I don't even recommend that you do what *I* did . . . I'm just saying that it's possible. There are people out there now that are going into the distribution business specifically looking for alternative DV venues, and they will create a relationship with theaters that will get you out there, on an indie DV cinema circuit, and they'll share the revenue with you, not ask you for exclusivity and not insist on owning your product in the future, through the entire interplanetary system, on all future media, for no money down. That's not going to happen anymore. One distributor told me half-kidding, "It's bastards like you that are going to put us out of business in five years." And they may be right, because they're barely in business now.

CHAPTER NINETEEN

AN INTERVIEW WITH MICHAEL ELLENBOGEN

At the time of this writing, Michael Ellenbogen informed me that Margarita Happy Hour, his latest feature film, had been held over in New York City. This is good news, and difficult to achieve for an indie producer. [It has gone on to open in Chicago; Washington, D.C.; Gainesville, Florida; Austin, Texas; Los Angeles; and Albany, New York, and was released on DVD/video by Wellspring on August 20, 2002; it has also just completed two screenings in the Cannes 2002 market sponsored by Orange World Film Sales of The Netherlands.] I spoke to him at Swift's Tavern on 4th Street, just past the Tower Video in the East Village.—RF

SHOOT ME: *What enabled you to make the educated choices about your career?*

ELLENBOGEN: I'd like to think they're educated, although I do sometimes have second opinions about that.

What really got me settled in this business was reading Larry Fessenden's script *No Telling*. I was visiting a friend down here and he was on a job one day, working as a production assistant on an independent film. I was just kicking around his apartment and I found the script, so I took it up to Central Park, lay down, and read it. It was a good script, and later I asked him if this guy needed anybody else working on his movie. I was living in upstate New York, trying to find a building in which I was going to open up a pizza restaurant, café, art gallery, and cinema. But I figured I might as well give this a shot. And when Larry and I met we immediately hit if off. I spent from 1990 to the middle of '93 working with him on *No Telling*, which didn't get a distribution deal, so there was no money coming in. My time with Larry kind of came to a halt. Not the friendship, we're still good friends today, but I felt it was time to do something else.

I got a 16mm projector and a screen and asked Limbo Café (which is no longer here) on Avenue A between 3rd and 4th Streets, if I could set up shop in there one night a month and show short movies. *Jack of Hearts* was the name of a short film I did in '92. So I called this event "Jack of Hearts: Full House." It was a night of movies. I brought three or four short films in once a month with the filmmakers, and they'd talk, and I'd always pack the place. It gave me the sense that people really do enjoy spending the night out watching short films.

And, of course, three months later, I went completely broke, because I'd pass the hat around and get $25–$30 on a good night.

So I moved back upstate, taking with me this idea of doing the short films, which immediately expanded into putting listings in the magazines and getting people to send in films, and traveling around the northeast with the program. I would book it at the colleges, making it into an evening event where I would show the films and discuss them afterward. I didn't bring the filmmakers to these; it was just an informal discussion with me and whoever wanted to stay behind. I was doing SUNY Albany, St. Rose, this old place in Saratoga where Bob Dylan started—Café Lena's, and several others. It was still called "Jack of Hearts" at this point. And I would keep coming down to New York, doing Limbo, a gig at Fez under Time Café, and a place in Williamsburg called Bar 612.

So I literally had the cinema in the trunk of my car, and every month I would put together a new show. I have an entrepreneurial mind, but not really a business sense. I remember keeping these little accounting books, and writing down $7.63 for gas, et cetera. And I would see if what I was spending every month would balance out what I was selling in tickets. And it came pretty close a few times, but it never actually broke even.

In '94, a year into doing this, I started a film festival in Albany. I originally called it the Albany International Film Festival, but then *Metroland Magazine*, an alternative newspaper, came in and wanted to give a lot of support for the festival, and they convinced me to call it the Metroland International Film Festival, that being the historical name for Albany. We wound up doing it at the Palace Theater, which used to be an RKO cinema, an old movie palace built probably in the thirties.

Everybody, at that point in the mid-Nineties, was talking about short films. It started to become the hip new thing. Short films, it seemed, were going to break out and be on all these new cable channels that wanted to get creative with their programming. There was talk about bringing them back before features. It never happened.

But at the time, with that first festival, I put out the call for submissions, which brought in about thirty-six films, out of which I picked about half. For what it was, it was a great event and it showed Albany that somebody was doing something. I still lost money on it but it wasn't about making money. I was thinking about building the audience and showing people the concept would work. So they went, though not in droves, and of course we're sitting in a theater that has 2,500 seats, and you're in there with 120 people, which would have actually been a great show anywhere else in the city.

That year ended and I immediately started working on the next year, and new things started picking up regarding the concept. "Jack of Hearts" just kind of went away, and my uncle Dave [Ellenbogen], brother [Jeffrey], and cousins launched a short-film business; Passport Cinemas became the business name that we incorporated. We started looking for short films to distribute, with the intention of building up a library to satisfy the demand that was sure to grow with all the cable outlets and broadband channels that were hungry for "king content." Meantime, I'm still doing the film festival, and when my uncle suggested we package these shorts on video and see if we could get them into stores, I was totally not into the idea. I felt that if *I* would never rent one, nobody was going to rent one. The whole point is that people enjoy going out and seeing these things in a social environment. So the idea of distribution was eventually squashed due to this difference of opinion, I just took the name and ran the Albany International Short Film Festival under Passport Cinemas.

The second year, I got very aggressive with my acquisition process. I invested money into it; I got film festivals to send me catalogues, I had an army of interns, and I ended up mailing three thousand applications out around the world. We had four to five hundred submissions and wound up showing around 120 of them. And this time I moved it to a more impressive theater—actually three of them—called the Empire Center at the Egg, up in Albany. It became an extremely impressive festival that year, and I was shocked that out of the 120 films shown, 60 of them were attended by their directors, producers, and actors. Some came with a whole entourage from twelve different countries. I couldn't believe that anybody would even think of coming to Albany for a short-film festival.

It was a three-day event and it was well run, the shows went off on time, the films were projected correctly. The parties were fun: I had three every day, a party in the afternoon, a cocktail reception in the evening, and then a party in the night. To me, a film festival isn't right without a party, again going back to the idea that film has got to be social. The comments from the filmmakers were extremely positive because the way I programmed was very personal. I did not program with a committee. I sat and watched everything and made decisions without any other voice of reason. They told me the politics of the European festivals got in the way, unlike mine. So, that felt good. However, again that year, it was a complete financial disaster for me.

After three months of depression, I woke up one day and said, "Well, if I'm doing it, I gotta start." And the third year, almost 1,000 films came in from thirty-three countries. That year I took it to four days, showed 170 films, and over 100 of those were represented by talent, again blowing my mind. The audience also grew substantially. The shows had funky names like "Visions of the Apocalypse," "Eyes Bright with Wonder" for the kids, "Late Night Erotic Café" for the prurient crowd. And I remember at the Saturday night "Laugh Out Loud" show, I sold out the nine-hundred-seat theater. I'd never seen anything like it before in Albany, or anywhere else for that matter, at least for short films.

And while the local papers had always been very good to the festival, writing articles leading up to it, reviewing certain packets of movies, and running whole schedules, the television stations would not come down and cover the event. I was indignant: I had a filmmaker from the Republic of Georgia, who got there because everybody at the film studio that he worked at, who make ten dollars a month, chipped in five dollars—half of their month's salary—so that they could get this guy over to Albany . . . and the TV people didn't come down. On the Saturday night during the "Laugh Out Loud" program, I went out, took a walk around the theater, and said, "Fuck it, I'm outta here." It had been another financial disaster for me, even though the audience was building. The city wasn't giving any support whatsoever. Radio stations were throwing in their marketing sense; papers were throwing in their editorials; but nobody was really putting any money into the festival. People would say, "It's such a great thing you're doing," and then they wouldn't come. And afterward, they would say, "Oh, I'm really sorry I couldn't make it this year, I'm really busy, but next year . . ."

Larry Fessenden at that time had made his second film, *Habit*, and nobody had picked it up. We talked about how much fun it is to do what we want to do, and how impossible it is, how it really affords you no leisure time. He said, "What would you think about coming back to New York and distributing *Habit*?" He knew that I was an insanely intense marketing person when it came to generating promotional pieces and tirelessly getting them out there. And once again, it was an instantaneous decision. I was back the next week and we were setting up shop in his offices down on Lafayette and getting *Habit* off the ground, which we wound up doing an excellent job of, getting it into about fifteen different markets: Chicago, Los Angeles, New York, Orlando, Austin, et cetera.

It was during this time that I met Jack Foley, the head film buyer from City Cinemas. We went out to dinner one night and had a great time: two personalities that sort of came together, discussions were lively, and he liked the movie, which I was trying to get into his theater. He wound up agreeing to let it be one of the opening films at their Angelika on Houston, and put it in midnights. And he also introduced me to a lot of other film buyers at the other exhibitor chains, and that's how I was able to go to Los Angeles and, unlike any other self-distributed movie ever, without much of a budget, get it in five theaters on opening weekend.

SHOOT ME: *The virtues of networking.*

ELLENGBOGEN: And after about a year it came to an end. It didn't generate much money . . . I think Larry did pretty well on a deal he made for home video. But it was a difficult time: I had just paid my last rent, and that was the last money I had. I was literally living out of a bucket of change. I had a lovely apartment in Brooklyn, brownstone floor, living by myself. But I didn't even want to buy a subway token into the city, because I could either eat or take the ride into Manhattan. So, I just sat home and wrote for six weeks, started and finished my first screenplay, which I am still rewriting today. Then I met somebody from Italy. She was here for a short period of time and then was going back, and I came to the conclusion that I was going to move to Italy and live with her and, you know, pull one of those disappearing acts.

I called Jack Foley and made plans to have lunch. We met in the city, I think my first time being in the city in about four weeks, and I told him my plans, and he said, "I'm changing, too. I just was hired as president of distribution for October Films." I stopped for a second, then I said to him, "That's interesting . . . I'm coming with you." He asked me what I meant, and I said, "I need a job; it's either that or moving to Italy." He said he had to check on it, and I've been working with him now for four years at USA Films.

That was in 1998. And, at the same time, I went back to my database. I'd kept a pretty intense system evaluating every short that I'd seen in the three years of the Albany film festival, a system of my own invention, formulaically driven, with different types of value systems, for everything from acting, to energy levels, emotional tones, writing for different kinds of stories, et cetera. The database sorted the results from high to low, and I called the top ten filmmakers and asked, "Do you guys have any feature screenplays that you're ready to make?" I got about seven screenplays and picked Ilya Chaiken's, which was *Margarita Happy Hour*.

So, simultaneously with working at USA Films full time, I was able to produce this movie with Susan Leber, who had previously been working for Hal Hartley. We made *Margarita* on a shoestring that ultimately reached the tune of about $250,000. We had a $400,000 budget to start with, then we cut it back. And when we got $35,000 from private investors, I just decided to make the movie.

SHOOT ME: *And, over the years, you'd learned a great deal more.*

ELLENBOGEN: Made a lot of friends, made a lot of enemies. I've got it all: a list of friends, a list of enemies. A list of people that never want to talk to me; a list of people that I never want to talk to.

SHOOT ME: *$35,000 is a huge cut compared with $400,000. How did you feel capable of making the film with such a reduced budget?*

ELLENGBOGEN: The $400,000 had everybody getting something. Nobody was going to get rich, but then again, you were talking about people out of film school, et cetera. If they're making $300 a week, it's not bad. It was based on a budget like that. With $35,000, we had enough to buy film and food and rent the equipment. We had all the locations . . . the most we paid for one was $600.

Once we got accepted into Sundance, we were able to raise another $70,000, and that got us through the blowup, providing the finished print we took to Sundance. And that was because all the labs agreed to some form of deferment. DuArt gave us 50 percent on the blowup, with six months to pay the other 50 percent. And they didn't charge interest. Spin Cycle did charge interest, but they're a smaller business and their cash flow is probably not the same as DuArt.

SHOOT ME: *What format did you shoot in?*

ELLENGBOGEN: Super 16. And if you're asking me how it was, if I were to direct a movie tomorrow which format would I go with, digital, film . . . I would shoot on 35mm. I think messing around with 16mm is messing around with your budget. It's basically admitting that you can't raise the money to shoot on 35, 'cause I don't think there is an artistic reason to use Super 16. I think it's a medium that just says, "We can shoot on a lower budget and deceive ourselves long enough to get deep in debt and stay enthused."

Going to digital would be a directorial question. It depends on what medium the director is comfortable working in. Digital is obviously a viable media format now. I don't think the audience really is so savvy that they're going to go in there and complain . . . or even notice in many cases. I don't think I would tell the public that it was a digital film. But Ilya has an aesthetic quality—works with colors and light—that is film-oriented, and that's why I say it's a directorial thing.

SHOOT ME: *Did USA help you with distribution, and what is it that you do there?*

ELLENGBOGEN: They're not hindering my efforts at self-distribution. As to what I do there, people have been trying to figure that out. Jack Foley is the only one who knows. He taught me what I know, which is to assist him in developing release strategies by studying the marketplace. So, I guess, I'm a market analyst. I do competitive studies, theater by theater, market by market. In a sense, it's demographics, knowing what neighborhood is going to play your movie. Every movie is going to play different: one movie might work at Sunshine, but the same movie might not work at Angelika. It literally gets that close: from the East Village to Greenwich Village, your audience will be different, and I have methods of studying this. I can paint a pretty accurate picture of where a film will work.

SHOOT ME: *Which USA films have you tried out based on these demographic studies?*

ELLENGBOGEN: *Traffic, Being John Malkovich, Gosford Park, Monsoon Wedding.* Whoever would have thought an all-ensemble period piece would do the kind of business *Gosford Park* has (as of this writing, it was up to $41 million). The Coen Brothers' black-and-white film *The Man Who Wasn't There*: That's about as niche an audience as you can get, and $7.5 million dollars later it's in the bracket where it's a successful art film. *Monsoon Wedding* is just expanding now.

SHOOT ME: *Have you been able to apply what you learned at USA to* Margarita Happy Hour?

ELLENBOGEN: I wasn't really able to because in order to do that you have to have not only a distribution plan, but a distribution budget. When you have no money to distribute, no money to advertise, no money even for a trailer . . . Then you really are at the mercy of what the theaters want to do with you, and *when* they're willing to do it with you. And that goes completely against what I've learned, which is to create your plan and stick to it. Because not only does it work neighborhood to neighborhood, but it's kind of like *Invasion of the Body Snatchers.* There are telepathic lines of communication that run through this country . . . that run through any country. A movie opens in New York, and it sends out little signals, up to Albany, out to Chicago, out to L.A., down to Atlanta, out to Philadelphia. If people are going in droves to see your movie here, there's all this intense activity, people talking about it, and now with e-mails people can tell each other about it much quicker . . . witness *The Blair Witch Project.* Word goes out from those cores.

If you had only one print, the best thing is to open in New York, then to open in L.A., and then Chicago. We're opening in New York on March 22. I have my Chicago booking May 10. It's too much space, because the reviews from New York will be forgotten by the time we go into Chicago, so then it's all up to the Chicago reviews to do it, which means we lost the momentum. But we're giving it our best effort. We got the Dobie Theater in Austin, Texas, June 7. The timing is off, but it's a calendar house, which is good. Nonetheless, we are going to accomplish what we need to with *Margarita* to make it successful. It will have played in movie theaters and gotten reviewed. We've sold it as a premiere to the Sundance channel. We have a video/DVD deal. We have a foreign sales rep who took it to Cannes. It's played all the best festivals that you could think of. And that leaves Europe and beyond. And it's time to wash the hands and move on. I've been doing *Margarita* since mid-1998.

SHOOT ME: *Are you getting your investors out on all these deals?*

ELLENBOGEN: I think there's a good chance that we can make good on the investors in time, at least on getting them back to ground zero.

SHOOT ME: *Many feel that would be good enough.*

ELLENGBOGEN: It would be a good token. I mean they'll probably get back to ground zero on their tax deductions at this point, from the losses.

SHOOT ME: *As a one-man distribution machine, you must have design skills . . .*

ELLENGBOGEN: Not exactly "one-man," as it is always a team effort . . . with *Margarita*, it is Susan Leber and Ilya Chaiken. After Larry's movie I decided I would never self-distribute again, because I had hoped to never have to open Photoshop or Quark XPress again . . . So what have I been doing? Designing postcards, posters for film festivals, everything now, and it never ends!

I'm focusing more on the distribution and graphic design because I can do it. Susan is focusing more on the publicity end of it. We just basically came up with our list; we've been doing screenings. We did bring somebody in who wanted to get experience working. They were doing publicity for some toothpaste company or whatever. Susan had posted a note on mandy.com, where people always look for jobs, saying "looking for publicist who wants to get experience in movies, no pay. Theatrical release coming up March 22nd, looking to do publicity in the New York area." And this woman came on for about two weeks, but then quit. She felt she had to spend her time looking for a job, which is totally understandable. But that's the way it's been. We had somebody doing our Web site free from the School of Visual Arts, in exchange for school credit. As of now, we've had about seven different people working on the Web site. Hey, at least we have one.

SHOOT ME: *How effective do you think it is, having a Web site to promote films? Certainly since the Millennium, it's been a big thing.*

ELLENGBOGEN: I personally never go to a movie Web site. I use the Internet for research purposes. But I also may be a different kind of Internet user.

SHOOT ME: *Well, then how would you prioritize effective ways of promoting your film? And that includes festivals.*

ELLENGBOGEN: Well, you have all sorts of different levels of art independent films now. You have art films with stars in them. Then the most effective way to advertise is put a big ad with their name in it. The audience is incredibly name-driven. Name- or concept-driven. You take a film like *The Blair Witch Project*, or *Crouching Tiger*, and it's not so much about the names as about the image that they created. The *Blair Witch* was a hard-won Internet campaign. They targeted the youth that's on the Internet with this compelling, riveting, offbeat horror concept, and it just went like rapid fire. With a film like *Wendigo*, or with a film like *Margarita Happy Hour*, I think publicity is our most important marketing tool. We're going to have an ad in the *Village Voice* and an ad in *Time Out*, but there's not going to be an ad in the *New York Times*. (At this time, after New York I can say this was a mistake, especially in second and third week, after getting very quotable reviews from most New York papers.)

As to festivals, when you go to Sundance, you hope that you're going to go there and make a deal. Same thing with Toronto. GenArt we did. I guess we just started doing it because we didn't make a deal and it's a good way to build recognition for your film. There's that plateau of people who follow independent film. And I'm not saying that's your core audience.

I think most people who make up the art audience these days are avid review readers. And it's important to have your name out there. I look at e-mail differently than I look at the Web because it's more like direct mailing. And as annoying as it may be to some people, it's an effective, inexpensive, grassroots way of getting people to spread the word, making them feel like, okay, I'm participating in this grass-roots thing by sending this on to ten people. And it's not going to be the selling thing to get them going, I don't think, but at least something with the title *Margarita Happy Hour* passes across their eyes, even if it's just on the way to hitting the delete key. And then, when a review comes out, or if they pass a poster on the street . . . and for the record, I just got arrested again, for the second time, on Saturday, for postering.

SHOOT ME: *Where?*

ELLENGBOGEN: On Houston Street. The other time, Larry (Fessenden) and I were postering for *Habit* back in '97. It was two o'clock in the morning and we were literally putting up the last poster. There wasn't even any glue left in the bucket, but Larry saw one pole that looked naked without a *Habit* poster on it. We were on Lafayette and Houston, and that was the one that clinched the deal, because no sooner did we slap the remaining iota of glue on the poster than the car pulled up and three policemen proceeded to get out. This was early Giuliani, when he was cleaning up the city. So, we got handcuffed and briefly imprisoned (see *www.glasseyepix.com* for photo of us in jail). And they were mocking us for being out there promoting our own movie, saying, "Guess you guys didn't get into Sundance." These were smart cops. However, this time that can't be said, because we *did* get into Sundance and I was still out doing it.

On the first one, we were booked and thrown in the tank with all the other drug dealers, murderers, rapists, and pimps. It was funny because Larry was handing them all postcards of the film. They were taking the postcards off to prison. We finally got out at 5:30 in the morning, after being photographed, fingerprinted, with a court date set, and we went back to court twice with a court-appointed attorney, and they got our sentence down to one day of community service. So we picked up cigarette butts in Tompkins Square Park on a beautiful day in the fall. Couldn't complain. However, this time around I did not get brought in to the precinct, or to prison. There weren't even any handcuffs. They just wrote me up a ticket for unlawful postering. I'm still trying to decide whether I'm pleading not guilty, because, technically, my staple gun did not work on the one I was arrested for, so they saw me attempt to put the poster up, and when my staple gun failed I started walking away, and that's when they came up. I tried plea-bargaining with them, explaining that even though I didn't actually put up a poster when they ticketed me, when I get to court I'll get the book thrown at me. I might as well have been holding an Uzi instead of a staple gun. And this was the East Village, a place of energetic artistic public expression. Throwing your stuff out there for the public to make a decision on is what the East Village represents, culturally speaking. And yet, I always get arrested in the East Village.

CHAPTER TWENTY

AN INTERVIEW WITH RICHARD DUTCHER

Not so long ago, homeless and finan-cially-strapped high schooler Richard Dutcher was living out of his beat-up '71 Mercury Comet. Later, he and his wife maxed out their credit cards to get his first film off the ground. (All they had left was their gas card, and they would buy their groceries at the gas station.) It took five years to complete this first film, which didn't break even. However, with his second feature, God's Army, *despite the naysayers, Dutcher found he had a hit on his hands, returning $2.6 million on a $300,000 investment. His next—* Brigham City—*was made for three times the cost of his previous one, and now, in*

© 2000 Zion Films.

2002, he's working with seven times that amount on his fourth feature.

Nothing unusual about all this, you're saying. An industry story not ter-ribly uncommon. But it's the niche market Dutcher believed in and fought for that makes his story unique; a market so untapped that he was literally the only person in the country who knew it would work.—RF

RICHARD DUTCHER: I got this from just being aware of the inde-pendent scene in Los Angeles, being aware of the different niche films, whether they were minority films, gay films, black films . . . Any film that's made not for the mainstream but for a particular audience. I knew from witnessing this firsthand that I had great stories to tell that might be somewhat specialized but also had a definite audience.

SHOOT ME: *How were you able to tap into that audience?*

RD: Well, it had its own particular challenges. It was easy to identify who the market was for *God's Army*, but at the same time, it was dif-ficult to reach them because the Mormon churches have a policy from the pulpit that you never talk about any kind of commercial projects. There's no marketing of any kind in the building, even bulletin boards. You don't put up anything that's for sale, and it's very rigorously enforced.

One of our main focuses was on Internet marketing. Getting the word out, building a list of Mormons throughout the country, throughout the continent actually, who we could keep appraised of the film and kind of enlist them to help us and get the word out. And then, although we personally couldn't go and put something on a bulletin board or put flyers on cars in church parking lots, the volunteers naturally could do whatever they wanted to do and some of them were very enthusiastic and did things that would have caused problems if *we* had done them.

We marketed very heavily . . . and one great thing about the Mormon population is that there are areas in Idaho, Utah, and Arizona, that have large populations that are predominantly Mormon and we were able to market in a very mainstream way there, and that word would then seep out because everybody here in Utah, for example, had Mormon relatives in Florida, or Washington, or wherever. And we were able to identify the audience, go after them, and enlist them to help us.

The entire budget of the film, including marketing, was $300,000. I had spent about $250,000 on making the film and then I had another $50,000 with which I was able to buy my thirteen prints and pay for the newspaper ads and stuff for the first couple of weeks. And then it would all be gone. Knowing that, I targeted the Salt Lake City and the Provo, Utah, areas, opened the film there, and put all thirteen prints out in those areas. I spent the rest of my money on the newspaper ads and the flyers, marketing it that way. And, fortunately, it worked the way that I believed that it would. It was even beating out the Hollywood product that was here. In fact, we ended up being, for Utah, one of the top grossing films of the year, which was really thrilling. But what that really did was enable me to use the success in this very small region and slowly expand into Idaho, then into Arizona, then into California, and eventually we were everywhere. But we had to build very slowly and we were restricted in some ways because we kept having to wait for the money to come in from the first couple of weeks before we could afford to do our newspaper ads in another city.

SHOOT ME: *So you had to be completely involved in the marketing for a long period of time?*

RD: Oh, absolutely. One thing I did which was very helpful was I would go out a couple of weeks before the movie would open, out to Oregon or wherever, and speak to a church group, try to organize something that would generate interest in the movie. There was a little anxiety about this film in the Mormon community because they didn't know what it was, and they were very touchy about how missionaries would be portrayed, and so it was important to let them hear me, even before they saw the film, to know what I was trying to do and what my take on it was, and that helped relax some of the anxieties. I noticed that in some cities where I was not able to go, there was definitely more suspicion about the film, and it often didn't play as well in those areas.

SHOOT ME: *How much of the film's 2.6 million theatrical gross was attributed to Mormon attendance?*

RD: For *God's Army* it was probably about 75 percent.

SHOOT ME: *Following* God's Army, *how did you go about raising money for the next project?*

RD: I joke about this, but it's completely true: it took me four years to raise the $300,000 for *God's Army* and it took me four weeks to raise the $900,000 for *Brigham City*. It was easier because I was coming right off the success of *God's Army* and the doors were much more open to me at that point.

The first significant investments that enabled me to make *God's Army* came from non-Mormons. I had a hard time convincing rich Mormons that there was actually a market out there for a movie like *God's Army*. And for some reason or another, non-Mormons could see that more accurately. There's 10 million Mormons out there and surely, if you made a good enough film, a lot of them would want to see it.

SHOOT ME: Brigham City's *story, of a serial killer in a Mormon community, coupled with the sense—almost like that in* The Wild Bunch—*that the community's time has passed, is a very troublesome concept.*

RD: Yes, it is. And I was very conscious with *Brigham City*, instead of having a 25 percent non-Mormon audience, to try to get a 50 percent non-Mormon audience, to do something that would be a little more approachable to non-Mormons. It was an interesting experiment.

I didn't tour and talk as much with *Brigham City*, because the subject matter was obviously different. I did do a lot of interviews and we used a lot of the connections that we had generated with *God's Army*. It was exactly the movie that I wanted to make, but some in the Mormon community had suggested that maybe it was five years before its time. I disagree with that but I see what they're saying. I think people were expecting something a little softer, maybe a *God's Army 2*, which it definitely wasn't.

SHOOT ME: *Wilford Brimley co-stars in* Brigham City. *I was curious if he was a Mormon?*

RD: He was born Mormon and he grew up Mormon, but he is not an active Mormon now. But he *is* a Utahan, actually, and in fact his brother, who played the mayor in the film, is an active Mormon, and I think Wilford's father was a bishop in the Mormon church. So, he definitely knows the terrain.

SHOOT ME: *Are there other Mormon filmmakers besides yourself working today?*

RD: There are, but they're not very well known, and they're not telling Mormon stories. Neil LaButte is probably the most well-known.

SHOOT ME: *Were the film festivals of any help to you with those films?*

RD: Not at all, in fact *God's Army* was not a festival film. I thought maybe it was a Sundance kind of thing because it's a unique American voice, and tried to enter it, but I found out very quickly that it was not the unique American voice they wanted to hear. It made no sense to me, especially with their festival being here in Utah. It would have been a packed house. But I see now, with a little bit of perspective, that it's not the kind of film that they really want to support.

But that was a good experience for me, too, because I walked away from it saying, "Yeah, well, who cares about festivals, I just want to get the film into theaters." I don't really care for that whole atmosphere. And Sundance was the only festival I really submitted it to. After that, I realized that I knew where the people who wanted to see it were, and I just needed to get it to them. Getting any kind of industry thumbs-up became meaningless. And with *Brigham City*, by that time I already had that attitude, so I didn't even think about doing it until the film had opened, and then just in some areas where it wasn't going to open. It was a way of getting it out there a bit more. And it's been curious to me that several of the smaller film festivals have picked it up and shown it even though it's already played in theaters.

SHOOT ME: *What about foreign sales for both films? How did that go for you?*

RD: Foreign sales on *Brigham City* are going very well. *God's Army* hasn't done well. I think there's a large segment of the population that really doesn't want anything with a strong religious tone to it.

SHOOT ME: *It sounds as if you control all markets.*

RD: Right, but I'm having to farm things out now because I'm working on a new film. The life of the films goes on, but I want to keep making films, I don't want to just worry about exploiting them in all markets, so I'm having to step away a lot from the marketing and the distribution and just concentrate on the next movie I want to make. I'm trying to find the best people to watch over these movies for me.

SHOOT ME: *Sounds like the natural evolution of having a career.*

RD: Yeah, it's nice to have such problems. The new one—*The Prophet: The Story of Joseph Smith Jr.—* is $6 million right now, though I'm trying to get a little more financing to make it $7.5 million. It'll still feel like a low-budget film, because I'm trying to pull off an epic for $7.5 million.

SHOOT ME: *I imagine you've built up a lot of good will in the community. Might this not get you a lot of free help, with locations . . .*

RD: Well, you'd think . . .

SHOOT ME: *Yeah. I guess I thought wrong.*

RD: I guess when people hear that it's a $6 million film, good will goes out the window.

SHOOT ME: *And also Utah has become a popular place to shoot Hollywood films on lower budgets. What was your schedule on Brigham City?*

RD: *Brigham City* was a thirty-day schedule. This one is a fifty-day schedule. *God's Army* I did in eighteen days. And that was rough. That's one thing; as I make more films I try to build in more days, and more footage. Of course, you never get to the point where you have all the time or all the film that you need, but someday I'd like to get there. In fact, it's my goal to do a Stanley Kubrick and do seventy takes on some guy walking through a door.

SHOOT ME: *And is there something you've learned along the way as an independent . . . a helpful word of advice or a pitfall you'd like to share?*

RD: Yeah, there is something I've learned, which is the opposite of what I thought I would learn. With *God's Army*, having written, directed, and produced it, by the time I got to the marketing, I had no money for anyone to help me, but I knew how I wanted to position the film, and I knew I had to be very creative in the marketing of it with very little money to make it work. With *Brigham City*, we got to that same point, only this time we had a little money and I thought, you know what, I'll trust the marketing people because this is after all their specialty, and just let them follow their instincts and see what they do.

And what I learned was that that's not really a good thing to do. I think in most films, especially independent films, there's kind of a father of the film, or a mother of the film, and they care about it more than anybody else. They recognize the weaknesses and the strengths, hopefully more than anybody else. And they know how to care for it. Most people in the marketing department go home at five o'clock and think about other things, or watch television. But the filmmaker can't stop thinking about it. He dreams about it. And that's good for the film, and it's important to trust that. In some ways, I wish I hadn't shared some of the decision-making with other people.

SHOOT ME: *I could be wrong about this, but I will say that the DVD I was sent on* Brigham City *had cover art that didn't represent the film properly.*

RD: You got the eyeball one.

SHOOT ME: *Yeah, which suggests something a lot more lurid and less intelligent than the film was.*

RF: And what worries me about that is that the audience that will like this movie may never rent it. And the audience that is renting that video box may not like the movie that they see. So, that's a good example of what I mean. I think it's naturally a filmmaker's tendency to try to control everything, and sometimes it's ego, but sometimes I think it's not. Sometimes your responsibility to the film is to really stick with it, all the way through, or at least as far as you can.

INDEX

About the Authors

Roy Frumkes and **Rocco Simonelli** have been writing, directing, producing, and teaching in their field for years. The team's story ideas, rewrites, and authorship include the hit feature film *The Substitute* (which has spawned three sequels) and the cult favorite *The Johnsons*. Their upcoming movie *The Sweet Life* will be released in New York in 2003.

Roy Frumkes's accomplishments as director, writer, or producer include the TV special *An Evening at Dangerfields*, the docudrama *Burt's Bikers*, the award-winning feature *Street Trash*, and the feature-length documentary *Document of the Dead*. As the owner of *Films in Review*, America's oldest and most prestigious film publication, Roy has brought the magazine online. The site, *www.filmsinreview.com*, draws thousands of hits daily. For the past twenty years, he has taught courses in film production and screenwriting at The School of Visual Arts, and he has lectured widely at such institutions as Harvard University and the Cornell Medical Center.

Rocco Simonelli has penned the scripts for the mystical thriller *The Johnsons* (based on a story by partner Roy Frumkes), the gangster comedy *Me and the Mob*, and the independent short *Swirlee*. His writing has appeared in *The Perfect Vision*, *Films in Review*, and *Expressions of Dread*. He teaches screenwriting at The School of Visual Arts, and has also taught and lectured at SUNY and Marymount College. *The Sweet Life* represents his directorial debut.

Books From Allworth Press

Technical Film and TV for Nontechnical People
by Drew Campbell (paperback, 6 × 9, 256 pages, $19.95)

Documentary Filmmakers Speak
by Liz Stubbs (paperback, 6 × 9, 240 pages, $19.95)

Producing for Hollywood: A Guide for Independent Producers
by Paul Mason and Don Gold (paperback, 6 × 9, 272 pages, $19.95)

Directing for Film and Television, Revised Edition
by Christopher Lukas (paperback, 6 × 9, 256 pages, $19.95)

Making Your Film for Less Outside the U.S.
by Mark DeWayne (6 × 9, 272 pages, $19.95)

Hollywood Dealmaking: Negotiating Talent Agreements
by Dina Appleton and Daniel Yankelevitz (paperback, 6 × 9, 256 pages, $19.95)

The Health & Safety Guide for Film, TV & Theater
by Monona Rossol (paperback, 6 × 9, 256 pages, $19.95)

The Filmmaker's Guide to Production Design
by Vincent LoBrutto (paperback, 6 × 9, 216 pages, $19.95)

The Screenwriter's Legal Guide, second edition
by Stephen F. Breimer (paperback, 6 × 9, 320 pages, $19.95)

Making Independent Films: Advice from the Filmmakers
by Liz Stubbs and Richard Rodriguez (paperback, 6 × 9, 224 pages, $16.95)

Writing Television Comedy
by Jerry Rannow (paperback, 6 × 9, 224 pages, $14.95)

Get the Picture? The Movie Lover's Guide to Watching Films
by Jim Piper (paperback, 6 × 9, 240 pages, $18.95)

The Directors: Take One
by Robert J. Emery (paperback, 6 × 9, 416 pages, $19.95)

The Directors: Take Two
by Robert J. Emery (paperback, 6 × 9, 384 pages, $19.95)

Please write to request our free catalog. To order by credit card, call 1-800-491-2808 or send a check or money order to Allworth Press, 10 East 23rd Street, Suite 210, New York, NY 10010. Include $5 for shipping and handling for the first book ordered and $1 for each additional book. Ten dollars plus $1 for each additional book if ordering from Canada. New York State residents must add sales tax.

To see our complete catalog on the World Wide Web, or to order online, you can find us at *www.allworth.com.*